90 0869993 4

D1759317

WITHDRAWN
FROM
UNIVERSITY OF PLYMOUTH
LIBRARY SERVICES

U
S

SELLING BEAUTY

THE JOHNS HOPKINS UNIVERSITY STUDIES
IN HISTORICAL AND POLITICAL SCIENCE
127th Series (2009)
1. Monique O'Connell, *Men of Empire: Power and Negotiation
in Venice's Maritime State*
2. Morag Martin, *Selling Beauty: Cosmetics, Commerce,
and French Society, 1750–1830*

Selling Beauty

Cosmetics, Commerce, and French Society, 1750–1830

MORAG MARTIN

The Johns Hopkins University Press

Baltimore

This book has been brought to publication with the generous assistance of the
Karl and Edith Pribram Endowment.

© 2009 The Johns Hopkins University Press
All rights reserved. Published 2009
Printed in the United States of America on acid-free paper
2   4   6   8   9   7   5   3   1

The Johns Hopkins University Press
2715 North Charles Street
Baltimore, Maryland 21218-4363
www.press.jhu.edu

Library of Congress Cataloging-in-Publication Data

Martin, Morag.
Selling beauty : cosmetics, commerce, and French society, 1750–1830 /
Morag Martin.
p. cm.
Includes bibliographical references and index.
ISBN-13: 978-0-8018-9309-4 (hardcover : alk. paper)
ISBN-10: 0-8018-9309-7 (hardcover : alk. paper)
1. Cosmetics industry—France—History.   I. Title.
HD9970.5.C673F866 2009
381'.4566850944—dc22   2008048621

A catalog record for this book is available from the British Library.

*Special discounts are available for bulk purchases of this book. For more information, please
contact Special Sales at 410-516-6936 or specialsales@press.jhu.edu.*

The Johns Hopkins University Press uses environmentally friendly book materials,
including recycled text paper that is composed of at least 30 percent post-consumer
waste, whenever possible. All of our book papers are acid-free, and our jackets and
covers are printed on paper with recycled content.

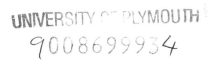

UNIVERSITY OF PLYMOUTH
9008699934

CONTENTS

ACKNOWLEDGMENTS

This book would not have been possible without the help of a large number of people. I am grateful to my dissertation advisor Tim Tackett at the University of California, Irvine, who provided a supportive and critical eye. I would like to gratefully acknowledge my debt to Colin Jones for inspiring the topic and then following me through to the end. Maxine Berg provided me with a research space and postdoctoral fellowship at the University of Warwick Eighteenth Century Centre. The Leverhulme Fund Special Research Fellowship helped me finish old strands of research and open new ones on the history of masculinity. Since 2000, the History Department at The College at Brockport, State University of New York, has been a highly welcoming and supportive environment for both a first job and writing my manuscript.

Thanks to colleagues who have helped me by reading my work, listening to my arguments, or giving me advice: Mary Salzman, Hazel Hahn, Peggy Waller, Cathy McClive, Dena Goodman, Tim Hitchcock, Natasha Coquery, Liliane Hilaire-Pérez, Catherine Lanoë, Caroline Fontaine, Katie Scott, Claire Walsh, Elizabeth Eger, Melissa Hyde, Melissa Percival, Michael Kwass, Robin Walz, Mary Gayne, Jenny Lloyd, Greta Niu, Carolyn Johnston, Lynn Sharp, Michael Lynn, Jem Axelrod, Christopher Forth, and David Kuchta. I would like to acknowledge especially the friendship and advice of Jean Pedersen, Rebecca Earle, and Yuki Takagaki.

My research trips to France would not have been possible without the support of family, friends, and institutions. Claudy Toche, Jean-Noel Sanson, Marie-Pierre Sanson, Karine Sarant, Lynn Sharp, and Marie-Paule Deslandes gave me their hospitality. My thanks to the Musée internationale du parfum and the Musée Fragonard in Grasse for allowing me access to their collections. I am also especially grateful to the archivists at the Archives de Paris, the Academie de médecine, the Chambre de commerce et d'industrie de Paris, and Valérie Marchal at the Institut national de la propriété industrielle.

In the final stages, Eleanore Dugan did an invaluable read-through of the whole manuscript; my father sharpened my writing, while my mother corrected my French. I picked the Johns Hopkins University Press because I had been told Henry Tom was a wonderful editor to be rejected by, furnishing useful advice for revision and alternate presses. He has proved to be an exceptional editor to be published by, along with the rest of the staff at the Press, especially Suzanne Flinchbaugh and Andre Barnett.

Part of chapter 4 and the conclusion were originally published as "Casanova and Mlle Clairon: Painting the Face in a World of Natural Fashion," *Fashion Theory Journal* 7, no. 1 (March 2003): 57–78. Chapter 5 was in part published as "Doctoring Beauty: The Medical Control of Women's *Toilettes* in France, 1750–1820," *Medical History* 49 (Spring 2005): 351–68. A much shorter version of chapter seven appeared as "French Harems: Images of the Orient in Cosmetic Advertisements, 1750–1815," *The Proceedings of the Western Society for French History* 31 (2003): 125–37.

Finally, for their constant support, I thank Carl Almer, Beatrix Almer Martin, and Rosalia Almer Martin. This book is dedicated to them.

SELLING BEAUTY

France has the well-earned reputation of being a center of luxury and fashion. Historians looking for the roots of high fashion have found key starting points during Louis XIV's reign in the seventeenth century and in Marie Antoinette's personal proclivities at the end of the eighteenth.[1] Despite this long history of luxurious excess, France is also the home of the radical revolutionary ethos; extremist Jacobins tried in the 1790s to destroy all representations of the frivolous Old Regime. The period from 1750 to 1830 that this book covers is one of disjuncture and change in the representation of France, fashion, gender roles, and ideals of beauty. This period starts with the extremes of Louis XV's court and ends with the simpler styles of respectable femininity during the Restoration. Court aristocrats in the 1750s wore thick layers of paint and rouge, while their Romantic counterparts wished to be naturally pale. Yet, despite this radical shift in fashion away from visible artifice, in the same period, French beauty culture transformed itself from an aristocratic luxury to a strong and vibrant sector of the economy.

The eighteenth century was first a century of artifice in court and in elite circles. From the reign of Louis XIV came lavish wigs and codes of dress. Louis XV's court was more frivolous; women's colorful silks grew in width, and men's wigs were powdered. Under Louis XVI, hair grew taller for women, while men luxuriated in flouncy sleeves. By the 1780s, the ideals of the Enlightenment reversed these trends, pushing fashion toward simpler dress touched by nature, illustrated by Marie Antoinette's *Hameau* at Versailles and Elisabeth Vigée-Lebrun's portraits of mothers and children. During the Revolution, honest self-presentation became essential to join the fraternity of citizens. With republicanism came the increased demarcation of fashion as a feminine and private pastime. Men were expelled from the toilette, adopting instead British-styled suits that presaged the development of the modern three-piece suit. The Revolution politicized fashion and emphasized transparency of presentation, while the Directory and Empire literally exposed women's bodies in see-through white sheaths to evoke antiquity.[2]

Focusing more specifically on the history of cosmetics, scholars have stressed the ways in which the use of face paint paralleled changes in the general use of fashion. Makeup gained great acceptance by the middle of the century, and then its popularity started to decline. The stark white skin, brilliant red cheeks, and black silk patches of Versailles were replaced by naturally flushed skin and an open, honest countenance free of artifice. By the 1760s, the use of makeup by men was on the decline, and by the 1780s, women outside the court eschewed rouge and turned to antiquity for their models of beauty. During the Revolution, natural fashions triumphed, and even afterward, cosmetics did not return to their Old Regime prominence.[3] The nineteenth century is often described as the century of repression, pallid faces, and respectability. Most historians of cosmetics have assumed that this was the end for makeup—leaving only actresses and prostitutes to wear rouge—until its slow rehabilitation in the twentieth century due to industrialization and mass marketing.[4]

While the downfall of paint is a compelling story, which fits well with the history of fashion, this book suggests that it is a superficial one. I focus not only on the anecdotes of elite use and the admonitions of journalists and advice writers but also on a broad range of archival sources and marketing tools to uncover the development of a complex and expanding beauty culture. Contrary to expectations and despite an onslaught of criticisms of artifice, the commerce of cosmetics expanded and prospered in the late eighteenth century, during the Revolutionary period, and into the nineteenth century, becoming, with the perfume industry, a key component in the world's conception of frenchness. I trace how cosmetics, at one time a typically aristocratic commodity, maintained their popularity among both male and female shoppers once taken up by ordinary people. To survive commercially, sellers repositioned what had been ostentatious elite products as purchases consistent with Enlightenment values. By validating their goods in a highly volatile market, sellers shifted the debate about beauty and artifice into the realm of commerce. Though makeup disappeared from public view by the Revolution, in France, it would remain a private and necessary part of many women's toilettes.

This book expands our conception of beauty products into the ranks of the urban populace, both as consumers and producers. I focus on three main groups of sources: (1) newspaper advertisements for cosmetics, which first appeared in the 1750s; (2) beauty manuals and medical treatises that provided recipes and advice; and (3) stories, poems, and anecdotes about beauty found in popular journalism and tracts. These three sets of often overlapping sources contain conflicting voices, all hoping to control the definition of beauty, femininity, and respectability. One group hoped to sell more makeup (the producers), one to control its uses (the medical practitioners), and the third to end all use of artifice by both men and women (the critics). While the voices of criticism were the loudest and most strident, this is a history of how the voices of compromise, promotion, and marketing made it possible for consumers to continue to buy and to use cosmetics despite a radical shift in the aesthetic criteria for beauty.

The study of cosmetics within the realm of fashion touches on a number of historiographies. The now well-accepted notion of a consumer revolution is at its center, along with the debate over why it occurred. My work intersects with the history of guilds and proto-luxury production. Central to these commercial concerns is the study of French systems of publicity and marketing. The history of cosmetics is also part of the history of fashion and luxury that has flourished in recent years. As a product that became increasingly associated with women, cosmetics are part of the larger shift in definitions of gender roles. My work, however, does not leave out the roles of men, joining a newer focus on the history of masculinity. Finally, and just as important, since cosmetics were a subset of medicines and were partially controlled by the medical profession, the history of the professionalization of medicine is part of its larger framework. What all these strands of historiography add up to is an investigation of how fashion changes, as radical as the shift away from ostentatious luxury to simple, natural styles, shaped and interacted with the commercial marketplace.

Neil McKendrick uncovered a revolution in English buying happening alongside the early Industrial Revolution. Studies of France point to a similar growth of purchasing that occurred not with industrialization but within the traditional artisanal and small-scale production of the Old Regime. Daniel Roche points to increases in the purchase of nonessential goods by Parisian servants and artisans. In her study of probate inventories, Annik Pardailhé-Galabrun finds a substantial number of pictures, wall-hangings, and mirrors in Parisian working-class homes by the end of the century. Cissie Fairchild's work supports both these studies by uncovering the development of a market for what she calls "populuxe" goods, cheap copies of luxury goods aimed at the urban working classes. Though beauty products do not show up in probate inventories because they are perishable and cheap, other sources point to an increase in the ownership of cosmetics. Unlike fancy silks and towering headdresses, a pot of rouge was affordable for a seamstress or maidservant.[5]

The consumer revolution has to be further investigated not just in terms of growth of consumer demand but through changes in production and methods of sale. My work investigates a breadth of products, from expensive luxury items, solely for the elite, to cheaper versions for broader commerce. Because they were easy to make and to transport, cosmetics were the ideal populuxe product. More than most artisans, however, makers of cosmetics were in a liminal, uncontrolled commercial space that allowed them to experiment with new techniques of production and selling. This work complements that of other historians who have uncovered thriving artisanal production of populuxe goods in a preindustrial context. Clare Crowston focuses on the seamstresses' guild, an all-female group, that similarly to cosmetics producers, helped shape patterns of consumption and definitions of femininity and fashion. Carolyn Sargenston's study of the elite guild of mercers uncovers the intricacy of the luxury trade market, linking tradespeople, entrepreneurs, and elite buyers in unorthodox ways. I am most indebted to Natacha Coquery, who has brought to light the complex market for luxury goods that resided between aristocratic house and public street corner. Her work illustrates how the budding consumer market existed alongside more traditional means of sale, such as barter and credit.[6] The work of Catherine Lanoë on a broader history of cosmetics and production methods most closely complements mine. I was not, however, able to integrate her recent book, *La poudre et le fard: Une histoire des cosmétiques de la Renaissance aux Lumières* into this work.[7]

Despite being firmly based in traditional means of production, the late eighteenth century was a period that promised invention and novelty, especially in the realm of beauty aids. Innovation was a main means for justifying new products, new fashions, and increased sales in the public marketplace. Marketing methods have been studied in detail for England: McKendrick's study of advertising illuminates a complex system of sales and promotion.[8] Few historians have taken French advertising systems as seriously. The French press was smaller, more regulated, and the guilds limited other forms of advertising. Historians of advertising have labeled French publicity as backward and strictly textual information, compared with the more complex selling mechanisms used in eighteenth-century England.[9] Colin Jones, however, opened up a new field of inquiry in his article on medical advertisements. He links the expansionist, bourgeois, commercial language of advertisements to the creation of a "civically minded consumerism" that would play a key role in the Revolution.[10] My work expands on Jones's research to focus more closely on methods of publicity by one set of sellers over a larger span of time. I do not claim that advertisers shaped the Revolution but rather that their campaigns helped shape commercial practices and consumer values. Advertising was central to creating the market that made the consumer revolution possible. Though most historians place the development of publicity campaigns in the nineteenth century, my study indicates that a culture of advertising developed earlier.

The worlds of production, shopping, and marketing encompassed an increasingly diverse set of buyers in a complex system of fashion and commerce. Until recently, historians explained this growth in consumer buying by using emulation theory, first posited by Thorstein Veblen.[11] The lower classes wanted to imitate their betters or, more threatening, aspired to "pass" for the aristocracy by donning their clothing and makeup. More recent historians have questioned the centrality of this explanation, arguing that there were many other overlapping reasons for the lesser orders to adopt proto-luxuries, not the least of which was the distinction between groups and ranks, as well as personal reasons such as pleasure, creation of legacy, and desire for novelty promoted through advertising and marketing techniques.[12] The growth of individualism and the democratization of taste before and during the Revolution allowed for larger numbers to participate openly in the processes of fashion and consumerism. Cosmetics were the ideal object of personal desire while fulfilling a number of social expectations. One pot of rouge could be bought by a shopgirl to seduce her lover, impersonate her betters, and gossip with her peers about new purchases.

Though emulation likely played a role in the consumer's choices, it is unlikely that many shopgirls could pass as duchesses. Nonetheless, the increased purchases by the lower orders led to fears among the elite of social upheaval and to intense criticism of luxury consumption.[13] Sara Maza attributes the "panic and outrage about *le luxe*" to both this increased consumerism and the effects of the desacralization of the French monarchy, which left the French with no central arbiter of rank.[14] Still wishing to justify their positions of power, the aristocracy turned to newer, more extreme forms of fashion to create distinctions between themselves and those below.[15] Greater luxury led to increased attacks against it. John Shovlin argues that "in the late eighteenth century . . . a luxury discourse that for centuries had been pro-noble shifted to being anti-aristocratic."[16] Attacks against the spendthrift aristocracy shifted the tenor of consumerism from the constant differentiation of the elite to avoid emulation to the creation of a new group of respectable elite whose taste could not be copied. The new elite defined themselves in opposition to both the aristocrats above them and the rabble below.

The meaning of luxury was redefined to justify this new social group of moral elites.[17] Though some commentators still argued against all forms of luxury, increasingly Enlightenment *philosophes* justified luxury by making a distinction between "ostentatious luxury" (*luxe de magnificence*) and "pragmatic luxury" (*luxe de commodité*), within which comfort could be accommodated without tying it to aristocratic indulgence.[18] This ideal of pragmatic luxury was highly politicized by Enlightenment thinkers. The new definition of fashion based on good taste allowed the elite to justify their positions of power and gave philosophes the ostensibly fairer political sphere they sought. Though couched in the language of truth and universality, this system of transparent social relations reinforced the traditional hierarchy while admitting bankers, lawyers, and philosophes into the salons of the aristocracy. Attacks against cosmetics as a mask for the face were central to creating the new society. Cosmetics, or lack thereof, allowed a visible means of proving differences "between upper and middling ranks, between court and city, between domestic and public spaces, between prostitutes and virtuous ladies."[19] If commodities stood for their owner's values, within the cultural context, then the rejection of cosmetics was central to the new citizen of France in the late Old Regime and into the Revolution.

This purer face was meant to disassociate the new elite from the old aristocracy. At the same time, critics of artifice defined luxuries and fashion as feminine, and thus frivolous and possibly even pernicious, pastimes.[20] What had been the flaws of the elite became those of women. Women were accused of uncontrolled buying that could lead to bankruptcy for their husbands and disgrace of the family name. Patricia Phillippy argues that cosmetics were a way for men to control women within "masculine standards for feminine beauty, virtue and vice" in the early modern period.[21] Men hoped that in redefining fashion they could discipline women's uses of artifice and their roles in society. Eighteenth-century literature on natural beauty reinforced the feminine private sphere as the only respectable place for the newly simplified fashion. In contrast, men were to give up the trappings of fashion, leaving their wives and daughters to signify their financial and social success through their clothing and leisure.[22]

Despite the feminization of fashion and beauty, practices of both men and women were slower to change. Amanda Vickery argues that, even though women shopped more for fashion and luxuries, this was not a degrading pastime. Other historians of fashion have found that the simplification of men's fashion did not occur until the Napoleonic period or later, and certain goods such as wigs, fancy waistcoats, and furniture remained masculine commodities.[23] Notwithstanding claims by J. C. Flügel that a masculine renunciation of fashion and beauty occurred in the late eighteenth century, many men continued to participate in the pleasures of the toilette and vanity. Men may no longer have worn wigs and rouge, but the expectations of masculinity still demanded subtle uses of cosmetics and hidden ministrations. Men were an important part of the marketing of fashion well into the nineteenth century.

For men to still wear cosmetics and for women to primp, beauty products had to be disassociated from the old system of rank. Michael Kwass argues that instead of reproducing aristocratic luxury, late eighteenth-century taste masters (self-proclaimed experts who defined what was in fashion) relied on images of "convenience, natural authenticity, and self-expression—to mediate the relationship between consumption and status."[24] These ideals helped redefine goods while marking consumers as educated, enlightened, and "modern." Yet, in the world of cosmetics, different taste masters battled one another to give meaning to these values. Critics of luxury and, thus, cosmetics were large in number and loud in their disapproval, promoting new natural aids to beauty. Another key group, professional physicians, defined itself as the sole authority over the private health, habits, and purchases of women and families based on their scientific credentials. Both of these groups attempted to discipline women within their own framework of acceptable natural beauty. A third group of taste masters, producers and sellers of beauty aids, however, both built on the arguments of these critics and hoped to supersede and invalidate them. Sellers of beauty adopted the language of science, Enlightenment, and respectability, but their goal was not to discipline (primarily female) buyers but to offer personal pleasure and satisfaction.

The desire for beautification made cosmetics an important part of individual quests for pleasure and novelty. Cosmetics were as much about gaining the attention of a loved one as social acceptance. Even if the limits to makeup and its uses were defined and controlled by male viewers, female wearers could construct their own faces in the privacy of their toilettes. Sociologist Colin Campbell argues that increased consumerism was a function of the romantic ethos, encouraging individuals into personal, imaginative pleasures created by shopping. Material pleasures, for Kwass, are more important than emulation in explaining the consumer revolution. Expanding the focus of consumerism to world trade, Maxine Berg focuses on the importance of novelty to explain why consumerism spread.[25] Novelty and desire motivated fashions that were made exotic by the spread of goods from Asia and the Americas, such as chocolate, tea, and porcelain. Cosmetics were the ideal novelty product because they were fairly cheap, disposable, and could evoke exotic locales by their names and properties.

Though critics called for an end to all artifice and doctors tried to rein in its uses, sellers helped create a space in which the commerce of cosmetics could thrive. On the one hand, sellers promoted their goods as luxuries, replete with values of seduction and exoticism linked to the elite. On the other, they also associated their goods with purity, regeneration, naturalness, and healthfulness. The market for cosmetics expanded because taste masters combined desire and respectability into one very appealing package. They gave choices within the complex system of male and female roles consumers had to navigate. Because of the flexibility in their marketing means, once the products left the store shelves, consumers did not need to adhere strictly to one set of uses. Makeup could be used to distinguish between groups, cross social lines, or simply to bring personal pleasure to both men and women.

This book is divided into three main parts. Chapters 1, 2, and 3 cover the consumption, production, and advertising of cosmetics at the end of the eighteenth century. Chapters 4 and 5 investigate the growing criticisms of cosmetics that occurred alongside and because of the growth in consumer availability from the point of view of aesthetics, morality, and medical science. In chapters 6, 7, and 8, I examine how producers and sellers of cosmetics attempted to be the key taste masters for the redefinition of beauty. The basic question for this section is how those whose livelihoods depended on selling beauty aids responded to a radical shift in fashion that threatened their products.

In chapter 1, I investigate the consumer revolution in the purchase of cosmetics, specifically in Paris. I first provide a short history of makeup, and I then trace types of cosmetics and their main uses at their height of popularity in the 1750s and 1760s. Depending primarily on advice manuals, recipe books, and account books of perfumers, I look at the shift from homemade to store-bought concoctions. I determine who made and bought cosmetics as the century progressed. I find an increase in purchases by servants and artisans, as well as a growing mix of male and female buyers. Finally, I use visual sources to investigate how cosmetics were worn on the face.

This expansion of consumerism was matched by developments in the structure of production and sales, discussed in chapter 2. Cosmetics were made and sold by the traditional system of guilds (primarily perfumers) as well as entrepreneurial outsiders. Cosmetic sellers were a diverse and rapidly changing group. Since many products defined as beauty aids were not linked to any one guild, their sellers could function in ambiguous spaces and adopt means of sale that challenged the guilds. I focus on the case of Antoine Claude Maille, maker of cosmetic vinegars, who, while tied to Old Regime systems of production, experimented with new methods of sales. Maille, and other beauty sellers, was among the first to build up brand names and loyalty in a national and even international arena. Despite this success story, those in the beauty business faced bankruptcy, like many trades, and economic difficulties, especially during the Revolution. By the beginning of the nineteenth century, a consolidated group of manufacturers had adapted to the changing market, ready to take on the industrial challenges to come.

One of the most innovative marketing developments of the eighteenth century was advertising. And, one of the most prolific groups of advertisers were makers of beauty products. Using a large database of newspaper advertisements, chapter 3 outlines a series of innovative marketing ploys used by these sellers, from guarantees to fixed prices, all of which were new to the second half of the eighteenth century. These advertisements created for their audience a language for commercial exchange. Advertisers (in a multitude of venues and formats) conjured up for their audience of buyers commodities that were both desirable and within reach.

In chapter 4, I trace the principal arguments against cosmetics found in tracts, journals, novels, poems, and memoirs. I survey the growing and virulent criticisms of cosmetics, not just from the works of well-known philosophes but also from popular journalism and anonymous sources. Despite many of these criticisms dating to the medieval period or Renaissance, their growing number and their tone were a key part of the Enlightenment attack on elite luxury. Critics attacked cosmetics as deceptive, turning women into monsters and men into women. The aesthetic falsity of artifice caused those who wore it to fall into lives of immorality and corruption. The solution to these ills was a return to the "natural." The cult of the shepherdess and Jean-Jacques Rousseau's depictions of unselfconscious young girls helped reinforce the new elite and their rejection of aristocratic values.

In the push for simpler fashion and better hygiene, the dangers of arsenic, lead, and mercury lurking in the jars of paint became the primary arguments against the use of artifice. In chapter 5, I investigate the role of doctors as advisors to the toilette. I look at advice manuals written by physicians as well as the files of the *Société royale de médecine* which oversaw the issuing of patents for cosmetics. Doctors advocated new ideals of health without the use of paint.[26] Yet the medicalization of the toilette did not always have the intended effect. Unwilling to place moral issues above scientific "truth," doctors often publicly approved of products they found to be safe through empirical analysis. In doing so, they succeeded in retaining control over the judging of cosmetics, but increasingly their testimonials justified the continued use of beauty aids by women who trusted their judgment.

In chapter 6, I look at how products seen as artificial, aristocratic, and destructive were redefined as natural, pure, and beneficial in public journals and advertisements. I focus on three main examples. First, I look at the adoption of medical language and patents (discussed in chapter 5) by advertisers. Second, I turn to the promotion of makeup as an enhancement of nature, focusing specifically on rouge. Both of these tactics responded directly to accusations often leveled at cosmetics in the same journals. Third, I turn to entrepreneurs who attempted to create a new monopoly for rouge, to stop or at least slow both the decline of the corporate system and the changing perception of their product. These campaigns promised that cosmetics were safe, could and did represent natural beauty, and functioned within a sphere of respectable commerce.

In chapter 7, I turn to the frequent marketing of cosmetics as foreign, innovative, and pleasurable objects, specifically the product of the Orient and its harems. I start by looking at the literature of the mythical harem, to analyze how it was transformed when it entered the sphere of marketing. What was originally a literary image of the exotic East, linked to the debauchery of the aristocracy, became a powerful marketing tool for promising unquestionable beauty. Advertisements for Oriental goods both exoticized prosaic products and linked beauty aids with feminine respectability rather than sensual excess. Under Napoleon, this exotic "other" was adopted as part of a French imperial project, further domesticating the products of the East for the consumption of respectable French women. Despite the lingering associations of cosmetics with sexual debauchery, advertisers successfully associated the East with individual self-beautification and personal gratification.

Just as advertisers revalued artifice to sell their products to respectable female buyers, they also catered openly and aggressively to male buyers and their beauty needs. For most men, the use of toiletries after the 1780s was private and personal, due in large part to the key shift in their fashionable dress: the loss of the wig. In chapter 8, I focus on this shift in male fashion to investigate how men and sellers of cosmetics coped with this loss. I use advertisements, medical tracts on hair loss, and patent applications to trace shifts in this market. The radical change in hairstyles brought down with it the commerce in hair powder, created a market for new lotions to stop hair loss, and encouraged the invention of new types of wigs. Baldness provided producers of cosmetics with a whole new, lucrative market for goods aimed at a desperate population. Rather than divorcing men from practices of beautification, the commerce of cosmetics actively recruited them as buyers and users.

If sellers of cosmetics were able to marshal ideals of nature, safety, exoticism, and masculinity to rehabilitate and, more important, to sell their products, the question of how buyers responded still remains. In the conclusion, I use two well-known eighteenth-century characters, the actress Mlle Clairon (Claire-Josèphe-Hippolyte Léris) and the painter Anne-Louis Girodet, to illustrate the changes mapped by the rest of my study on the lives of individuals. Cosmetics and artifice after the 1780s continued to play a role in private relationships but also had a key function in public presentation. Clairon disavowed using gaudy paint on stage to legitimate her profession, while still wearing rouge in private. Girodet depended on artifice to depict himself as part of a coterie of new republican artists to validate his professional career, despite the movement toward natural masculinity. Both Clairon and Girodet struggled with the contradictions inherent in the new standards of beauty, hoping to create a presentable self with naturalized (and invisible) artifice.

At the center of this book is the production, marketing, selling, and buying of cosmetics in late eighteenth and early nineteenth-century France. Those who sold cosmetics rehabilitated these goods by altering their meanings and redefining the links between beauty, femininity, and status that in turn affected the practices of their buyers. Though much of the language they adopted was borrowed from philosophes and doctors, when associated with the growing consumer market, it was irreversibly altered to fit the needs of commerce and consumers. The consumer culture that arose was distinct from both the aristocratic court and the Enlightenment salon. Sellers emphasized their goods' luxury and pleasurable aspects (thus promoting a subtle emulation of the elite or the Orient) alongside the simple, useful, and affordable aspects (thus promoting individual needs and Enlightenment values). They hoped to educate women and promote their purchases within the dominant aesthetic set mostly by men, while still allowing women spaces in which to make choices. The makers of cosmetics in the late eighteenth century responded to female and male consumers' needs and, in doing so, were able to shape their buyers' desires.

The Practices of Beauty

The Creation of a Consumer Market

Many historians assume that only the wealthy and the social elite wore the trappings of artifice in the eighteenth century.[1] General histories of cosmetics are principally built on anecdotes about the rich and famous. One oft-told story is about nineteen-year-old Marie Therese of Spain who came to the French court in 1745 to marry the dauphin. She reluctantly complied with the court rule to wear rouge only when she found out it would please the future king. Louis XV wore rouge around his eyes and may have wanted a well-rouged companion.[2] Napoleon was said to have told Josephine, "Go put on rouge, Madame, you look like a cadaver."[3] Rouge in these stories indicated assimilation into court culture, representing aristocratic privileges. Outsiders to the court often made opposing comments, finding the rituals of makeup excessive and ugly. After the educator Mme Stéphanie de Genlis was made-up for court, a courtier commented that "she has too much powder and too much rouge; she was a hundred times prettier yesterday."[4]

Going beyond court habits allows us better understanding of day-to-day (or at least evening) use of an array of beauty practices. It is also a difficult task for a historian of material culture and consumption. The court was highly scrutinized and analyzed (albeit most often in catty tones), while eighteenth-century memoirs, novels, and letters do not spend much time on physical presentation. Portraits allow for a glimpse of the sitter or the artist's preferred presentation of the face but are only available for the upper bourgeoisie and aristocrats. The practices of the middling and working classes, however, are to be found in the account books, death inventories, and advice manuals of the period. These sources give a sense of who wore cosmetics, what they purchased, and how they wore their makeup. By matching these archival sources with the commentary of observers and the portraits of the elite, we can start to put together a picture of cosmetic practices in the time before their banishment from visible public use in and around 1780. It becomes clear from this overview that there was a growing market for beauty products, but that these products did not conform to a single set of practices. Cosmetics use by the bourgeoisie, by artisans, and by servants was worn neither strictly to emulate the elites nor to reinforce social lines. Rather, cosmetics created different aesthetic models of beauty from among which each individual buyer could choose, depending on the person's social setting, age, or financial circumstances.

A Short History of Makeup

Cosmetics were hardly new to the eighteenth century. The history of cosmetics is tied to the development of perfumes that first flourished in ancient Egypt and Greece but which mostly disappeared during the medieval period. In the twelfth century, perfumes made of both animal and flower essences were brought to Europe from Arabia. Perfumes were meant to purify, to cleanse, and to scent one's environment. They were applied to clothing and furnishings and not directly to the skin. These *eaux,* distillations of scents in alcohol or oil, were made with fruit essences and flowers. The scents of orange blossoms, jasmine, lavender, cloves, and the well-known rosemary *Eau de la Reine d'Hongrie* were popular.[5] The elite burned incense perfumed with roses or other flowers in their houses. Perfumers also made breath sweeteners from such exotic animals and plants as ambergris (the bile of sperm whales), acacia wood (*catechou*), and cinnamon.[6]

As perfumery grew in the sixteenth century other products also developed. In 1533, Catherine de' Medici brought with her from Italy the practice of wearing rouge and face paint, which was quickly adopted by the French court. Throughout the sixteenth and seventeenth centuries, cosmetics were used only sparingly, but with the reign of Louis XIV new practices arose. Louis XIV reinforced wearing wigs for his courtiers. Though hair powder had been used under Henri III, it wasn't until the early eighteenth century that elites applied white powder to color wigs and natural hair rather than as a degreaser. White-haired wigs' popularity (because they were the most expensive and rarest) led to this cheaper imitation. White and gray powders created uniformity and were less destructive than hair dye. By the early eighteenth century, court ladies had adopted this practice as well, though they sometimes wore colored powders to enhance their complexions.[7] To contrast with white hair and to emphasize the wearer's nobility, face paint, rouge, and patches increased dramatically for both men and women under Louis XIV and continued in popularity under Louis XV.

Though cosmetics were first commercialized in Italy, by the eighteenth century, France had become the center of both the fashion and production of perfumes and cosmetics. French fashions spread to other European courts and elites. It was widely worn in the German courts and in Russia under Catherine the Great. Maria Theresa, however, forbade the archduchesses and courtiers to wear makeup, implying that there were fashionable reasons to ignore her injunction.[8] In Germany, more advice manuals on beauty were published than anywhere else in Europe: eighty-nine for the eighteenth century, with more than half coming in the last decades.[9] In England, critics compared the restraint (or expectation of it) of their own women to the excesses of the French. As Lynn Festa shows, cosmetics were the ultimate form of distinction between nations. English commentators attacked the French use of makeup and felt that it made all French women look the same, taking the individual face and turning it into a symbol of the nation.[10] The French, however, found English women's faces too pale: "Their faces look like their breasts, they are sallow due to whitening."[11] A 1798 poem equated frenchness with a playful coquette, whose beauty is enhanced by cosmetics, while foreigners and their countries have vices with "nothing covering their hideousness."[12]

The French woman defined by her paint and primping had many products to choose from. Advice manuals, advertisements, and articles in journals used the term *cosmétique* for both makeup and creams, which distinguished it from *parfumerie,* which included only products meant to add scent (to skin or to clothing). Cosmetics, in contrast, were products to clean or beautify the skin.[13] Cosmetics entailed more specifically the art of "beautifying the body; of combating ugliness, of diminishing faults which can cause . . . repulsion; of hiding natural imperfections . . . ; and even of preventing infirmities."[14] Within this wide definition of cosmetics, contemporaries included the subcategory *fard,* which consisted of "all compositions, be they of white face paint or rouge, which women and even a few men use to embellish their complexions, to imitate the colors of youth, or to repair them by artifice."[15] Thus, cosmetics were essentially divided between those that embellished beauty through improvement, such as creams and lotions, and those that masked imperfections and created the illusion of color.

In this second category of fard, two types of makeup were most popular: *blanc* and *rouge.* The dominant aesthetic in eighteenth-century France was for women and men to show their respectability and class through the whiteness of their skin. Fashionable women took many precautions to preserve fair skin, such as using parasols and hats to keep the sun out. People not born with flawless features (and few were) covered their faces with heavy makeup, which became over time more respectable than naturally light skin. Elites applied white face paint in thick layers across the entire face and shoulders to erase signs of aging, disease, and freckles. This mask could be made with a variety of ingredients. Some recipes called for bismuth or vinegar, while others preferred the white chalk of lead (*céruse*).[16] Since white lead was expensive, most perfumers preferred alum (aluminium sulfate) instead. Alum could be turned into white powder and added to a number of oils for application.[17]

If face paint was the foundation of all elite toilettes, rouge was the finishing touch, meant to highlight the wearer's shiny white skin. Red cheeks were the ideal to which both fashionable men and women aspired, but because most had their faces already masked in white, they had to turn to artificial means. Recipes called for rouge to be made of minerals such as cinnabar (mercuric sulfide, called vermillion) or red lead. It could also be made from vegetable matter, such as safflowers (*catharme*), saffron, gum benzoin (wood resin), sandalwood, and brazilwood. One of the most expensive dyes was carmine that came from female cochineal insects found in Latin America. These dyes were originally combined with vinegar or lemon, precipitated on powder using alum, and then scented with flowers. This powder could be mixed with rose water or grease for easy application with a brush. Another type of rouge was *au crépon,* dying a cloth or paper with cochineal that could be moistened and rubbed on the face. Liquid vinegar rouges were also popular because they dyed the face for longer periods, were not greasy, and were considerably cheaper to make and buy. By the middle of the eighteenth century, perfumers started selling *rouge en pot* (pots of rouge) as a simpler and more portable means of applying makeup.[18] The most common recipe for these types of products was a mixture of talcum powder, safflowers or saffron, lemon juice, and oil, a much more affordable product than rouge made with minerals.[19] Lips, however, were not necessarily reddened; instead, they were treated with almond oil or goose grease to keep them smooth and shiny.[20] If color was desired, women dabbed their lips with distilled alcohol or vinegar. By midcentury, some recipe books and sellers proposed red pomades for the lips, some were even sold in stick form.[21]

In addition to rouge and blanc, women and some men wore *mouches,* black silk beauty spots, or patches, held on by glue to highlight the skin's whiteness. Elites wore patches in a variety of positions, each one associated with a form of flirtation. For example, a patch on the forehead was called the "assassin"; a patch on the cheek was called the "gallant," and one near the lips was called the "coquette."[22] Numerous sizes and shapes suited almost any taste. One perfumer ordered an assortment of patches, varying from the size of a pea to the size of a half dollar.[23] To gain attention, court ladies organized their patches in designs, such as trees or birds on their cheeks and forehead. In England, patches took on political meaning; female supporters of Whigs and Tories sported patches on opposite sides of their faces.[24] To accentuate their whiteness, would-be or real aristocrats traced the veins of their necks and bosoms with blue coloring.[25]

Other facial alterations were used to contain natural hairlines. Men used depilatory creams to lengthen their foreheads, which was especially necessary when they
wore wigs that sat on the back of the head.[26] Women used the same creams to erad-
icate signs of facial hair and to thin their eyebrows.[27] In the late seventeenth century, both women and men plucked and painted their eyebrows, and some wore false
ones made out of mouse fur.[28] Though these forms of grooming probably continued into the eighteenth century, they were never popular beyond the court. Instead
women were told to rub their eyebrows with ripe elderberries or burnt cork to keep
them black, and a few perfumers sold more complex eye makeup.[29] Women and
men could dye their eyebrows with the same dyes used for their hair, using a small
comb or brush. Since red hair was never in fashion and blond hair not in favor until Marie-Antoinette's reign, black or brown hair dyes were popular. The safer recipes
included nuts and roots, but others contained white lead, litharge, quicklime, and
salt. A sample of white hair dyed brown and blond, found in good condition at the
archives of the Académie nationale de médecine, shows that deep auburns and strawberry blonds were possible using the chemistry of the time.[30] Even though some
men and women chose to dye their hair, most members of the economic elite wore
hair powder over either their natural hair or on a wig. As a by-product of starch,
powder was also relatively affordable, though large quantities were needed to cover
the hair. Powders came in a variety of qualities, from basic to fine, and were perfumed with orange blossom, jasmine, roses, and jonquils. Wigmakers or private individuals applied powder by blowing it onto the hair while covering the face with a
mask.

If fards were products meant to cover up blemishes or to create false color, the
purpose of other cosmetics was to enhance attractiveness by curing skin problems
and lightening the skin. Creams, lotions, and essences were touted for their cleans-
ing and whitening effects.[31] *Pommades* referred to creams made from a grease base
of either animal fat (such as pigs' hooves, butter, whale fat) or vegetable (such as olive
oil or almond oil). Their main uses were to preserve hair (and wigs) and to embellish the face. Pommades were applied to the hair to soften and clean it but were also
used for thickening and strengthening as well as helping the powder to adhere.[32]
Pommades for the face cleaned, polished, whitened, and moisturized. Specific types
were touted to remove freckles, wrinkles, and smallpox scars.[33] Fashionable women
desiring soft white hands also slept wearing gloves dipped in fat.

Another category of products was the eaux that were both scented waters and
effective cosmetics. These distillations were complicated to make but had a variety
of uses. Simple aromatic eaux, such as orange flower, jasmine, lavender, and rose,
were used to perfume clothing and the home and to wash the mouth, skin, and hair.

These essences were also used to cure illnesses such as epilepsy, lethargy, and va-
pors.[34] Other recipes were aimed at whitening the skin and reducing wrinkles. Many
of these concoctions were not even distillations but mixtures of common ingredients. Saltpeter and water, for example, were touted as an acne remedy. Men and
women used egg yolks, lemon, and balsam of Peru (a sap derived from a Central
American tree) to wash their skin. Urine, rose water, and wine supposedly eliminated
redness.[35] A distillation of pigeon, milk, and almond oil was also a popular cure.[36]

At the heart of the promises of white and unmarked skin was a fear of aging in a
society where old age came in the thirties. To postpone or mask the rapid destruction of youth, cosmetics evoked miracles. A common recipe for combating wrinkles
combined calves feet, river water, white bread, fresh butter, and ten fresh eggs.[37] To
combat wrinkles, women wore headbands around their foreheads during the night.
Perfumers also sold a popular *eau virginale* (made with vinegar), which promised to
return women to their virginal state by contracting the vaginal muscles. There were
also many mentions of *lait virginale* aimed solely at the hands and face.[38] Women
and men also feared signs of illness. Cures for acne, pockmarks, and syphilis scars
were common, as were remedies for freckles and sunburn.

Teeth, too, were to be sparkling white. Opiates, not all of which contained opium,
were meant to keep the teeth attractive.[39] Recipe books touted *dentifrice* (tooth-
paste) made of coal and sugar or orange peel and honey. Aromatic tablets made of
plants were recommended for bad breath, and scraping knives eliminated food
from the tongue and gums. Perfumers sold powders meant to whiten the teeth and
alcohol-based eaux to strengthen them.[40] When all else failed, eighteenth-century
elite turned to false teeth made of ivory, human teeth, porcelain, or even hippo-
potamus teeth. These were not perfect solutions to the increasingly gaping smiles of
the French elite because animal teeth smelled over time and porcelain turned black.

Although early seventeenth-century elite men and women washed their hair and
bodies in water, by the end of the century, water was replaced by powder, grease, and
perfume.[41] Doctors believed that water weakened the body and should be avoided
unless absolutely necessary. Fear of immersion was based on the theory that liquids
penetrated the body and could potentially harm the internal organs. The elite only
washed their face and hands regularly, dipping them every other day in aromatic waters or distilled alcohol, though some aristocrats did take full baths for sensual pleasure rather than for hygiene.[42] To fend off unwanted smells, sachets of dried flowers were carried inside one's clothes and aromatic incense was burned in the house.
The elite's attempts to mask body odors, however, would have had little effect on
the highly noxious smells of the city. Since clean water was expensive, Paris's working-
class citizens could not afford to use water for hygiene even if they had desired it.[43]

Soap was available during the eighteenth century, but bar soap made of quick-lime, soda ash, or potash served primarily as a laundry detergent. Cosmetic soap was thought to be "pernicious for the skin" because it dried it out. "Light *savonettes* made of pure cream of soap" were preferable. *Savonettes* differed from soap by the addition of perfumes and powder that dissolved in water to create a thick white paste with which to shave or to wash the face.[44] Even so, these products were not widely used until the nineteenth-century promotion of perfumed toilette soap, especially those imported from England. Instead of soaps, liquid almond paste was used to clean and to moisten the hands and face without water. Though better hygiene was a growing concern in the eighteenth century, its solutions were slow to spread, and water still remained suspect to many.

Most of the elite's toiletry efforts took place away from washbasins and in an atmosphere filled with perfume, powder, and paint. The location of this ceremony evolved over the course of the eighteenth century, with the process becoming as important as the jars of rouge themselves. In the early part of the century, no special space was set aside in the homes of the rich for beautification. Furniture sets called *coiffeuse* were marketed to provide women with appropriate toilette surroundings. Elites created new rooms for these tables whose windows faced north to avoid unwanted sunlight.[45] Men were less likely to have their own rooms for this purpose but set up toiletry tables in their bedrooms. The very wealthy constructed special wig closets to store and powder their hairpieces.

A woman's coiffeuse was decorated with many ornate boxes and bottles. Porcelain containers at the beginning of the eighteenth century helped elevate cosmetics to luxury goods. With the invention of *rouge en pot,* the wealthy could show off their taste and wealth by purchasing decorative containers. A porcelain jar from the Goncourt factory cost four gold louis, much more than the rouge stored in it.[46] Porcelain perfume bottles shaped like dogs, birds, or pretty girls, and boxes made of sweet-smelling orange peels (*bergamot*) filled with powder graced the tables of fashionable toilettes, making their contents seem more valuable. *Boites à mouches* were de rigueur for male and female outings, as well as discreet but expensive, compacts for rouge. Made of porcelain, enamel, or wood, the most expensive of these boxes were decorated with portraits or pastoral scenes.[47] A wealthy woman never left home without her traveling case, or *nécessaire,* which held her perfumes and toiletries. Marie-Antoinette commissioned a new nécessaire just before the flight to Varennes, prompting her maid to suspect that she was about to take an important trip.[48] Women carried *nécessaires de poche,* which housed one or two important bottles and brushes for emergency application, deep in the many pockets of their voluminous gowns.[49]

This detailed description of what men and women wore on their faces and hair in the eighteenth century is derived primarily from the habits of the elite. Cosmetics were essential accessories to the pomp and ceremony of the court, integral to the maintenance of its power and prestige. These fashions then spread slowly to the urban and provincial elite, which included the wealthier ranks of the Third Estate as well as the nobility. The spread of cosmetic beauty manuals and the accessibility of products meant that a much larger population was capable of adopting some if not all these practices.

Homemade to Store Bought: The Function of Beauty Manuals

Most cosmetics before the eighteenth century were homemade creations, with recipes culled from published or oral sources. This tradition was crucial in the sixteenth and seventeenth centuries when selling prefabricated perfumery goods was less common and not accessible to those living outside France's main cities. Recipes provided both men and women with the basic information to shape and to create their own toiletries. By the end of the seventeenth century, however, an increase in both perfumers and noncorporate manufacturers of cosmetics made the lengthy process of home creation less necessary, though still potentially entertaining and money saving. This development shifted production from the privacy of the home to the workshops of professionals. Recipes were no longer aimed at amateur distillers but at a budding group of literate artisans whose professional skills could be perfected and shaped. The public might still amuse themselves with home concoctions, but they now were primarily buyers.

Recipes for home remedies and beauty enhancements have a long history, dating back to the Greeks and Romans. Most of these recipes did not survive the medieval period; however, advice books became popular with the spread of cosmetics in the sixteenth century. Cosmetics recipes first appeared in *livres de secrets,* which promised readers effective love potions, stain removals, medicinal cures, and beautifying creams.[50] These early books were distinctly influenced by magic; one recipe for the darkening of the skin (an unusual desire) recommended the use of water from an alchemist's still.[51] A typical cosmetics recipe demanded large quantities of costly ingredients and much patience. Only the aristocracy and royalty had the tools to create most of the cosmetics and perfumes described in these manuals. For instance, Louis XIII made his own perfumes, while Louis XIV enjoyed watching them being made.[52]

As home distillation became popular and the use of perfume grew in the late seventeenth century, manuals started including more easily reproducible recipes. These books differed from earlier works because they depended on medical knowledge rather than folklore. Their authors were often well-known physicians or elite per-fumers. For instance, the king's doctor Lazare Meyssonnier, in *Introduction à la belle magie,* specified that he would provide memorable descriptions of all the important recipes for beauty.[53] Likely the most influential author at the end of the seventeenth century was Louis XIV's perfumer Simon Barbe who published *Le parfumeur fran-çais* in 1693 and *Le parfumeur royal* in 1699. Both works were reprinted during the eighteenth century and helped spread the popularity of home creations among the nobility.[54]

This tradition of specialized beauty books continued into the eighteenth century. Esoteric recipes, however, all but disappeared, leaving prosaic lists of ingredients that most middle-class readers could assemble. Women were singled out as the primary audience for these home creations. Simple, straightforward recipes ensured they would not endanger themselves. One female author stated that she would "facilitate the creation and explain it as comprehensively as possible, to teach women to make the products that they need."[55] Authors advocated using edible ingredients, espe-cially those found in the home. Bread was turned into skin creams and milk was mixed with eggs to create face whiteners.[56] Lemons made effective skin toners; vine-gars functioned as astringents and rouges, while almonds, honey, and fruits were guaranteed skin softeners. Indeed, because food was commonly used to create reme-dies, some people criticized recipes for their wastefulness.[57] Emphasis on foodstuffs tied these published recipes to the oral tradition and to feminine pastimes. Most eighteenth-century recipes provided only lists of ingredients, with few details on how to make or to apply the product. Even in the early nineteenth century, most recipes were vague and differed widely in their proportions. The tradition of orally trans-mitted instructions meant that women could provide the missing steps of the process, depending only on the published work for reminders of ingredients or new formulations.[58]

For each desired effect, a number of solutions were given, allowing the reader to choose between different techniques. For instance, face whitening could be achieved by various ingredients, including donkey's milk, egg whites, lemons, wheat, one's own urine, and wine.[59] Solutions for freckles, acne, dull skin, and wrinkles were even more common.[60] The lack of specific instructions allowed readers to tailor their con-coctions to available ingredients and tools. The names given to each recipe reinforced practicality by providing descriptions of cures rather than fanciful monikers. For in-stance, one list of recipes included

5th virginal milk for the embellishment of the face
6th virginal milk for the whitening of the complexion

To make spots disappear from the face

To make redness disappear.[61]

Readers could easily find what they were looking for by subject and then choose between the different options. These simple recipes continued to be reprinted throughout the eighteenth century and into the nineteenth century.

Yet during the second half of the eighteenth century, no new books of recipes aimed solely at laypeople were published, and the tone of advice changed. Manuals aimed at the public primarily focused on teaching women how to apply products properly rather than how to make them, while recipe books transformed into commercial manuals to educate professional artisans. Writers no longer expected women to be capable of producing cosmetics in the home. Instructions now made a clear distinction between recipes for the public and those for artisans. Antoine Hornot, in his manual on distillation, listed only simpler recipes for decoctions rather than the more complex *eaux cosmétiques* to make them comprehensible to the general public.[62] The division between homemade and professional products was also evident in the ingredients included: chemical ingredients were primarily the privilege of perfumers and distillers, while edible goods and plants were safer for amateurs. These authors, aware of the growing complications of chemistry and distillation, hoped to control and supervise attempts at home production. Hornot had "particularly paid attention to being clear and exact so . . . no individual can be without these ministrations, by practicing exactly what" he specified.[63] He believed that the practice of making cosmetics was not to be taken lightly and should be attempted only with proper guidance. This concern indicated a fundamental change in who could best benefit from recipes and advice. Previously authors tailored their works for lay readers, but Hornot's work was dedicated to perfumers, who though "not the only ones it can serve as a guide" made up most of its expected audience. Buc'hoz's *Toilette de Flore,* though it could teach womankind "the means of preserving their charms," was specifically a "useful work for perfumers."[64] Female readers were secondary as the market for cosmetics expanded.

During the eighteenth century, wearers of cosmetics were transformed from producers and controllers of their own concoctions to buyers of prefabricated goods. The division between simple homemade recipes and complex chemical potions reinforced the growing market for commercial cosmetics. The ease of purchasing ready-made goods was touted over the complications of private fabrication. Late eighteenth-century advice manuals distinguished between the artisans who could be better trained in their profession and the literate public who should purchase these goods in the proper market spaces. Though home production remained popular throughout the nineteenth century and into the twentieth century, it was a minor aspect of the ever-expanding cosmetics market. This shift in emphasis redefined the sphere of beauty: the manufacturers of cosmetics were increasingly seen as professionals, while the wider public was defined as consumers of proto-luxury goods.

Those Who Wore It:
Changing Patterns of Cosmetics Consumption

As the production of cosmetics shifted out of the home and into manufacturing spaces, the audience of buyers widened to include a diversity of social classes. Cosmetics became available to this larger public by the middle of the eighteenth century because of the progressive decline in the price of these goods and their increased availability throughout France. Aristocrats may have had private toilettes and porcelain jars, but cheap paper containers of rouge and powder were available in corner shops. Their buyers may not have entertained visitors in their private boudoirs, but they could purchase the same basic goods and adapt them to their lifestyles.

Historians studying probate inventories have found that mirrors were increasingly common in the homes of urban artisans and servants, suggesting their use in private practices of beautification. The ownership of brushes, dressing tables, and other accouterments of the toilette also signify a growing concern with personal appearance.[65] Though cosmetics were not listed in these inventories because of their perishable nature and low cost, plain white porcelain containers might indicate the ownership of cosmetics with cheaper and thus less ostentatious packaging. These traces of the toilette indicate that many of the lower orders followed a similar regime of ablutions than their betters.

Though the ownership of cosmetics cannot be definitively ascertained from probate inventories, the seized account books of bankrupt perfumers supply lists of their clientele. Thirty-one such books were included in this study, all from Paris. Only one book remains from the first half of the eighteenth century, with the majority of the rest coming from the 1770s and 1780s. César Robin's account book from 1737 to 1741 indicates he mostly sold to a female and aristocratic clientele. Among these women were duchesses, marquesses, the "Princesse de Bégue au Palais de Bourbon," and even the queen's servants. He strengthened his network of connections by carefully noting which clients recommended new patrons. These noblewomen bought large amounts of powder and creams, spending up to sixty livres a year on these items alone. Men were also on his client list. One especially spendthrift gentleman owed 315 livres for one year's worth of perfumes and powders.[66]

The ledgers of perfumers in the 1770s contain a greater diversity of buyers, though the lack of earlier sources does not allow any firm conclusions about a shift in clientele. The perfumer Du Haulant sold to both countesses and butchers, and Miraux had mercers, surgeons, grocers, and milkmaids on his client list.[67] Often perfumers did not even know the names of their clients, so they simply listed professions or descriptions. One was owed money by "a female servant, the husband of the market fruit-monger, the male cousin of the count, the fat female neighbor living on Verrou street, a lady with big breasts, the mother of the cask-maker, my charming female neighbor from the hôtel de Nevers, the miss with the tender eyes, a female neighbor with a sick child."[68] Artisans and servants were among those who could thus buy cosmetics. This list illustrates clearly a diversity of cosmetic buying.

If we can ascertain how much and what types of cosmetics these individuals bought, we can also surmise with what frequency cosmetics were worn. The most typical perfumer's client bought large amounts of powder and pommades but not much else. They bought one or two pounds of powder at a time and a few sticks of pommade, which could be worn as hair grease or as a cream to soften and lighten the face. The most popular cosmetics were ultimately not for the face but for the upkeep of prominent wigs. In the available records, white face paint was hardly ever mentioned as an item for sale. Mouches were more common, but neither of these items of aristocratic artifice truly crossed over into the realm of popular cosmetics. Instead, most customers bought whitening creams or continued to make these products at home.

The quantities bought by consumers varied greatly. For example, M. Brevigny purchased forty-one livres worth of cosmetics and gloves over ten months. He bought perfumes, soaps, powder, creams, and even borrowed money from his perfumer to buy a turkey![69] Over one month, Mlle and Mme Rocuchon bought fifteen livres of powder and little else.[70] Either this mother and daughter bought the rest of their cosmetics elsewhere, or they only wore a dignified amount of powder and no paint. In a much larger order, Mlle Lahaye bought fifty livres worth of powder, creams, gloves, rouge, patches, fake teeth, and perfume all in one day but failed to pay her bill on time. Other buyers returned multiple times in a month to buy small amounts of powder and creams, the two items that were consumed the fastest.[71] The account books of perfumers indicate a diversity of practices and a clientele who probably shared their spending between various shops and outlets. Though it is difficult to generalize from these books, the impression is of a clientele who bought certain core goods regularly and periodically splurged for more expensive items.

Though these lists of clients do not tell us much about the day-to-day beauty practices of individuals, they do indicate whether men and women bought different products. One merchant sold both weaponry and hair powder to his male clientele.[72] The fard that appealed to both sexes, at least for a time, was rouge. A detailed inventory from 1768 shows both men and women buying rouge one pot at a time.[73] One provincial gentleman ordered "theater rouge," while another complained that his shipment of face paint and rouge was delayed.[74] It is difficult, however, to judge whether these men were buying for their wives or for themselves. It would be safe to say that up until the 1780s, some men purchased rouge for their own use. Though few account books for the 1780–1800 period remain, perfumer Nager's book shows a growing division between women's and men's purchases, with women purchasing most of the rouge and pomades and men continuing to buy perfumes and powder.[75] Rouge was only 1 percent to 7 percent of the total sales of official perfumers. Rouge undoubtedly made up a larger percentage of purchases since numerous specialized rouge sellers operated outside guild strictures.[76]

Historians of consumerism and gender have argued that a growing differentiation among male and female fashion habits had occurred by the end of the century, anchored in the "cult of domesticity." The discussion of fashion had become feminized and trivialized, as Jennifer Jones has shown convincingly, which implied rejection of cosmetics by men.[77] Though this is definitively the case in texts, it does not relate as directly to the purchases of consumers. A shift certainly occurred around 1780 that pushed men away from using visible makeup. Men continued to buy other toiletries, such as powder, creams, and perfumes in large quantities. By the early nineteenth century, as wigs became less popular, hair tonics and oils aimed primarily at men became the most prominent cosmetics on the market. The feminization of makeup still left room for men to participate in the practices of the toilette.

Even if men and women bought similar amounts, the cost of cosmetics circumscribed which classes could afford them. Prices varied greatly, depending both on quality and on reputation of the seller. Most perfumers offered wholesale discounts to other artisans, such as wigmakers and hairdressers. For instance, Méry sold his powder number six (of lesser quality) for one livre nineteen sols to wigmakers but to other clients for two livres two sols.[78] One ounce of good powder typically sold for eight sols to clients.[79] Two ounces of pommades sold for between two and five sols, though up to one livre for fancier scented ones.[80] However, if these creams were marketed as special cures, they were among the most expensive purchases. A pommade made with snails sold to eliminate freckles cost one livre five sols for a two-ounce bottle, and the famous *Pommade de Ninon,* meant to eliminate wrinkles, cost three livres.[81] Rouge had the most varied prices of any product. A jar of rouge might be sold for one sol sixteen deniers to sixty livres, depending on its quality. Leaving aside the luxury rouge sold by Mme Martin, which sold for sixty to eighty livres, most sellers sold their "superfine" rouge for between ten sols and three livres, depending on the packaging.[82]

One commentator felt that these prices were "so cheap, that the smallest *grisettes* can lay out as much as a person of the highest birth."[83] Yet an anecdote by Giacomo Casanova indicates what these prices really signified to a less-privileged cosmetics buyer. Having gone to visit a young girl whom he was helping financially (and found attractive), he watched her toilette in awe of her beauty. The spell was broken when the beauty's maid chastised her for spending on "combs, powder and creams the three livres that she had been given."[84] Three livres was not a large sum for the rich, but it represented half of a laborer's weekly wages.[85] The wages of journeymen would have been considerably higher, ranging from ten to fifty livres a week, with most falling somewhere in-between.[86] Master artisans earned more, but independent businesspeople risked more as well. Women workers tended to earn less then men, though those running their own businesses could rise to the level of master artisans. Most of the working classes could not indulge in rouge and powder every day, but they could on special occasions. In small quantities, artisans and the wealthier working classes could buy most of these products. Many, like their noble counterparts, ran up substantial debts in the account books of perfumers.

Wages for servants and wage earners increased over the course of the eighteenth century, allowing a greater proportion to go to consumer goods.[87] Amid rising wages, however, was an even sharper increase in the cost of living.[88] Though this circumstance increased poverty among the rural peasantry, the Parisian working classes managed to survive and even purchase nonessential goods. Jan de Vries explains this contradiction by arguing that an "industrious revolution" occurred before the Industrial Revolution, starting in the mid-seventeenth century in the Netherlands and Britain.[89] More time was spent at work and less at leisure, allowing for a shift by the eighteenth century in the purchases of the working classes in France, from everyday objects to consumer goods such as fashionable clothing. Daniel Roche has found proof that even poorer workers exchanged "durable investments for consumer objects." Though their economic situations did not necessarily improve, the working classes of Paris did not forgo buying consumer goods enjoyed by the wealthier around them. Instead, they gave up household necessities such as pots and pans to buy mirrors, dresses, and, as indicated in the account books of perfumers, cosmetics.[90]

The rich did not often have to leave the privacy of their boudoirs to increase their beauty, enlisting the services of hairdressers, servants, and *modistes*. The middle and artisanal classes purchased these same services in shops specializing in the toilette.

Male customers frequented the stores of wigmakers who powdered wigs for a small fee. Louis-Sébastien Mercier described these shops as dirty, disgusting places, filled with putrid powder. The clients of these establishments were the neighborhood artisans who came on Sundays to have their wigs prepared for the evening's opera.[91] Men of all classes also paid to have themselves shaved by barbers, though in Paris shaving became increasingly a private ritual.[92] Nicolas-Edmé Restif de la Bretonne lamented that "I was the only man in Paris who still went to have himself shaved . . . in the wigmaker's store."[93] Women of the lower orders could have their hair done by hairdressers or they could do it themselves. The shops of perfumers also provided the tools for applying makeup and related practices, such as removing hair.

Shopping was increasingly a form of entertainment in the second half of the eighteenth century. For browsers and consumers, perfume stores, like those of other luxury trade, were part of the pleasure of public outings. The rue St Honoré and rue Richelieu attracted high-end buyers. Yet Restif de La Bretonne compared the rue St Honoré to a bazaar, where luxury and commerce mingled with prostitution and charlatanism.[94] Similarly, Mercier described the shopping in the Palais-Royal as both the most opulent and the most deceptive. The "eyes are fascinated by all the exterior decorations, which dupe the curious, who realize the trickery . . . only too late."[95] Though a pleasure ground for the elite, "debauched youths, thieves, *petits maîtres,* swindlers, prostitutes, and financiers" patronized the infamous *galeries de bois,* less permanent structures with cheaper rents.[96] Shopping was a perilous pastime that allowed for the intermingling of men and women in public, creating arenas for deception. Both male and female shoppers endangered the viability of the family: pretty shopgirls tempted men, while tempting products led women into financial excesses.[97] Casanova was more forgiving, describing the Palais-Royal as "a rather nice garden, . . . numerous men and women strolling" with "benches here and there where one sells new pamphlets, perfumed scents, tooth-picks, and knick-knacks."[98] Over time the threats to respectability diminished. Stores developed window displays, visiting areas, and lighting. Women may have shunned nighttime excursions, but during the daytime, the streets and fairs of Paris were filled with the intermingling of genders and ranks. In particular, the wives and daughters of artisans, often owners of their own businesses, had no fear of visiting neighboring stores for purchases.

Cosmetics could also be purchased in locales aimed at the working classes. Restif de la Bretonne described the atmosphere at the Foire Saint-Laurent as an ideal place for foisting unsaleable products onto unsuspecting consumers. There he saw "a few miserly, badly furnished stores; fortune-hunters laying out fashions like spiders arranging their webs."[99] The fair atmosphere allowed for more freedom in buying and thus more possibilities of lower prices and bargains. Street-corner sellers and itinerants also allowed the poorer urban classes to purchase products in their neighborhoods. Though there were no used cosmetics on the market (food was sold half-eaten, so why not rouge?), there were numerous venues that allowed working-class consumers to participate in the joy of purchasing beauty.

According to these same commentators, each social class had their own method of brightening their complexions. Court ladies wore rouge in uneven swaths across the face, from the corner of the eyes to the corner of the lips, to put sparkle in the gaze. Casanova argued that this intentionally artificial style was meant to invoke past dalliances and future escapades.[100] As a schoolboy, the Count of Fersen observed the Countess of Brionne putting on her makeup. After applying powder, she used a small knife to scrape off any that had landed on her face. Then one of her servants brought her a box containing six pots of rouge and one that seemed to contain something black. After she applied it, he realized it contained "the most beautiful red one could see." She then added to this first layer from the other six pots, two at a time.[101] The countess's many hues indicate the expensive and artistic (or artificial) nature of the toilette for the elite. While visiting Paris, Henri Walpole stated that the princesses of the blood wore their rouge in the deepest red, "though all use it extravagantly."[102] In contrast, women of the bourgeoisie and the provincial nobility wore neat, circular dabs at the center of their cheeks while men sported theirs in small circles high on their cheekbones. The different hues of rouge were associated with specific social groups: the lighter pinks with the bourgeoisie and the darker reds with prostitutes and actresses.[103] Yet Mercier condemned the "ghastly mistresses of apprentice butchers" who wore rouge the color of blood and compared them to the "loose courtesans of the Palais Royal" who wore "rose colored" rouge.[104] Thus, in his description, it was the wives of artisans who copied the elites and the courtesans who wished to mimic the bourgeoisie. In this confusion, both emulation and distinction are present, but neither one seems to be definitive. While court rouge was set in tone and style, other forms and tones of rouge seem to have shifted meanings, depending on context, wearer, and, even more important, the commentator's opinion.

Anecdotes, such as Mercier's numerous snapshots of life in Paris, help us better understand what options were available for consumers of makeup. Like many available sources, however, they are the generalized witty observations of a few opinionated men. To visualize the wearing of rouge, face paint, patches, and powder, it is useful to turn to the iconography of the period. I have studied a variety of paintings and engravings, focusing especially on portraiture. There are inherent problems with using painting to reflect the use of cosmetics. First, paintings represent idealized versions of beauty and the individual tastes of the painter as much as the reality of daily life. When a client complained that her complexion was painted inaccurately, Hyacinthe Rigaud responded, "It's astonishing—for my rouge comes from the same merchant as yours."[105] Even when the sitter had a say in how the painting looked, she (or he) was likely to pick a flattering pose and a mythologized version of herself. The popularity of allegorical portraits makes reading the fashion of the face even more difficult. Second, many paintings, especially after 1770, which show red cheeks and white skin, were attempting not to create the dissimulation of paint with paint but instead to reproduce the ideal of a natural beauty.

Genre paintings by François Boucher, Jean-Honoré Fragonard, and their followers depict young, beautiful women almost always with blushing cheeks and pale skin. Denis Diderot criticized Boucher for his "affectation, romantic gallantry, coquetry . . . rouged flesh tones, and debauchery."[106] Boucher's paintings, especially *Le dejeuner* (1739) and *La toilette* (1742), depict the full panoply of cosmetics available: hair powder, face paint, mouches, rouge, lip pomade, and black for the eyebrows. Fragonard tones down this excess in his paintings from the 1750s through the 1770s, emphasizing instead creamy skin and well-rouged cheeks. Yet even his shepherds and shepherdesses are highly made-up.[107] Jean-Baptiste-Siméon Chardin's more restrained images depict servants and bourgeois mothers with rosy cheeks, though only the later have whitened skin.[108] These scenes reflect the beauty aesthetic of the period and, in many instances (especially the scenes of amorous tryst), imply a virginal blush rather than applied artifice.

Indicative of what elite women wore are portraits painted from 1750 to 1775. Jean-Marc Nattier's extremely flattering portraits of the royal family, high aristocracy, and *arrivistes* show women with bright, deep pink color applied in a wide circle across the cheek. For example, a 1749 portrait of Mme Marsollier, the social-climbing wife of a silk merchant, with her daughter, shows them at the toilette table in dishabille but fully made-up. As a rich woman with low social status, the sitter adopted the conventions of aristocratic makeup and pastimes (the extended toilette) to associate herself with and thus emulate her betters.[109] The style that she was emulating can be found in a number of portraits of Louis XV's daughters, depicted as enchanting and well-rouged virtuous members of the royal family.

The six hundred or so watercolor profile portraits of aristocrats, artists, and scientists by Louis Carrogis Carmontelle provide a wider snapshot of cosmetic practices. Carmontelle painted quickly while the sitters busied themselves with their everyday activities. Almost all of Carmontelle's women, no matter what age, rank, or profession, sport round, deep orange pink rouge, which takes up almost the entire cheek from ear to eye to mouth (figure 1). Only a few wear mouches, and the skin is pure white (unpainted on the page). Carmontelle's men are a more diverse

Figure 1. Carmontelle, *Madame la comtesse de Rochechouart* (1759), Réunion des musées nationaux/Art Resource, NY

group. Some wear no distinctive color, while others sport shades of pink along the cheekbone of a tanned face. Those in court dress are more likely to be depicted with rouge than those in less formal garb.[110] Overall, paintings of the royal family, aristocracy and bourgeois elite by a variety of artists generally depict them as wearing round daubs of color, from orange to pink, with little bright red represented. These portraits emphasize the uniformity of paint among the elite, while downplaying the extreme color and stripes described by commentators.

A second group of portraits shows a different ideal of cosmetic beauty. Portraits of older aristocrats (outside of Carmontelle's oeuvre), nobility living outside the court spotlight, and the upper bourgeoisie depict much more subtle use of color, with no clear demarcation between the skin and the makeup. In Nattier's portraits of Marie Leszcysnka, the Queen of France, and the Comtesse de Tessin in private settings, both women sport light-colored rouge (or the symbol of natural color) spread out across their faces. These two older women, certain of their social positions, chose to be pictured in informal garb.[111] Similarly, Jean-Baptiste Greuze's 1749 portrait of Mme Léger de Sorbet depicts her with a generally flushed face rather than the distinct lines of makeup. Joseph-Siffrid Duplessis' painting of Mme Lenoir, wife of a stocking merchant and mother of Alexandre Lenoir, the painter and founder of the museum of French monuments, shows a good *bourgeoise* with slightly rosy cheeks on pale but not whitened skin. Jacques Louis David's portrait of his cousin Mlle Buron (1769) portrays her with flushed pink cheeks on mottled, apricot-toned skin, not the bright white face of an aristocrat.[112] The elderly Mme Faventines, painted by Jean Valade, was a wealthy aristocrat, but her manner (doing needlework), dress, and face show her as a dignified matron who no longer painted her face.

These images show the diversity of fashions available for women outside the court. Young and old could wear paint many ways that were not categorized as described by commentators such as Mercier. The amount, color, and application of makeup depended as much on age and circumstance as on status. Court expectations dictated the use of makeup in a specific setting, but many aristocrats and up-and-coming *bourgeoises* chose not to depict themselves so obviously in their portraits. Rouge and face paint were the norm, but their application (on canvas) varied. Consumers who shopped the stores of the Palais Royale had choices: they could emulate their betters for an evening at the theater with thick dabs of rouge, be commemorated in painting with a rosy blush, and spend their private hours at home with no makeup on.

Conclusion

The growth of a population with a disposable income made possible the market of cheap luxury goods. Luxury goods could enter the homes of artisans and servants, allowing them to participate in fashion on a larger scale. This economic development represented a shift in the *mentalité* of the working classes. Luxury goods became necessities for those who had previously owned only a few essential items. Wearing cosmetics enacted in a visible way the new consumerism. Even though cosmetics were associated with the court and aristocracy, members of the lower nobility and middle class adopted rouge and face paint, with a new emphasis. The porcelain jars of nobles were rivaled by stoneware or paper cones of rouge in the homes of artisans. The swaths of thick rouge of courtiers lived alongside the round rosy cheeks of the urban matron, though neither style was limited to one specific group.

As Mercier stated, it was not so much the rouge that changed, but the price and thus the image each class had of it: "women of the court, who play a high stakes game, pay one louis for a small pot; women of quality, six francs; courtesans twelve francs; and the bourgeoises, who wear it imperceptibly, do not haggle."[113] Rather than indicating a rampant emulation of elites, wearing makeup by a broader base of consumers helped delimit rank, occupation, age, and gender, while at the same time keeping these categories malleable. Because makeup could both delimit classes and provide hope of emulation, along with private self-fashioning, it was a cheap and available way for women and men to participate in the consumer revolution.

CHAPTER TWO

A Market for Beauty

The Production of Cosmetics

Merchants in shops . . . are entrepreneurs who buy at a set price and who resell in their stores or in public places at an uncertain price. What encourages and maintains these types of entrepreneurs is that consumers . . . will pay a little more to buy what they need in retail.   —Richard Cantillon, *Essai sur la nature du commerce*

Cantillon's 1755 essay on commerce posited the development of a consumer public that looked to fulfill their needs in the stores of entrepreneurs selling both necessities and luxuries such as cosmetics. His basic understanding of supply and demand reflects an eighteenth-century shift in market representations. Enlightenment ideals stressed the need for "production, free trade, and a balanced budget . . . Consumption would no longer be decided by rank, but by the market."[1] Mercantilism, guild protectionism, monopoly, and product control were slowly being replaced by laissez-faire, independent producers, free enterprise, and consumer choices. In this shift, the essential relationship was between the buyer and the seller, rather than within guilds or privileged bodies. The change in the eighteenth century was not only in market perception, but in its function. At the end of the century, the increase in buyers of cosmetics transformed the retail world and the relationship between sellers and buyers.

Like all merchants of nonessentials, cosmetic entrepreneurs had to learn to sell their goods in a freer market that catered to increasingly savvy and demanding customers. As we have seen, men and women of the upper and middle classes no longer made all their own cosmetic products at home but turned to purchasing them in stores. At the same time, artisans and servants began to purchase luxury and fashion goods, which had been previously limited to the elites. These intertwined developments enlarged the possibilities for commerce. Artisans had to increase the scope of their offerings and lower their prices to cater to both the shopping elite and the working classes. Producers responded to consumer demand and helped create it. The close-knit world of Parisian trades conceived and created the populuxe goods, which altered the lives of those who made them as much as those who bought them. Sellers of cosmetics helped make available products at reasonable prices, sold in accessible locations, and appealed to a diverse consumer base. The development of a responsive and reactive production economy was essential for creating a consumer society. A consumer revolution may have occurred before the Industrial Revolution, but, without the conscious interaction of supply and demand, the desire to consume would have had no outlet or shape.

The "bazaar economy" of the late eighteenth century consisted of a hodgepodge of artisanal goods, not yet industrialized, but no longer strictly based on systems of patronage and guild monopoly. Luxuries aimed at the elite were sold alongside reproductions fabricated with cheaper materials or ingredients. Artisans continued to work within guild regulations by providing the quality and tradition associated with luxury goods. But, as Gail Bossenga shows, guilds were "transformed by merchants into flexible instruments that served mercantile interests in the competitive world of commercial capitalism."[2] Manufacturers often ignored or broke from guild strictures to make a diversity of cheap populuxe goods available to the larger public of buyers.[3] Cosmetics made ideal populuxe consumer products because they could be manufactured without large expense, and their perishable nature meant constant demand. The techniques for producing cosmetics were widely available in manuals or through oral tradition, and little capital was required to enter the trade. Such conditions made it largely impossible for the guilds to control prices, quality, and output. The possibility of quick and easy financial profit attracted numerous noncorporate sellers, who promoted the purchase of their goods over homemade production. The growing demand for affordable luxuries, the decline of guild monopolies, and the ease with which cosmetics could be manufactured encouraged the development of a thriving market for *fards* and perfumes. In turn, the creation of new forms of production and selling further promoted consumer demand, encouraging people to shop for their needs and desires. Though still functioning within artisanal modes of production and the structures of guild finance, the commerce of cosmetics at the end of the century expanded its scope and established new selling methods. Those producers who separated themselves from the guild structure and branded their name and image as accessible to all consumers succeeded in the highly competitive world of the beauty trades.

Creating a Free Market: The Perfumers' Guild and Its Rivals

The transformation of the public from producers to consumers and the entrance of the working classes into the market profoundly affected the professional production of cosmetics. With cosmetics' newfound popularity came competition among sellers, pitting those with guild privileges against those without, with each hoping to make a profit from artifice. Under guild rules, the manufacture and sale of goods was traditionally controlled by masters. The guilds of perfumers, mercers, wigmakers, vinegar makers, and apothecaries monopolized different facets of the toilette. As products and their fabrication evolved, guilds were unable to control the illicit production and sale of goods, as well as the publication of secrets, by a diverse set of independent entrepreneurs. Yet it was precisely this race—pursued by both guild members and illegal producers—to dominate constantly changing fashions that turned the commerce of cosmetics into a thriving, innovative branch of the larger luxury market.

Under the corporate system of the Old Regime, each guild's council supervised goods for price and quality. Guild regulations were meant to foster equality of enterprise for the seller and safety for the buyer.[4] Regulations also limited the number of masters and ensured profits for those who gained this valued title. The guilds' overall concern was to maintain skills, rights, and morality. Luxury trades, however, held a privileged position within the hierarchy of professions. They supplied the aristocracy with finery, and their members could become quite wealthy. Michael Sonenscher argues that the luxury trades represented both labor diversification and potential commercial innovations outside guild control. Artisans from different professions worked together to make sumptuous *chinoiserie* and textiles for the French court and nobility. Because of the diversity of tasks and the patronage of the aristocracy, makers of luxury goods were free to negotiate prices, to set levels of quality, and to gain financial wealth.[5]

Cosmetics, however, did not necessitate large outputs of labor or capital and were not sold solely to the aristocracy. Yet cosmetics producers were as much a part of the commercialization of luxury as other manufacturers. Though their profits were never as high as furniture makers, their customer base had greater potential. One reason for their commercial potential was that cosmetics never truly functioned within guild strictures. Cosmetics were easy to define as an overarching concept but hard to enumerate, as new potions were invented regularly. This meant that most cosmetic products were not assigned to any one guild and could be legally produced by any artisan or independent producer. The low cost of cosmetics, compared with other luxury goods, meant that they were sold by street sellers, in specialty stores, or directly to the aristocracy by private hairdressers and seamstresses. Ultimately, the ill-defined nature of cosmetics meant that guild members constantly struggled to enforce their own monopolies and definitions of their goods. These struggles allowed for a diversity of commercial possibilities that increased the production of beauty goods.

The main contender for the production of cosmetics was the perfumers' guild, first established as the leather glove makers guild in 1190. In the sixteenth century, French chemists developed methods for macerating plants in vegetable oil and animal greases, which shifted the commerce of perfumes away from the southern Mediterranean to the flower-growing centers of Grasse and Montpellier and from there to the shops of Parisian glove makers who started perfuming gloves and other leather goods.[6] Because of this connection, the glove makers were given a monopoly over perfume in 1614.[7] Throughout the seventeenth century, gloves remained the guild's principal trade, but it also produced "smells and scents . . . for the commodity of their estate and profession."[8] By the eighteenth century, wearing gloves had declined but fragrances for scenting clothing and houses remained popular. New technological advances, such as distilling essential oils and extracting essences using fats—a process that allowed the flowers' scents to be transferred directly to creams and other greases—helped broaden the use of perfumes in cosmetics.[9] Because of their past association with perfume, glove makers argued for their legitimate right to control this growing market. The glove maker–perfumers fought legal battles against the manufacture and selling of cosmetics by other guilds, provincial perfumers, itinerant hawkers, and independent producers. Court rulings throughout the eighteenth century favored the perfumers as the rightful producers of cosmetics.

The most prominent and dangerous rival the perfumers faced were the mercers, members of the elite *Six corps* of guilds.[10] In both 1689 and 1754, court rulings reiterated the perfumers' right to sell perfumes and soaps to the exclusion of the mercers.[11] In 1766, the mercers took the glove makers and perfumers to court for seizing cases of creams and essences a mercer brought from Grasse.[12] The mercers pleaded "artisans such as the glove-makers are not meant to be the inspectors of commerce to real trades people."[13] Though the perfumers won the case, they did not have the clout to enforce their claims against the more powerful mercers. Throughout the eighteenth century, mercers continued openly to sell creams, makeup, and other cosmetics.

Other guilds also threatened the perfumers. The wigmakers, who constantly battled the hairdressers, encroached on the perfumers' monopoly over hair powder and pomades. A 1726 edict maintained the

> master perfumers in the right to make pastes, scented oils, essences, powders,
> soaps, and other merchandise and perfumes dependant of their state as glove-
> makers and perfumers and to sell to the public this merchandise; permits the

barber-wigmakers to make at their own locations powder, soaps, opiates, essences, pastes to wash the hands and other perfumes used for ornamentation, cleanliness, and neatness of the human body, for their own use only and to be used and consumed in their stores and houses.[14]

This specific enumeration of products to be sold, displayed, and employed by the different guilds was a triumph for the perfumers. It reinforced their right to sell to the public all goods pertaining to their profession and limited the wigmakers to making cosmetics for their business use only. More important, this ruling specified what constituted cosmetics as a consumer item to be sold in the perfumer's store. This edict clearly defined the perfumers' control over the cosmetics market, but the wigmakers, like the mercers, most likely ignored it.

Rulings against the production of powder by starch makers also attempted to reinforce the perfumers' control over private consumption. Starch makers supplied perfumers and wigmakers with the basis for making perfumed hair powder. In 1751, the guild seized the property and fined a master starch maker 120 livres for producing hair powder out of starch and talcum.[15] The court ruled in favor of the perfumers, strengthening their control over the sale of cosmetics and also defining the appropriate sphere for consumption. According to the ruling, the illegal creation and sale of powder by an untrained starch maker was not a legitimate venue for creating specialty goods meant to represent the highest fashions of France. Scented powder should be created publicly and by those who had the know-how to make it well.

Even more indicative of the permeability of the perfumers' empire was the vinegar makers' legal right to make cosmetic vinegars. In 1750, the vinegar guild had the scented vinegars of a perfumer seized. The police ruling of 1752 sided with the perfumers, giving them the right to make scented vinegars out of products bought from vinegar makers, limiting the vinegar makers to condiments. But in 1754, the vinegar guild regained their right to make scented vinegars, banning the perfumers from doing so. Finally, in 1756, they reached a compromise. Both could sell scented vinegars, but they had to purchase the necessary guild-controlled ingredients from one another.[16] Though the perfumers lost this battle, allowing vinegar makers to sell cosmetics expanded the market for new and more complex products.

The Parisian perfumers faced other competitors besides rival guilds. Provincial perfumers and itinerant sellers competed for the Parisian market. Most provincial perfumers or wholesalers came from Grasse, the main center for cultivating and distilling flowers. Grasse wholesalers had the right to sell their goods to Parisian perfumers only after registering them at the guild office, located on the rue de la Pelleterie on the Left Bank. There, a clerk from the guild inventoried the goods to assess their quality and price. Frequently, itinerant merchants without registration papers were caught selling goods to perfumers or, worse, directly to the public. The Parisian guild most often won these cases, but their number indicates the extent of the problem and suggests that other hawkers most likely succeeded in cheating the guild.[17] There were other means for outsiders to gain protection. One seller of cosmetic cleansers gained access to other cities through the approval not only of various guilds but also of "the magistrates of the principal cities of France."[18] The police commissioner issued permissions to hawkers from both Paris and the provinces.[19] This approval was especially important for artisans who were entering into the territory of another guild. For instance, a grocer placed his police protection before his advertisement for perfumes.[20] The department of commerce could issue similar endorsement to bypass guild approval.

Local small-time operators were even more troublesome than provincial peddlers because they saw cosmetics as the means of making a living. The many rulings on cosmetics, passed down by the courts to the guild, never specifically included the fabrication of rouge. This lacuna allowed a thriving, unregulated business to emerge within the Parisian working class. This free market was especially tempting to women who could fabricate and sell their own products to either support themselves or supplement their husbands' incomes. In 1778, the perfumers' guild threatened Mme Martin, who sold the most expensive rouge in Paris, but she won because its statutes did not specify the sale of that product.[21] In addition to rouge, other products were also only nominally associated with perfumers. Hair dye, magical whitening potions, and any product labeled "new" could not be controlled by the guilds' archaic system of classification. After 1776, women were allowed to enter the guilds. Steven Kaplan finds that between 1785 and 1788, twenty women became glove makers, some of whom might have also been perfumers.[22] Thus, from street corners, doorways, and stores, new female entrepreneurial retailers sold goods of their own invention in opposition to and in competition with reigning and more visible male perfumers.

Like the *marchandes de mode* studied by Jennifer Jones, these women used "cracks in the corporate system of production and retailing for their own advantage."[23] And as with clothing, contemporaries increasingly saw rouge and makeup as the prerogative of women, both in terms of consumption and production. Cosmetic creation was an acceptable feminine trade, especially when it could be depicted as a frivolous pastime. Clare Crowston traces the feminization of the women's clothing trade based on the argument that sewing was a female pastime.[24] Yet female artisans were often labeled immoral, easily seduced by both luxury and debauched upper-class men. Contemporaries depicted shopping for luxury goods and fashion as a courtship between the male buyer and the immoral shopgirls. The lowly artisan could also become corrupted by her own power within the fashion world by wanting to purchase the goods that she produced.[25] Female rouge makers may have suffered from this denigration of their commerce, but ultimately they benefited from participating in a trade that was less hierarchical or grueling than the sewing trades.

The profitable market of cosmetics could be entered by anyone with a little know-how. Commercial manuals, which supplanted recipe books, allowed a growing population of literate workers to gain skills previously controlled by the guilds. Artisans willing to divulge trade secrets, seemingly in opposition to guild protectionism, were commonplace in the second half of the eighteenth century as corporate control declined. The publication of Diderot's *Encyclopédie* (1751–1777) and the *Dictionnaire universel de commerce* (1759–1765) also helped establish the writing of commercial manuals as a legitimate scientific pursuit. Yet no eighteenth-century perfumer chose to divulge his secrets, and few seemed to have owned or used such manuals.[26] Instead, distillers, apothecaries, or doctors published recipes for cosmetics.[27] Those who published advice or recipes promoted their works as trustworthy means of gaining skills far surpassing those of the corner charlatan or even the master artisan.

Because perfumers produced goods that depended on the whims of fashion, the definition and control of their products were difficult. Though the guild was able to define the creation and sale of private goods in a public marketplace, they were ultimately unable to prevent others from profiting from the growing market. Guild members were increasingly alienated from their own system of regulations. It was impossible for the perfumers' guild to get enough past officials (*jurés*) to serve on their assembly, and it became harder over time to get experienced members to serve or to pay their fees.[28] Successful guild members did not feel pressured to participate actively in the corporate system. Because of its financial difficulties, the guild opened up its ranks to larger numbers of outsiders through the system of selling masterships for 500 livres to those outside the apprentice system, which allowed unofficial sellers to legitimize themselves but strengthened the free market rather than guild traditions.[29]

Never fully in control of their products, the perfumers' guild was further weakened by Turgot's abolishment of the guilds from January to August 1776. Turgot argued that the guilds' control over who could manufacture and sell goods restricted commerce, inflated consumer prices, and retarded progress. Turgot's reforms did not last, and most guilds were reinstituted until their dissolution during the Revolution.[30] Yet after August 1776, women were allowed to participate, and those who opened shops during the brief period of liberty were allowed, for a fee, to remain in business.[31] In the already fractured world of cosmetics sales, this moment of liberty reinforced the power of outsiders. The constant pressure of competition, though divisive for the guild structure, forced cosmetics producers to turn to new forms of legitimacy and marketing, which became the basis for the commercial development of beauty.

The Making of Artifice: The System of Production and Sales

As the popularity of home production and the power of the guilds declined, space opened up for educating and promoting a new kind of artisan. Successful retailers presented themselves to the public as the antithesis of the decried charlatan whose only aim was to cheat the public with shoddy goods. Instead, the new artisans were literate, professionally trained artists whose goods and services were not so much legitimated by their corporate affiliation as by their own merit. To survive in the highly competitive yet thriving market for artifice, luxury artisans had to position themselves as purveyors of recognizable commodities with a respectable clientele but also deal with changing fashions and innovations. In the small world of cosmetics manufacture and retail, entrepreneurs jockeyed to get ahead in an economy that often led to bankruptcy and instability. Some who succeeded did so because of traditional patronage of the court and aristocracy that bound them to the trade as well as to a regular clientele. Other retailers, however, thrived by using new forms of production and selling beyond the realms of patronage. By the late eighteenth century, a few manufacturers had even established large-scale industries that evolved into the factories of the nineteenth century.

The production and selling of cosmetics was based on a complex system of interrelations between producers and sellers. Some manufacturers fabricated products to be sold wholesale; others simply sold their products directly to the public. Most enterprises mixed retail and wholesale, production, and selling. Perfumers might buy rouge and creams from other perfumers, while selling their own wholesale powder to wigmakers and mercers.[32] Wholesalers and retailers in Paris received their perfumes and flower essences from manufacturers in Grasse either directly or through itinerant hawkers. Trade also took place between artisans in other parts of France. The Parisian perfumer Tellier sold goods to glove makers in Dauphiné and Grenoble and bought products from a merchant in Lyon and a starch maker from Lorraine.[33]

Sellers who aimed their goods at the public could also cater to a variety of price ranges and audiences. However, three main groups of retailers can be identified in the eighteenth century: (1) those who sold solely to the aristocracy, some even limiting themselves to the court; (2) those who catered to the lower classes in more informal settings; and (3) those who aimed to bridge the gap between the elite and urban bourgeois consumers through the establishment of respectable stores. Of the three, the most likely to succeed were the last. Itinerant sellers did not have job security. And those who sold solely to the aristocracy were dependent on systems of patronage and credit that could be highly profitable but had little room for expansion and presented considerable risks. The third group, who sought public renown with a broad-based clientele, had the best chance of surviving and becoming recognizable brand names by the nineteenth century.[34]

The most elite perfumers were well-known names to members of the eighteenth-century aristocracy, but their presence in the wider market was minimal. Houbigant, Lubin, and Fargeon were celebrated court perfumers under both the Old Regime and the Napoleonic period, and their trademarks are still in use today. Fargeon was Louis XV's official perfumer, and Houbigant opened *À la corbeille de fleurs* on the faubourg Saint-Honoré in 1775 with the patronage of the Duchesse de Charoste.[35] The Baronne d'Oberkirch visited Mme Martin's rouge store in 1776 and reported that "Mme Martin, approved of by the Queen and all the female royalty in Europe, is a real power . . . she sends her jars of rouge to queens; rarely does a duchess get hold of one by mistake. We made fun of her self-importance."[36] An artisan's snobbery, even one with an elite client list, seemed ridiculous and uncalled for to the aristocracy. Yet Martin, Lubin, and Fargeon were able to gain financial if not social standing and, like other luxury artisans, may have associated themselves and their families with merchants, professionals, and even the lower nobility.[37]

Retailers who aimed their wares at the lower echelons of society were more influential in developing a diverse buying public. Fairchild argues that illegal producers of lesser-quality populuxe goods were responsible for the growth of consumerism in the late eighteenth century.[38] These retailers enabled artisans, servants, and actresses to afford rouge and powder. They often did not own their own shops, setting up ad hoc sales spaces with friends or relations, selling goods from doorways, or, using networks of servants, taking their goods directly to clients' homes. All these retailers needed was a home workshop or a simple connection to a wholesaler. Hawkers were threatening to perfumers because they had direct access to the public. The itinerant "comes to the best parts of town, laying out his wares as openly and as tranquilly as the citizen merchant exposes and sells in his store, having an even greater advantage over the merchant, by knocking on the doors of houses liberally and is often led as far as the toilettes of ladies."[39] Though merchants feared the influence of itinerant sellers on respectable ladies, the lower echelons of Parisian retailers mostly sold their goods to the working classes, especially other artisans and servants.

Between these two extremes were sellers who catered to a wide swathe of customers and who relied principally on their storefronts as a visible sign of their commerce. Though some of these sellers focused their energies mostly on catering to the urban middling classes, most attempted to make their products and shops appealing to all ranks. First businesses needed a storefront. Perfumers' shops varied as much as their clientele. Successful businesses presented luxurious fronts to the public. Mirrors, mahogany, and gilding framed the items for sale in opulent surroundings. Elite perfumers set up display cases, both in their windows and inside to best present their wares, using counters and chairs for the comfort of customers. Mme Cradock, visiting from England, was impressed by a pharmacy in Lyon that occupied five rooms and sold products she had not seen elsewhere.[40] The outsides of these shops were no less eye catching. Artisans set up boards (*tapis*) on which to pin their wares for exterior display, hoping to lure customers inside the store. Distinctive signs, which identified stores by name, were also essential to the promotion of a luxury shop. Luxury artisans spent considerable sums to have their own personal emblem painted and hung.[41] By the end of the century, shop owners had added lights at night to illuminate displays.

Stores with especially ornate décors could become tourist landmarks. Lafaye, a perfumer on the rue Plâtrières near the Père Lachaise cemetery, ran a shop that "merits being seen by foreigners."[42] The perfumer Tessier was singled out as having "the most beautiful store in Paris. At night, due to its lights, it offers a charming sight. The little pots of rouge, of paint, those of cream, of essences, are all categorized and arranged with much art."[43] Most elite perfumers stuck to the neighborhoods around the rue Saint-Honoré, and, by the eighteenth century, the Palais Royale had also become popular despite its inordinately high rents. The right bank housed 71 percent of Paris's perfume stores, with the rest across the Seine where the population was smaller and less elite.[44] Paris was known for its luxury shopping and stores that "metamorphosed themselves into splendidly decorated salons, sparkling with mirrors and gold, illuminated every night like magical palaces."[45]

Most perfumers rented storefronts and backroom workshops that were much simpler and less visible than those of the elite luxury tradespeople.[46] Though artisans and commoners might visit these shops, wealthy patrons were served in their private *hôtels*.[47] The workspace, thus, could remain functional. A typical perfume shops was small, and retailers used their attics and basements to store their goods, having no access or need for warehouses or laboratories.[48] One lucrative perfume business advertised as having a store, a storeroom, a large basement, a nice living space, and two wooden cases.[49] The son of a perfumer left a similar legacy when he died in 1784. His store contained a counter with a locking cash box, numerous shelves for wares, a display window, and a mirror.[50] His holdings indicate an attempt at display, while not achieving the showy décor of the shops along the rue Saint-Honoré. From the complete list of Mme Geoffroy's business holdings after her bankruptcy, we can visualize the interior of an even more modest perfume store. Her inventory contained small numbers of different products: from complexion water, to powder, to toothpicks. As for furnishings, she had two stools, two tables, nine planks of wood, and nine drawers in which to store her goods. Geoffroy probably bought most of her products ready made, mixing scents to her clients' liking, not using her small shop as either a factory or a site for customer browsing. Her inventory indicates a functional sense of commerce that did not include flattering or entertaining clients.[51]

A master artisan traditionally ran his store, whether large or small, with the help of his wife, family, and apprentice. Richer perfumers hired servants to help in their business. For instance, a perfumer to the king hired a *garçon de boutique,* a servant, a maid, and a cook.[52] Those who sold their own concoctions or made gloves needed more assistance than those who simply sold the products of others. Businesses were traditionally passed down to sons or apprentices, but it was not unusual for widows as well as other female family members to take over.[53] Unofficial businesses had little need for apprentices, though they might enlist family members to help. For instance, in the same space, Frénehard sold coffee and powder, his sister, a hairdresser, sold hair dye she had invented.[54] Women, generally, did not run large stores unless they were widows of perfumers, but many sold products out of their homes, stores run by their husbands (or other family members), or in outlets in a variety of locations.

Many creators of perfumes and cosmetics attempted to expand their businesses beyond their own retail spaces by adopting the potentially unstable system of outlets. Though protectionism constituted the eighteenth-century commercial ethos, entrepreneurs who wanted to succeed realized the need for national expansion. These attempts were not without risk. The rouge maker Joseph Collin set up outlets all over Paris in which clients could acquire his specially patented rouge. Though he had his own manufactory store on the rue de Vaugirard, he left his product with, among others, Mlle Heran at the gate of the Gobelins and with Mlle Sadous, a *marchande de mode,* who sold it out of the shops of furriers and jewelers "for the commodity of ladies." Yet Collin's outlets caused him trouble. In 1779, he took Ringard, a wigmaker, to court for selling his rouge at a higher price than agreed on. Ringard was forbidden to manufacturer or sell rouge for ten years and had to pay Collin 1,200 livres in damages. After this, Collin learned his lesson and limited himself to only one outlet in Paris.[55]

Outlets were more profitable for smaller producers because producers had less to lose if their reputations were tarnished. Often these resellers and manufacturers did not have their own shops and depended on outlets to promote their goods. When a ship's captain brought back from Canada "authentic pure and natural bear grease" to stop baldness, he told the public to purchase it from the concierge at the Hôtel des Postes, two grocers, a tobacconist, or a store owner in the Tuilleries.[56] Possibly, the same merchant set up outlets in Versailles, Lyon, Chartres, Dijon, and Rouen.[57] The most successful distributor was probably Dubost, who sold his lotion in six outlets in Paris and in nineteen provincial cities. His outlets varied from a bookstore to a director of carriages to the office of the local *affiches*.[58] Those who chose to set up outlets presaged the development of retail networks, described by Balzac in *César Birotteau* as the essential means of conquering the backward provinces.

Though one Parisian wag felt that the overabundant wearing of cosmetics meant that "the profession of perfumer is now the most profitable in Paris," most perfumers and cosmetics retailers were small artisans trying to get by. The average perfumer was worth only 2,500 livres at his or her death, less than the average for tailors.[59] After 1770, the number of bankruptcies for Parisian perfumers increased from an average of three per decade to thirty-nine in the 1770s and forty-four in the 1780s.[60] These bankruptcies were not due to lack of demand but were due to unpaid bills by customers who bought more than they could pay for or were loath to pay their debts.[61] The aristocratic client, though he granted prestige, was often the least willing to pay bills and used all types of ruses to delay or cancel payments. Extending credit was essential to a successful perfumer, who feared that a dissatisfied client would buy elsewhere, but it could take years to be repaid.[62] Delinquent customers were not the only reason perfumers were liable to lose their businesses at the end of the century. Many perfumers made extravagant purchases to elevate their social positions. Perfumers borrowed money from other artisans or family members to expand their businesses and to buy nicer furnishings. Not unlike César Birotteau, the failed entrepreneur in Honoré de Balzac's novel, perfumers wished to elevate their status among other luxury artisans such as the wealthier jewelers. They were participating in the consumer revolution both as producers and consumers, and many got caught up in the frenzy to own new luxuries. Outrageous spending and overdue bills left some with little choice but bankruptcy.

Another cause of bankruptcy was unhonored debts between artisans. The possibility of obtaining raw materials on credit made it easy for artisans to start a business, but sometimes without real knowledge of the market or the goods they sold. Many who went bankrupt in the 1780s created a domino effect. They owed money to others who were in turn forced into financial insolvency.[63] Wigmakers who extended credit to their clients did not pay off their debts to the perfumers who sold them powder, and in turn, these perfumers did not pay off the starch makers who provided the raw materials. Artisans tried to help one another with loans, which often were not repaid. These small artisans benefited from a boom in private borrowing facilitated by the intermediary of notaries, though many seem to have defaulted because of the interconnectedness of the loans.[64] Jean Louis Fargeon, one of Louis XV's perfumers, declared bankruptcy in 1778 because of Louis XVI's unwillingness to pay his predecessor's debts. When he reopened his business, Fargeon was soon owed huge sums by a number of bankrupt perfumers. Neither the patronage of kings nor links with other artisans could ensure financial security. Though the family name continued to be associated with perfumes into the nineteenth century, two other Fargeon's went bankrupt as well.[65]

The case of the rouge maker Collin can illustrate the tenuous nature of the trade. Collin had outlets around Paris, his own factory store, and sold high volumes of rouge starting in 1772. Yet he went bankrupt in 1786. Two clues to his bankruptcy survive: (1) a book of his daily spending on food and wine and (2) a list of his creditors. The former shows a widower spending small sums each day (on average four to six livres) on bread, wine, and small amounts of meat, along with candles, soap, and powder. Nothing in this book indicates that Collin was a spendthrift. The second says more about his business dealings. He owed large sums to a number of artisans and professionals, including members of the elite Parlement court. These debts probably represent professional loans held either directly by those involved or bought by others after the fact. The sums, a few over one thousand livres, indicate that Collin hoped to set up a much larger enterprise than a small rouge workshop. He also owed money to a printer (presumably for leaflets or trade cards) and a maker of porcelain (for his rouge pots). His biggest creditors were four different landlords. Not surprisingly, Collin constantly changed addresses (his factory store moved from rue Vaugirard to Franc Bourgeois and after his bankruptcy from rue St. Michel to Mathurin). Yet despite a bankruptcy, he managed to reorganize his debt and start over.[66]

Collin was not a member of a guild, but like perfumers, he was caught up in dependent system of artisanal finance. The declining number of perfumers also points to the fragility of the commerce of cosmetics. Similarly to other trades in the eighteenth century, there was a consolidation of businesses in the 1770s–1780s, with many smaller shops not surviving. According to official guild listings, between 1776 and 1789, there was a 34 percent drop in perfumers practicing in Paris. This drop can be partially explained by holdouts who did not reenlist in the guild after Turgot's reforms. These members may have still continued to practice without a visible guild presence. They joined the ranks of independent producers, further weakening the guilds' power. Yet after 1776, anyone willing to pay could become a master, which created a rush of new guild members.[67] Some of the decline of perfumers, thus, should also be attributed to the declining popularity of gloves and wealth consolidation in a few larger enterprises.[68]

The market for cosmetics and beauty products may have allowed a few perfumers to expand and innovate, but most were in precarious positions. The perfumer's business was not only constantly under threat by other guilds and sellers but also all retailers of cosmetics were at risk because of their dependence on changing fashions. Fashion meant that the corporate values of trust, quality, and control were less important than newness, fantasy, and publicity. To succeed in the world of Parisian luxury crafts, cosmetics retailers had to be able to market their products to a broader customer base than just the aristocracy, whose buying patterns were as irregular as their payment. By making certain cosmetics cheaper for wider consumption, retailers could hope to create a reliable market, as long as the fashion for artifice and toiletries was maintained. Under such conditions, few succeeded in the long term, but those who did were adept at mastering new markets and products.

Il n'y à que Maille qui m'aille: Creating an Entrepreneur

The most striking example of such an adept and successful entrepreneur was Antoine-Claude Maille, vinegar maker *extraordinaire,* whose name today still graces bottles of fine French mustard. Maille was a member of the vinegar guild and specialized in high-end vinegar and luxury cosmetic products made of both vinegar and mustard. He invented up to 180 different types of aromatic vinegars with cosmetic, medicinal, and dietary uses.[69] He began his career in 1747 and on July 27, 1769, was named *vinaigrier du roi.* He also had the approbation of the King of England, the Emperor of Austria, and Catherine the Great, who gave him her stamp after he donated vinegar to fight the 1771 plague in Moscow.[70] Besides royal patronage, Maille's industry received testimonials from such Enlightenment figures as Casanova, Mme de Genlis, and Mercier.

In 1788 Genlis, then governess of the king's children, took her charges to visit the Maille factory as their first stop in an educational tour of Paris to teach "her students different branches of industry."[71] Genlis wanted the royal children to learn about the production and commercialization of goods, and her trip to Maille's workshop was meant to highlight the development of French industry. A journalist from *L'année littéraire* was also greatly impressed by his visit to Maille's store. He praised Maille as an example of "the height of perfection that all types of industry in this kingdom have reached."[72] Maille and his mustards and vinegars represented the rising productivity and inventiveness of French commerce, one of the enlightened monarchy's greatest feats.

Yet Maille also represented the antithesis of royal privileges. Mercier adopted Maille as the model for the humble entrepreneur in his play *La brouette du vinaigrier*.[73] The play told the story of a poor vinegar maker whose thrift and labor allowed his son, a learned young clerk, to marry above his rank. The play celebrated classes mixing, the artisan's hard work, and fathers' selfless and accepting love. The vinegar maker, in Mercier's vision, represented the unflinching commercial hero, capable, with truthful entrepreneurial acumen, and unwavering hard work to turn misery into wealth. Even a simple vinegar maker, Mercier felt, could become a self-made success story in the commercial sphere freed from guild rules and caste constraints.

Maille was more than an artisan to Mercier and others. He ranked as an artist and scientist who should not be associated with other more prosaic vinegar makers. In the *Tableau de Paris*, Mercier reinforced this vision by calling Maille "the leader of vinegar-makers" and "the most inventive genius in the world of mustard."[74] For Mercier, Maille also played the important, if humorous, role of uniting husbands and wives by selling a vinegar capable of recreating virginity. Blushing young maidens visited Maille to purchase a product called "virgin vinegar for the ladies." Maille's artistry in this case became science because "all is regeneration due to the laws of chemistry; the happiness of the spouses is linked to this sublime science which I idolize."[75] Maille, thus, was an artist, scientist, magician, and marriage counselor all in one. He specialized in luxurious versions of food items as well as less respectable and highly dubious concoctions. Though the basis of his products was vinegar and mustard, the outcomes did not fit neatly into the definition of the trade.

He also differed from other elite manufacturers in his attempts to reach out to a larger audience. Maille did not just depend on the good will of the king. He used new methods to sell his wares and saw the potential of appealing to a larger consumer base that would allow him to increase his output and influence. One indication that Maille hoped to secure a larger customer base was his charity work. In the winter months, he offered his mustard plasters free to the poor and to any priest who wished to make his way to Paris.[76] He would thus supply the parishes of France with free cures while promoting their sale to those who could afford them.

Maille was not aiming his products at the poor, however. His prices were high, though still within the range of the urban middling classes who might want to splurge on his well-known products. Maille's many scented vinegars sold for three livres a bottle in the 1750s, relatively cheap compared with the sixteen livres charged for a small bottle of eau de toilette by the king's perfumer.[77] His rouge vinegars sold for one livre each, which was cheaper than most high-end rouge, but the price of the packaging was extra. Though none of his rouge containers have survived, many of his mustard pots have. The many options for materials, lettering (in gold or plain black), and decoration indicate the variety of prices and clientele that Maille catered to.

To attract a larger and more diverse buying public, Maille also offered a variety of ways to buy his goods. He had a storefront on the rue Saint André des Arts for his elite clientele. He also ran a warehouse in Sèvres, a suburb of Paris, where he produced both his liquors and aromatic creams, products that were not included in the privileges of his guild and thus needed to be made outside the boundaries of the city. In this way, Maille could maintain both a thriving vinegar and mustard enterprise and expand his business to other products without upsetting guild rules. Maille also put the postal system to use for his own expansion. He sent his products to both the provinces and foreign countries.[78] He had ties with foreign courts that helped spread his goods throughout Europe. He was not the only cosmetic seller to do so. Dubois, inventor of a face cream, sold his product in numerous European cities, including Amsterdam, Constantinople, Hamburg, Leipzig, and London.[79] Most manufacturers were not as ambitious, but they did send their products to the provinces. The growing postal system, though slow and unpredictable, allowed both buyers and sellers to depend less on local markets.[80]

Maille represented a new type of artisan, one who was both a respected master of a guild dependent on royal privileges and also an independent artist and inventor. He was an entrepreneur above all, attempting, as Mercier saw it, to elevate his trade through hard work and exceptional skills. He broke from a purely elite clientele and sold goods at a fixed price to all who entered his stores. Others, whose names have not lasted as long as Maille's, also bridged the gap between aristocratic patronage and innovations in production and sales. These entrepreneurs broke from tradition by attempting to widen the scope of their enterprise, breaking down limits to both their customer base and their methods of production. They became part of a growing proto-industrial urban manufacture that had strong ties to rural agriculture (in this case, growing flowers) even while they focused primarily on the demands of city life.[81] In doing so, they also created a different sort of shopping experience. The elite still had their products delivered to their homes, but, by the end of the century, luxury shops increasingly invited browsers as well as serious clients. Shop windows and displays lent added appeal to the neighborhood perfumer's shop. Mercier may have criticized the "race of little merchants who had neither integrity, honor, nor scruples," but he praised their shining window displays and had only positive things to say about Maille.[82] Elite merchants catered to the homes of the rich, street sellers expanded the reach of consumerism to the lower rungs of society, and, significantly, actual shops became the physical representations of this new consumerism available to anyone with extra money or credit.

A Fashionable Revolution: The Perfumer as Hero or Traitor

The developments in production and retail started in the eighteenth century did not continue without interruption during the Revolution. Since cosmetics and perfumes like fashionable dress and wigs were associated with aristocratic luxury goods, their makers were likely to be suspect in the eyes of ardent revolutionaries. Balzac's César Birotteau was a perfumer whose Royalist ties brought him trouble during the Revolution and prestige after the Restoration. He hated the Revolution because it "forbade powder, and was thus responsible for the fashion of wearing hair *à la Titus*," a short hair cut favored by both men and women.[83] The loss of income due to changing styles became a political cause for Birotteau and thus for the profession. Perfumers' oft-precarious position in the Old Regime was further threatened by a Revolution that put little stake in the trappings of artifice and the refinement of bodily odors.

The real story of the counterrevolutionary Antoine Caron inspired the image of the royalist perfumer created by Balzac. From 1778, Caron ran a perfume shop called *La reine des fleurs* on the Four-Saint-Germain. Virulently royalist, he hid counterrevolutionaries in his attic. Caron's conservatism may also have been sparked by changes in revolutionary fashions because his business "no longer prospered since the Revolution."[84] In 1804 Caron was caught attempting to hide George Cadoual, the infamous *Chouan* rebel sought by Napoleon. Caron was jailed for this crime, but the Restoration brought him a medal for his services and a position in the Palais Bourbon. A lucrative government post amply compensated the loss of his struggling perfume business. Caron is not the only example of a royalist perfumer. Maille's student and successor, Aclocque, a commander-general in the national guard, helped protect the king when the monarchy fell on August 10, 1792, an action for which he was arrested during the Terror.[85]

The royalist perfumers and their fictional counterpart Birotteau reinforced the notion that successful artisans, especially luxury tradespeople who depended on the patronage of the nobility, were either expatriates or ardent antirevolutionaries.[86] Yet of the 2,598 French shopkeepers and tradesmen who emigrated, only six were perfumers. Overall, the artisans from each occupational group who fled represented a cross section of society, rather than an exodus of luxury craftspeople.[87] Though they did not leave the country, some perfumers either suspended their trade or moved to the provinces for the duration of the Revolution. Fargeon, the king's perfumer, closed his shop in 1794 and did not reopen it until 1797.[88] Bourgeois, the first perfumer to call himself *citoyen* in 1792, sold the contents of his store in August 1794 and returned permanently to his hometown.[89] The reasons for these absences are not completely clear. Having lived through the Terror, Fargeon chose to abandon his business at a time of financial rather than political hardship. The period between 1794 and 1797 was probably the hardest for luxury artisans because of the growing economic instability and trade blockages brought on by war. For others it may have been safer to spend the worse years of the Terror in the provinces than to be the butt of ridicule and possible attacks in the capital.

An anecdote poking fun at the revolutionary government provides a glimpse into the dangers present in revolutionary Paris for perfumers who stayed. In 1793, a representative from the revolutionary committees spotted a large crate marked *Eau de la Reine de Hongrie*. The crate was seized and its owner, a perfumer, was labeled a traitor, conspirator, and counterrevolutionary for having corresponded with a foreign court. The uneducated revolutionaries were unaware that this popular perfume with a foreign moniker was actually made in Draguignan, a provincial city. After the perfumer promised to change the name of his product and send the committee samples of his wares, he was allowed to go free.[90] Perfumers had to tread lightly during the Revolution because in their fervor its representatives looked for and found traitors everywhere. It was not the link between perfume and aristocrats that made this business suspect but the inability of uneducated revolutionary officials to correctly comprehend the culture of elite luxury goods.

Though some perfumers felt threatened by revolutionary enthusiasts, most were more keenly concerned with the financial strains brought by the Revolution. The rapidly changing concept of fashion and the revolutionary wars and embargoes took a toll on many perfumers' already precarious financial positions. Commercial activity was paralyzed by stagnation: "In general little business is done. Prices on many articles vary little and, despite deliveries, stocks are low."[91] The importation of foreign ingredients was greatly constrained by the blockade of French ports and revolts in the colonies. The overall spending capacity of consumers decreased because of this economic instability. Mercier described the commerce of the Revolution as full of fancy storefronts meant to mask the emptiness inside, where shopkeepers employed mirrors to enlarge their holdings.[92] Yet perfumers attempted to reassure their customers and continued to do business as best they could. Labrierre informed "his co-citizens that he never gave up his commerce as a few persons had rumored; he only canceled certain items." He also assured his clientele that, although ingredients were scarce, the quality and prices of his products were not affected.[93] Another retailer proudly announced the arrival of new stock to his store, noting that otherwise "creams are very rare."[94]

Financial times were unstable for all professions. Perfumers had to make do with the stock they managed to acquire but they did not close down shop. The economic hardships had only a minimal effect on the number of Parisian perfumers who continued to eke out a living from their trade. Though not entirely accurate, lists of artisans found in commercial almanacs indicate only an 8 percent decline in Parisian perfumers between 1789 and 1798.[95] If we can trust these numbers to represent actual practitioners, this is actually a lower rate of decline than the prerevolutionary years. Only 28 percent of named perfumers practicing in 1789 are represented in the 1798 almanac, but this disappearance is similar to the next decade, indicating not a massive turnover among perfumers but a normal pattern that may have as much to do with the way the almanacs were edited as actual disappearances of specific perfumers.[96] The Revolution, thus, did not substantially weaken a profession that had already faced retrenchment.

By 1798, the perfumer trade was once again profitable. New luxury shops opened and flourished. The fashionable shop of *Laugier père et fils* on rue Bourg l'Abbé doubled the number of its staff and opened a factory in Grasse.[97] Laugier, the company's owner, petitioned for forty-two trademarks for his products in 1806, insisting that cosmetic names were equivalent to other industrial products.[98] By 1811, Laugier had 140 workers but had to ask Napoleon for a loan of 100,000 francs to avoid bankruptcy.[99] Despite this temporary setback, Laugier's store and factories continued to gain recognition throughout the 1820s. These large entrepreneurs competed with small retailers for visibility. In 1827, the approximate one-year total of sales of soap and perfume produced in Paris was 8,250,000 francs, of which four manufacturers sold 1,875,000, thus dominating the market. One of these four, Auger, employed twenty-five to thirty workers in his soap manufacture, which was said to rival the quality of British soap.[100]

Production capacity developments and marketing technique transformations used by cosmetics manufacturers intensified in the 1820s, by which time a few elite perfumers ran pristine luxury stores and complex factories. By 1825, the industry was centralized in Paris, with Grasse as primarily an agricultural center. In the 1830s, the discovery of distillation with steam allowed perfumery to become a veritable industry that could produce large quantities at low unit costs. Thereafter, both the industries of flower extraction in Grasse and the factories for perfume distillation in Paris expanded rapidly, making it more expensive for small retailers to keep up with new developments.[101] To run a competitive business, a perfumer needed a store, a workroom to mix the products for sale, two laboratories to make oils and soap, a studio for making labels and engravings, and a storage space.[102] These spaces needed to be fully furnished with the proper (and expensive) equipment.

Though not fully industrialized until the 1850s, the production of cosmetics and perfumes had become a stable and profitable national industry firmly based in the chic shopping quarters of Paris and other provincial cities. After the Revolution, the industry came to represent French pride in ingenuity and quality, especially in competition with British goods. Rouge sellers, perfumers, and soap makers were represented at the Expositions des produits de l'industrie française starting in 1806, winning prizes for their inventions.[103] Having survived both the strict controls of the Old Regime and the commercial morass of the Revolution, nineteenth-century luxury commerce hoped to rise from the ashes and conquer new markets.

Conclusion

In mostly dimly lit, unglamorous surroundings, perfumers concocted potions and creams to gain customers and patronage. These same perfumers were constantly at odds with the development of different outlets for cosmetics, such as the vinegar makers' array of aromatic rouges and the mercers' stock of eau de Cologne. From this bustle of competition and contention emerged a few thriving businesses and many less successful ones. Stores rapidly opened, closed, were taken over, and were renamed. A few institutions remained the same, while most struggled to make their mark on the faces and purses of the Parisian coquette. The increase in potential customers fueled both the rising number of sellers and in turn caused the insecurity present in the profession. Retailers diversified to meet the needs and desires of the working classes as well as the elite, hoping to gain stability. Competition between retailers for customer attention created the necessary push for developing new and innovative means of sales and, by the nineteenth century, production. Trademarks, factories, and diversification of products allowed certain producers to retain a regular and loyal clientele while attracting new customers away from smaller shops. Though it would not be until the twentieth century that large corporations would be created around cosmetics, the move toward national brands had already started.

CHAPTER THREE

Advertising Beauty

The Culture of Publicity

The growing diversity of shops, the rising popularity of store-bought beauty goods among the working classes, and the disintegration of guild control all point to a thriving market for cosmetics in the second half of the eighteenth century. Yet this expanding market was also precarious, the whims of fashion dictating success or failure. To ensure their survival, small entrepreneurs turned to public promotion of their goods, and, in doing so, attempted to control fashion trends themselves. By using new forms of marketing, they hoped both to inform buyers about their goods and to ensure that their vision of fashion dominated the highly volatile market. These strategies were not always successful and often clashed with traditional means of selling controlled by the guilds. Though advertising campaigns were not common until the 1830s, sellers of creams, rouge, and powder were early pioneers whose efforts would help construct the commercial practices of a free-market economy after the Revolution.

The printed journal advertisements that flourished in the second half of the eighteenth century provided an ideal medium for marketing cheap beauty products. Advertising sheets, called *affiches,* represent the flourishing activity of the Old Regime "bazaar economy," which catered to all tastes. Affiches were defined as "small periodical papers where one learns about all marvelous creations, either in merchandise or in crafts . . . They put on the right path those who are desirous to buy, and all types of baubles are sold with the greatest of success."[1] In these useful papers, announcements of scientific discoveries jostled with pleas for employment and advertisements for used furniture. Notices of lost pets were found alongside those selling luxuries or simple foodstuffs. Bourgeois families sold their houses while nobles auctioned off expensive carriages. All aspects of the Old Regime clashed and cohabited in the pages of the affiches.

From 1750 to 1799, the number of cosmetics advertisements found in this bazaar grew steadily, indicating an increased concern for promotion and publicity. Before the creation of newsprint advertising, sellers had a more limited audience of buyers, *le monde*, who were patrons to well-known perfumers and set the rules for using makeup at court. With the growth of consumerism, new producers and new buyers needed outlets to communicate with one another. Sellers needed a means to educate the growing and diverse public of buyers, and buyers needed ways to access available products. The publicity used to raise public awareness of goods was not only more visible but also distinctive in its aims and methods. Unlike the inserts placed for lost cats, used carriage, and even the sale of foodstuffs, beauty product advertisements marshaled complex, aggressive publicity techniques. Advertisers knowingly constructed their texts to sway buyers with culturally recognizable symbols of trust and quality, while stressing buyers' dreams and desires. This mix of the practical and the ephemeral created a distinct culture of advertising that placed traditional categories of legitimacy within an expanded marketplace.

Shaping French Publicity: A History of the Affiches

Advertising was not new to the eighteenth century. Posters (affiches), itinerant hawkers, trade cards, and explanatory pamphlets were used from the late sixteenth century. In the streets of Paris, government decrees, signs for lost pets, and publicity for cosmetics and plays competed for the most visible spots. The only security against having expensive posters unceremoniously ripped off the walls was to petition the Lieutenant of Police for a special permission. The expense and difficulty of such a process meant that street posters were not the most efficient means of promotion.[2] Another visible means of advertising was handing out of leaflets to passersby. Guild regulations, however, made such promotion illegal for members of the elite *Six corps*, the most privileged and powerful guilds. To counter the spread of publicity, they called on the police to censor the material published by others. An added difficulty for cosmetic makers was they needed the Medical Academy's permission before their texts could be legally distributed. This complexity of bureaucratic authorization meant that many chose to produce illegal pamphlets. The fear of a 300 livres fine for the first offense and forced closure for a second were not enough to stop this practice. Though these pamphlets and posters were likely the most common form of advertising during the eighteenth century, few survive. Those that do have texts that mimic newspaper advertisements; sellers used one language of publicity, no matter the format.[3]

By the 1750s, sellers had another less supervised option for promotional purposes. The affiches had been created to provide the public with useful information, but retailers quickly adopted them as a perfect space to promote their wares. Though censored for political content, journals were not breaking the laws against promotion by printing such advertisements. The ability of newsprint to circumvent guild and government regulations against promotional material did not go unnoticed. The members of the *Six corps de Paris* argued that these journals went against corporate rights by printing advertisements for charlatans. They felt that the public "by finding their announcements in the periodic journals" would be tricked into thinking that the state had authorized these unofficial sellers. These journals were more dangerous than leaflets handed to pedestrians because they "entered into all houses and cabinets." The guilds called for a government crackdown on all forms of advertising to save their own prestige and business. Ultimately, however, the guilds' ability to control and restrict public forms of promotion failed. The Lieutenant of Police never enforced censorship of the affiches, focusing on the public display of publicity over the private reading of journals.[4]

As the main uncensored and unregulated means of promotion, newspaper advertisements experienced a huge growth in the second half of the eighteenth century. Despite Théophraste Renaudot's failure in 1631 to start an advertising *Gazette*, in 1745 Antoine Boudet inaugurated the *Affiches de Paris*.[5] In 1751, it was transformed into the *Annonces, affiches et avis divers* (known as the *Petites affiches*, but I will refer to them as the *Affiches*) by the Chevalier de Meslé as a subsidiary of the *Gazette de France*. A year later, a provincial equivalent using the same name started, which I will refer to as the *Affiches de province*.[6] These journals welcomed free inserts, which allowed advertisers to spread their renown outside the boundaries of their neighborhood and even outside the boundaries of Paris. Along with the official *Affiches* of Paris and the *Affiches de province*, there were soon numerous local affiches published in the larger cities of France copying the capital's format.[7] The many versions of affiches were the most numerous sites for advertising but by no means the only ones. As early as 1742, the *Mercure de France* published advertisements for new books as well as other products under the rubric "avis." Other journals, such as the *Avant coureur*, the *Journal de Paris*, and the *Journal des dames*, also included advertisements. The appearance of these numerous advertising sites accompanied the development of weekly and daily newspapers aimed at a growing literate public that hungered for commercial, political, and literary information.[8] Not until the late 1820s, when catalogs and illustrated posters became popular, did the means of publicity broaden.[9]

Upon their inception, both the Parisian and provincial affiches struggled to find subscribers for a journal solely aimed at announcements. Ultimately, they added reviews of literary works, political news, and philosophy to attract readers. By the Revolution, the provincial affiches focused strictly on political news, while the Parisian version remained an advertising journal.[10] In another effort to gain revenue, journals started charging for inserts. Many of the local sheets, such as the *Affiches de Mar-*

seilles, Toulouse, and *Orleans* charged between ten to twelve sols per insert.[11] On November 1, 1788, the *Affiches de Paris* began charging three livres for each lost item notice and one livre four sols for requests for services because their proliferation threatened to take over the paper.[12] By the 1790s, because of financial difficulties, the *Affiches* started to charge for all inserts, giving a subscriber's discount to compete with the *Petites affiches* that gave them away for free.[13]

In the eighteenth and into the early nineteenth century, the affiches' publishers had limited success selling subscriptions because of their high price. For example, a subscription to the daily Parisian affiches cost thirty livres a year in 1782, well out of the range of artisans. The local provincial affiches cost from six livres to seven-and-a-half livres, cheaper but still out of reach of most.[14] In 1789, only three thousand people subscribed to the Parisian affiches and thirteen thousand to the provincial version.[15] These small figures, however, do not represent the potential readership that used the information available in these advertising sheets. Colin Jones estimates that between four and ten people perused each copy of the local affiches through networks of reading rooms, borrowing, and family ties.[16] This estimate suggests a total readership of between twelve thousand and forty thousand for Paris and between fifty-two thousand and one hundred thirty thousand for the provinces in the eighteenth century. The numbers become larger if added to the subscribers of other journals that contained advertisements. The *Mercure* had fifteen thousand subscribers per year in the late 1780s while the *Avant coureur* had as many as seven thousand in the same period.[17] Thus, even though the format of the advertising journals was not a huge success, their contents were useful to a large group of people looking for both goods and services.

Not only was the dissemination of advertisements potentially wide but the readership also included a broad spectrum of society. The *Année littéraire* stated that its potential audience for advertisements were "manufacturers, who will know to whom to offer the product of their factories, and merchants, who will know to whom to address themselves for the buying and supplying of their stores."[18] Yet readers could include consumers as well as producers. Colin Jones argues that the majority of readers were "merchants, traders, businessmen, and the middling professions . . . 'the middling sort.'"[19] The middling sort included women as well as men. Special articles on fashion were tailored for this readership. The usefulness of the affiches spread even farther than the middle classes, as announcements were also aimed and placed by artisans and servants, looking for business or work. The numerous sales of *chateaux*, heraldry, carriages, and other luxuries indicated that the nobility also perused the affiches. Essentially, the affiches' hodgepodge nature meant they could appeal to any literate urban dweller looking for information or bargains. As Restif de la Bretonne noted of the *Petites affiches*, "Everything is in it that should be . . . here is a useful journal!"[20]

Though other journals contained advertisements, the affiches were the dominant space for inserts, especially when other journals changed editors and thus policies toward advertising, as did the *Avant coureur* in 1777 and the *Mercure* in 1778. The *Affiches* evolved in 1783 from a biweekly to a daily, which allowed commercial inserts to increase. Indicative of its status as a publicity sheet was a new focus in the *avis divers* section that went from focusing on lost property and individuals looking for work during the 1750s and 1760s to stressing commercial goods for sale during the 1770s and 1780s. The fees imposed on inserts by 1788 benefited commercial interests. By the Revolution, only merchants and artisans could afford to place an ad because they might recoup the costs. The prominence of the *Affiches* and its provincial equivalents by the 1770s clearly defined advertisements as linked to the world of commerce and consumerism. By focusing advertisements in a specific journal, retailers and publishers were defining publicity as a marketing tool and not simply as a subset of the political and literary gossip found in other journals. The reign of the affiches was a sign of changing concepts of both marketing and buying, giving Parisian as well as provincial shopkeepers and artisans their own journals in which to promote their wares.

By the early nineteenth century, other journals started realizing that they could use advertisements to raise money, rather than as a free service. Paid inserts allowed more specialized journals, such as women's magazines or medical journals, to lower their subscription rates and attract more buyers. The affiches format lost popularity because of rising competition from other journals for the same group of advertisers. There were not enough paying advertisers to support a journal solely funded by their inserts. When the editor Panckoucke tried this in 1792 with the *Aviseur national*, he failed within a few months.[21] According to one historian, in 1803, the three main Parisian advertising journals had only seventy-four subscribers, which if accurate represents a considerable drop in their popularity.[22] In an even greater blow, in 1811, the government consolidated the *Affiches de Paris* and the *Journal général d'annonces*, two main advertising sheets, into the *Petites affiches* to better protect the public from fraudulent inserts.[23] Napoleon cracked down on other journals that printed advertisements, leaving only four (*Le moniteur, Journal de l'empire, Gazette de France,* and the *Journal de Paris*) that had considerable scope and room for publicity.[24] One artisan complained that this consolidation and limitation of venues meant an increase in prices and a lack of competition. The price of inserts went up to one franc fifty centimes, making it too expensive for small businesses to advertise frequently.[25]

Shrinking advertising spaces did not last; new specialized journals printed paid

advertisements despite regulations, and by 1827, even political journals were printing paid advertisements to make up for increases in the price of mailings.[26] In this
period, pictorial newspaper advertisements appeared more frequently and billboards
flourished in city streets, which meant that the simple, strictly textual format of the
affiches was once again relegated to listings for lost dogs and the sale of used furniture. By 1825, a journalist for the *Petites affiches*, a successor of the *affiches* style, complained that its advertisements were being poached by other journals, forcing it to
publish political and literary articles instead.[27] And publicity space continued to expand.[28] In 1831, *L'office-correspondance* was founded. Along with articles, it distributed the advertisements of Parisian businesses to provincial newspapers, allowing
them to reach a national audience. Marc Martin argues that despite the creation of
national publicity by 1836 the economy remained regional, creating a discrepancy
between the reality and the image of brands that were being sold in these journals.[29]
Yet advertising had become a ubiquitous means of self-promotion for entrepreneurs
and for France. And this publicity would from now on be paid for and would increasingly be targeted at specific audiences to create brand recognition and profit.

The Rhetoric of Promise: New Methods of Marketing

As the *affiches* added advertising space, those who sold cosmetics took advantage of
this free publicity. The number of cosmetics advertisements grew during the second
half of the eighteenth century, indicating a new relationship between retailers and
publicity.[30] In this same period, cosmetics retailers used increasingly complex and
sophisticated marketing ploys to make their inserts stand out. The quantity and the
quality of inserts indicate the development of an aggressive and sophisticated conception of publicity by artisans and merchants of beauty. These marketing tools
came to represent a distinct culture of publicity.

   This culture of publicity, however, existed alongside a much more prosaic use of
inserts that dominated the eighteenth- and early nineteenth-century presses. All
journal advertisements remained purely textual throughout the eighteenth century.
Visual representations of goods for sale were not common until the 1830s, though
they were already present in the English press.[31] Most French advertising texts had
basic information, employing the same format as personal notices for services or lost
objects. Advertisements for cosmetics were primarily lists of information. They contained the name of the seller, his or her occupation, address, and sometimes a short
description of products. For example, a typical insert read: "The Sieur Guet, Perfumer, Chabanois St., has received from Germany very beautiful powder cones and
continues to sell his flowered paste which whitens hands and stops them from crack-

ing."[32] Editors probably composed most of these inserts from information provided by the retailer, thus limiting their language and individuality. Overall, the number of advertisers was also small (for example, approximately 101 sellers advertised cosmetics during the 1780s) compared with the numerous stores present in Paris and other cities. There was a limited variety of categories represented, with medicinal goods and books dominating.

Historians of advertisement have judged print advertisements as neither the most innovative or successful form used in the eighteenth century. Claire Walsh, writing about England, argues that most advertisement was done in the shop. Customers would browse multiple shops and would be sold on goods by the shopkeeper's patter. Similarly, Natasha Coquery finds that the invoices of luxury stores (often called trade cards) contained visuals and long texts meant to entice shoppers to return. Katie Scott argues that trade cards functioned as a memory of shopping, a reminder of the pleasures and novelty experienced.[33] Unlike newspaper ads, trade cards often contained artistic renderings of the shops or images of the goods sold, calling on an iconography of the decorative arts that was meant to seduce the buyer. Trade cards, however, were advertising after the fact. Attached to the product itself or to the top of the invoice, shopkeepers gave them to customers when they made their purchase. Though some surviving trade cards for cosmetics have added imagery, their texts are the same as that found in newspaper advertisements (figure 2).

Other historians who have studied newspaper advertisements in detail argue that the simple and repetitive nature of inserts signified the French economy's unsophisticated nature. Marc Martin argues that the affiches' simple texts and small subscription numbers signaled the lack of a capitalist market in France. In his view, French advertisements were a straightforward means of disseminating information. He also believes that the guilds' complaints stopped advertisements from being more commercial. Alain Descombes supports this view, arguing that eighteenth-century advertising was the work of unimaginative men stifled by strong guild control. These historians take for granted the guild system's viability, the French economy's backwardness, and the monarchy's strength to explain the rudimentary uses of the press.[34]

Recent studies argue, on the contrary, that the straightforward wording was a sign of a nascent capitalist market. For Colin Jones, the simple texts represent the editors' belief in the viability and perfection of the market, which led them to pick a repetitive, anonymous format that could promote free enterprise while still allowing a forum for the editors' growing political consciousness. The affiches' editors created a world defined by economics and consumerism rather than social rank and hierarchy. They focused on a burgeoning capitalist market rather than on increas-

Figure 2. À la renomée des parfums, Bibliothèque nationale estampes

ingly irrelevant Old Regime corporate privileges. Jack Censer supports this argument by showing that the journals' editors participated enthusiastically "in the outpouring of criticism against the Old Regime manners and mores." Contentious political articles by the editors were reinforced by advertisements that put all things, from royal offices to cures for pockmarks, up for sale to the highest bidder, thus threatening the Old Regime system of privilege by creating an alternate civil society based on a new set of values.[35] The editors' political beliefs allowed for retailers and merchants to promote their wares in a language of equality.

Thus, editors promoted a utopian, laissez-faire vision of the market that allowed for "ingenious inventions of all kinds" to clash happily on the pages of journals.[36] This editorial openness to advertisement may have allowed for the placement of commercial inserts, but it did not limit or determine their content. Christopher Todd explains the preponderance of informational inserts by arguing that self-promotion was in bad taste in the eighteenth century.[37] Yet this does not explain the flowering of a different, much more elaborate and showy form of publicity. Editors may have supported the ideals of the *philosophes*, the free-market economy, and bourgeois capitalist values, but their advertisements presented the reader with an array of aristocratic beauty goods trumpeted as the sole vision of entrepreneurs. Once the prerogative of the wealthy, these goods were now made available to all by sellers who wished to expand their status, commerce, and wealth beyond the boundaries of elite society. The advertisers, even if they got help writing their inserts, consciously chose to break corporate rules or commercial manners. The advertisements for cosmetics in the affiches, *Mercure*, and other journals did not just mimic the "serious" content of these journals or reinforce the editor's belief in a free market but, by adopting contemporary discourses created a distinct language of commercial advertising that formed the basis for complex marketing strategies for luxury goods.

Cosmetic advertisements first broke from marketing tradition in their proliferation. From their inception in the 1750s, cosmetic inserts steadily grew.[38] Rather than indicate an increase in advertisers, this rise was primarily created by the use of repeat publicity. Advertisers realized the profitability of repetition, placing not just one insert to inform buyers of changes in their store, but multiple inserts in various journals. By the Revolution, repeat commercial advertising dominated, which emphasized brand-name awareness rather than simply the dissemination of information. This rise did not apply to other types of products, however. Cosmetics made up an increasingly large part of all commercial advertisements, sharing the space with the popular listings for medicines and new books. Most surprisingly, the largest gain came during the revolutionary years, with an overall increase of 70 percent, despite the expected dips during the years of the Terror. Loosening of guild regulations and the rise in repeat publicity due to discounts for subscribers help explain this growth.[39] The continued presence of cosmetics retailers indicates their faith in advertising even as it grew more expensive and the commerce of luxury goods became more precarious. Just as political and economic forces threatened their livelihoods, perfumers saw the need to further reinforce their presence in the market by reminding customers of their continued commercial existence. Speeding up a change that had already started in the 1780s, nonartisans selling perfumery products entered the market after the destruction of the guilds. Eighty percent of those who advertised during the Revolutionary years were new to publicity. The Revolution's support of free trade allowed advertising methods to bloom whose roots had been firmly planted during the Old Regime.

Compared with England, the number of advertisements is small. English advertisements also contained imagery much earlier than French advertisements did. Yet when their texts and ploys are compared, they have a similar tone to French advertisements.[40] As advertisements became common in France, more sophisticated and aggressive marketing ploys appeared. A growing number of eighteenth-century advertisers viewed advertising spaces available to them not just as a means of passing on basic information. Instead, they adopted distinct methods of marketing to distinguish their seemingly common goods from other perfumers and cosmetics sellers. Retailers and producers adopted strategies meant to appeal to buyers. They mobilized recognized forms of legitimacy, such as the king's seal. Yet they also broke with tradition and aggressively courted clients by describing in detail the usage and reliability of the product for sale as well. Using such strategies, cosmetics sellers sought to bring to life in the pages of the *affiches* a plethora of consumer goods that buyers could imagine and desire well before purchase. In consciously constructing their marketing campaigns, eighteenth-century advertisers showed how acutely aware they were of their market and of the importance of publicity in the success of their enterprise.

An analysis of the publicity campaigns of two of the most ambitious self-promoters of the eighteenth century—Maille and Collin—can illustrate the new forms of marketing. Both of these entrepreneurs took it upon themselves to promote their own names as well as their goods and wares in an expanding consumer market. Both were willing to adopt any means necessary to gain the recognition of the court and nobility as well as that of the larger public of buyers. Others adopted similar marketing ploys, but Maille and Collin stand out for their entrepreneurial vigor. They represent a new type of advertiser, though neither was necessarily successful financially.

Collin went bankrupt in 1786 but never closed his business, and Maille divided his property from his wife's in 1783, which implies he was worried about insolvency.[41]

A salient characteristic of Maille and Collin's strategy was the frequency and longevity of their inserts. Though most retailers advertised only once or twice before the Revolution, a few established a regular presence in journals. Maille was one of the most persistent, coordinating his advertisements with the seasons. He inserted the same ad in five or six different journals at the same time, targeting New Year's gift giving or the Parisian balls. He publicized his wares from 1754 to 1785, keeping his customers abreast of his new inventions for more than thirty years. A half-dozen other sellers of cosmetics, including Collin, advertised regularly for over ten years. The longest of these, even surpassing Maille, was the Onfroy family who sold the famous Farina eau de Cologne for fifty-three years, from 1762 to 1806. Though these cases are exceptional, numerous other retailers formulated organized campaigns within shorter time spans.

Maille's inserts were also much longer than the majority found in journals. He regularly placed four-page advertisements in the *Mercure*, one even used an engraving of distillation equipment surrounding his initials, something almost unheard of for the time.[42] These long texts described numerous products in detail, reading more like prospectuses than pithy advertisements. Maille reproduced these same texts as leaflets given out with purchases (a form of trade card that went beyond the invoice). Providing buyers with instructions for using goods they had just bought makes business sense, but inserting these same lengthy descriptions in journals seems unnecessary and dull. There is no catchy slogan, no clear promotion, and hardly any imagery to entice those who might be scanning the journal.

The standards of twenty-first-century advertising, however, cannot be used to judge the effectiveness of eighteenth-century inserts. Maille's and other's verbosity about their products produced a sense of competence, discovery, and transparency. With the expansion of consumerism came new buyers who did not have any experience or knowledge of how and where to purchase the new goods available to them. Advertising functioned as an education in consumerism. For those who had never entered his store, the insert provided a cornucopia of sensuous experiences as well as a veritable surfeit of useful information and advice about grooming. Though the majority of advertisements remained pithy, the lengthy ones were probably those that gained the most attention from readers.

Length, frequency, and persistence were important, but the advertisements' contents determined customer response to products. The initial step to gain public recognition was the establishment of a name. The French elite recognized Maille's products early. Collin was less well known, but he too acquired a reputation that he could translate into a marketing ploy. To promote their renown in their advertisements, both made frequent reference to the titles and patents they acquired. Among the most common inducements were patents and permissions issued by the king, medical commission, or the police lieutenant that retailers needed to advertise legally but that also functioned as consumer guarantees.

The most obvious title advertisers' adopted was a corporate occupation, such as perfumer, vinegar maker, or pharmacist. Because cosmetics were not controlled by any one guild, such titles did more to undermine corporate monopolies than reinforce them. Pharmacists sold rouge, perfumers sold chocolate, and mercers sold anything they pleased. These crossovers were intrinsic to the weakened guild system, but they also represented the freedom of the "bazaar economy" found in the pages of the *affiches* and elsewhere. By announcing their positions, guild members may have gained status in the eyes of buyers, but they also distanced themselves from the guild by entering the world of advertising. As the century progressed, a master vinegar maker or a perfumer was not enough to guarantee quality and reliability.

The king's privilege, bestowed to a few elite masters of every guild, endowed the holder with particular prestige. The number of perfumers named *artisans suivant la cour* was limited to eight throughout the reigns of Louis XV and Louis XVI. Aspiring owners petitioned or sought out members of the royal family.[43] Traditionally, court artisans were literally supposed to serve the king's needs, but the titles were also useful for marketing goods to the larger public. For instance, when Maille first received the title *vinaigrier du roi*, he used his newfound prestige to affirm his position.[44] Maille had competition from his predecessor's student, who felt the title should rightfully belong to him.[45] A struggle for recognition ensued and Maille warned that there were "different individuals who, using [his predecessor's] name and the false title of the King's vinegar maker, hoped to dupe the public."[46] The advertisements of this "fake" quickly disappeared and Maille triumphed as the official vinegar maker to both the court and the literate public. Collin, too, gained royal privileges, calling himself "producer-seller to the Queen, patented by his Majesty." Collin was not a member of a guild, which made him more dependent on royal privilege. Manufacturers could also turn to aristocratic patrons for prestige, even though these ties did not provide them with legal protection. The Duke of Orleans, the Duchess of Chartres, and the Prince of Condé, among others, lent their names to their favorite goods. Collin alluded to garnering the patronage of an archbishop, the Marquis of Rubel, and the Empress of Russia.[47]

Neither Maille nor Collin rested on their laurels, hoping to base their renown on more than just institutional recognition. Both wished to associate their names with the production of high-quality luxury products. Maille advertised his vinegars as "invented by the Sieur Maille" and Collin called himself "author of vegetable rouge." In every advertisement, Maille made sure he mentioned the 180 different vinegars he created, while Collin asserted that his vegetable rouge was of higher quality than any other. Both stressed their own innovations above any other form of recognition. Because of their inventiveness, their creations were guaranteed to be unique and respected. Innovation rather than tradition became the central tenet of commerce and consumerism, a necessity for a thriving business in the luxury trades. These luxury tradespeople were no longer ordinary artisans and portrayed themselves as genuine creators.

Growing emphasis on invention and authorship in beauty product advertisements directly opposed guild production methods. In the traditional guild workshop, the corporation set standards for artisans to follow, encouraging perfection but not innovation. Invention and individual publicity clashed with the corporate ethos of community and religious confraternity. The spirit of invention was touted by the philosophes, specifically Diderot, for perfecting the mechanical arts outside corporate restrictions.[48] Promoting innovation was clearly marked out in the pages of the affiches, where both master artisans and independent producers labeled themselves as creators rather than as members of a larger system of production. Invention was the keystone of recognition, fomented by the hunger for fashionable novelty. In a trade built on change, advertisers knew they had to reject the ideals of traditional corporate production, instead promoting themselves and their goods as representing fresh standards.

The new standards of innovation could garner both government titles and public recognition. Publicity and renown gained ground at the end of the eighteenth century as artisans hoped to build reputations. Maille claimed to be a "celebrated distiller, whose compositions have long possessed the favor of the public."[49] Bully evoked his public support to woo new buyers. Because of "the praise that he has received from people who use it," he was determined to give his hair vinegar "a greater amount of publicity."[50] Though the term *publicité* would not be tied to methods of advertising until the second half of the nineteenth century, Bully was well aware of the importance of gaining public approval for his products.

Successful inventors constantly had to defend the quality and authenticity of their products because of public fears of charlatanism. The eighteenth-century marketplace was depicted as filled with uncouth sellers ready to dupe the public for their own profit. This imagery put sellers on the defensive but also allowed them to define themselves in opposition to imagined or real hucksters. Accusations of theft and copying were numerous. For example, Raymond, a seller of suspect cosmetics, was publicly attacked for copying *citoyen* Charière's products. Raymond responded by accusing Charière of acting out of "animosity and detestable jealousy." He would "wait in silence, confident of his almond milk's merits."[51] The reading public probably was well aware that Raymond remained all but "silent" about this affair. Perhaps the most public and contentious battle was between Jean-Marie Farina, the inheritor of the original eau de Cologne recipe, and countless "unofficial" retailers who abused his name to market their goods. In 1762, Farina, living in Cologne, placed inserts in the *Affiches* and the *Mercure*, stating that he would set up only one outlet in Paris and that all other claimants to his name were fakes. In 1786, he squelched rumors of his own death and reassured the public that he was still producing eau de Cologne.[52] This disclaimer was repeated regularly, appearing in the *Affiches* as late as 1809.[53] Farina's name and its association with quality needed to be regularly reaffirmed to reassure clients and discredit counterfeiters.

Fear of being copied was widespread. To ensure that their products were of the highest quality, advertisers warned clients to beware of falsification. The citizeness Lachantrie hoped her clients would not confuse her beauty cream "with all the creams [and] beauty potions that some so-called chemists and other manipulators of the same caliber have pompously announced as their discovery."[54] Worried that her reputation would be tarnished "the widow Dupré, seller of rouge for the Queen and court, warns the public that there is sold daily in Paris and the provinces rouge marked and numbered as coming from her factory that can only harm her favorably established reputation, seeing that these different sellers or makers falsify her rouge or make it themselves with harmful ingredients." To stop this counterfeiting, she proposed to sign all her packaging and to send samples to selected ladies of the capital.[55] Dupré ensured that her public knew directly of these changes from her, through both the press and her own links to aristocratic clients. Collin reneged on responsibility for any jars of his rouge that had been tampered with, and, like many other retailers, he signed and sealed all his creations.[56] These advertisers were acutely aware that faulty products could irrevocably endanger their reputations.

One way of guaranteeing the quality of goods was for creators strictly to limit their sale. Outlets were becoming common in the late eighteenth century, but they needed to be advertised as controlled. Farina insisted over and over that his eau de Cologne would only be sold by one outlet in Paris. Other Parisian retailers were adamant that they would protect their customers by never opening outlets throughout Paris and the provinces. Mme Josse made clear "that she has authorized no one, neither in Paris nor in the provinces, to distribute her rouge, which will be sold only at her store." By 1781, however, she had changed her mind and set up one authorized

Parisian outlet.[57] By signing their products and promising to control their output themselves, these retailers hoped to convince buyers that their goods were reliable and pure.

Entrepreneurs not only promoted their products as legitimate but also promised satisfaction for their clients. Advertisements included instructions on how to apply products and descriptions of packaging. The goal of this detail was both to indicate the ease of use and to ensure that buyers would not misuse products. One cream to whiten the face was touted as highly successful because "the method of use is not difficult; one need only scrub the face, the neck, and the hands."[58] Concerned with her customers' satisfaction, Mme Sadous, a rouge manufacturer, would "convey herself immediately to their houses" to demonstrate its application.[59] Eighteenth-century artisans were well aware that the market was competitive and that they must promise the best services possible.

Maille clearly identified himself as more reliable than his competitors by offering foolproof products. He touted that his rouge could travel across oceans and would not run even in the hottest weather.[60] A few retailers went further than Maille and actually guaranteed satisfaction. For example, the owner of the "store and manufacture of super fine vegetable rouge, *à la Reine*," guaranteed that her rouge would last "for ten years, as beautiful at the end as at the beginning of the jar."[61] Desparo was so "certain of the beneficial effects of his potion, he proposed to receive no money from customers unless they were satisfied."[62] A seller of face whitener allowed the public "to experience the cream before buying it: in less than two minutes they shall see the effects."[63] The avid advertiser Dubost even offered free three-month trials of his newest product.[64] These money-back guarantees reinforced the commercial ethos of trust and reliability. Because cosmetic sellers were not producing recognizable commodities, such as foodstuffs or furnishings whose value could be tested rapidly, they turned to promising results. Guarantees from a commerce renowned for its falsity were worth more than a multitude of royal titles.

An essential part of good customer relations in addition to guaranteeing quality was listing prices. By publishing their prices, shopkeepers rejected the traditional system of bargaining or the guild regulated *prix juste*. Some artisans saw publishing fixed prices in journals as damaging to their reputation as "it risked creating false pretenses for those who buy and causing those who sell to look suspicious."[65] Yet as early as 1742, prices for products appeared in advertisements, which customers would have expected to be fixed. Rather than render the seller suspect, these prices were meant to reassure the client. Collin insisted that the price for his rouge would "never vary and would always be written on each container."[66] During the Revolution, one store even changed its name to *Au prix fixe* to make its policy clear.[67] Published prices meant that the buyer knew what to expect when entering a store and could ask for it by name and cost rather than be at the mercy of the shopkeeper.

Fixed prices also meant that customers could compare costs and choose to buy from the lowest or, if attempting to mimic the elite, highest bidder. Collin sold his jars of rouge at different prices, depending on the quality of the packaging—from porcelain (twenty-four livres) to crockery (six livres)—and on that of the rouge itself.[68] This allowed him to present his product as both an expensive luxury and a fairly affordable high-quality necessity. As we have seen, Maille's tactic was to list all vinegar rouge at the same price (one livre) but to charge separately for the packaging.[69] Another seller proposed to sell his cream with or without a jar and gave discounts to those who returned their jars, thus allowing for a wide range of prices.[70] Advertisers positioned themselves by stating their prices. Along with references to the courts of Europe, high prices signified an elite clientele, though the publication of these prices was a means to woo the wealthier commoners who hoped to gain in social status. Manufacturers such as Maille and Collin published their relatively flexible prices alongside their impressive titles to encapsulate a much larger customer base.

Signatures, guarantees, and set prices were some of the many ways retailers hoped to compete with one another and the home market. Advertisers benefited from the rise in consumption, positioning themselves as the perfect replacements to home creations. Instead of creating totally new products, some insisted that the goods they sold were just as reliable as homemade varieties. One advertisement began with a description of a recipe made of potatoes and almonds, which "makes a very economical and sweet smelling liquid paste." The insert then gave the address at which such a product could be bought.[71] Other ads, however, stressed the huge gap between homemade and store bought. Advertisers knew well that with the development of a thriving industry of perfumes and cosmetics it was no longer viable for women to spend time and money making goods they could just as easily buy from the local perfumer, preferably one that catered to their needs.

To supplant homemade goods, advertisers had to make theirs seem exceptional. Naming products was important to formulate a consumer product, in opposition to a lowly generic home creation. Retailers and manufacturers named their products in association with culturally recognizable symbols of taste and beauty. The most prominent types of labels adopted were those tying the product directly to its effects, such as *Crème de beauté*, *Eau de jouvence*, and *Essence virginale*. More suggestive of elite approval were royal and noble monikers. There were cosmetics named *Pâte d'amande royale*, *Blanc à la reine*, *L'eau du roi*, and *Essence royale et virginale*. None of these names referred to actual monarchs, at least not recent ones. Uncontroversial historical figures, such as Ninon de l'Enclos, were conjured up, but there was no *Pommade de Pompadour* or *Eau de Marie-Antoinette*. Consumers could distinguish between the "noble" past monarchies with the present state of affairs under first the lecherous Louis XV and the cuckolded Louis XVI.[72]

Staying away from current politics, retailers turned to names that evoked the past, especially antiquity or the exotic Near East. Maille sold his famous *Vinaigre romain* as well as a *Vinaigre de Cypres*, which was meant to dye hair brown.[73] There was an *Eau grecque* and an *Eau de Perse* with the same functions, evoking the dark beauties of the East. Though Collin's rouge did not have a fancy name, each of his jars was decorated with a classical head to associate his goods with the ancients.[74] There was also rose water from China, powder from Turkey, and, closer to home, honey cream from England, soap from Naples, perfume from Portugal, and, of course, the famous eau de Cologne.

The naming process was part of the larger definition and description of a product's potential. Unlike eighteenth-century novels that kept physical descriptions to a minimum, advertisers attempted to illustrate their goods with descriptive phrases. This growing art of description gave depth to advertisements that went beyond simple declarations of information. The seller's task was to appeal to the buyers' senses with evocations of scents and textures. Creams could be perfumed with "rose, jasmine, orange, vanilla, heliotrope, jonquil, violet, hyacinth, carnation, millefleurs, or pot-pourri."[75] Rouges were touted for their softness and fineness. Hair dyes could re-create a myriad of natural colors while eliminating unwanted ones. These advertisements evoked abundance, a cornucopia of goods ready and waiting for consumers of all tastes. Purchasing these products was as much about their sensuousness as about their uses. Affordable luxuries brought pleasurable responses from their new owners.

Advertisers listed characteristics for their goods to attempt to seduce the buyer by their miraculous properties and promises. Maille's vinegar rouge was "a singular and useful discovery . . . that gives the skin the most beautiful tone, the color of the rose, the complexion of youth."[76] Evocative advertisements described cosmetics in terms of the fantasy they could provide. Buyers were told in detail of the transformations that would occur once they bought and used their products. Hair dyes provided not only better color but also an end to hair loss and even regrowth. Rouge could re-create the lost bloom of youth, and creams could return to the skin its former elasticity. Advertisements tempted readers with promises of rebirth and, most important, beauty. Cosmetics advertisements created the possibility of both desirable and useful consumer objects. An insert that advertised twenty different products offered a plethora of heady scents and physical gratification, alongside solutions to all kinds of personal ills to all types of people.

Though not everyone would have the need for rouge or powder, most inserts did not specify for whom they were intended. Advertisements often addressed their readers as "mesdames" and "messieurs," implying that they wanted respectable clients. Their adoption of royal patrons and titles also implied emulation of the elite on the part of their buyers. But their other strategies highlighted the role of individual needs and desires. Pleasure and individual choice had an important place alongside emulation to explain the appeal of these new goods.[77] The stress on useful miracles allowed the readers of the affiches, even the servants and artisans, to identify with products and determine whether they fit their price range and lifestyle. Even those who could or would never buy luxury goods might read the affiches and partake vicariously in consumerism. Only the poorest and illiterate, who did not have access to the affiches, were not expected to need the services and products it provided. Because the products were defined as essential and useful, all others should be able to buy them. The format of publicity implied the means necessary for purchase and, without openly excluding anyone, circumscribed the sphere of consumerism.

Cosmetics advertisements, however started to address men and women differently. Most advertisements did not specify which gender their products pertained to, but some made references to differences in men's and women's toilettes by noting exceptions in the possible applications of products that were already gendered by the reader. One hair growth cream was "almost as precious for women, and consequently for men."[78] The discovery of a new rouge might be "interesting for all women and even for a few men."[79] Most advertisers did not need to specify who they were addressing because, by the end of the century, readers most likely assumed that women were the main audience for most makeup and cosmetics. Fashion magazines, which had previously contained equal coverage of male and female fashion, were increasingly focused on women's clothing and hair. Men's fashions were still part of the discussion, but they necessitated less time and thus less print space.[80] Yet by not openly defining the gender of the customer, advertisers allowed men nonetheless to identify with them. Though cosmetics had been defined as anathema for the new male by the 1770s, the ownership of products that could reduce wrinkles, whiten the skin, and renew color may have resonated with them as much as with women.

Conclusion

"By bringing producers and consumers of goods and services together in mutually beneficial markets and exchanges . . . by establishing new links that transcended geographical localism, social particularism, gender exclusivity and occupational restrictiveness, the *affiches* played a considerable role as agents of the commercialization of *ancien régime* society. They activated and simultaneously legitimated market exchange; they both boosted demand and fashioned the reader as a consumer."[81] Colin Jones gives the affiches an important role in the growing consumerism of the eighteenth century and even in the motivations for the Revolution to come. The newspapers' format allowed the editors, the advertisers, and the readers of the journal to shape the development of an advertising culture. Ultimately, advertisements helped create a consumer object that in turn allowed the general public of literate French citizens to participate in the consumer market. Cheap and expendable consumer objects, such as rouge vinegars and bear greases, transformed the pages of journals into symbolic storehouses filled with wondrous goods. Eighteenth-century advertising may have started as a simple means of passing on information based in the ideals of corporate privilege and protectionism, but it flowered into a sophisticated means of publicity. Though not all advertisers used aggressive methods of selling, those who did positioned themselves and their products outside the traditional means of production and sale.

These retailers used both accepted forms of commercial exchange and new marketing methods. They continued to associate their products with royalty while defining their shops as separate from corporate entities. They depended on recognized titles, while asserting their right to list prices and provide individual guarantees that seem inconceivable in a corporate setting. They stressed their own vulnerability as members of a respectable profession amid growing fears of charlatanism. Yet by publicly announcing their names, in opposition to guild regulations, they placed themselves alongside the long tradition of street hawkers and shady vendors. Tradition and innovation coexisted in the advertisements of the eighteenth century, as those who used it clung to age-old means of selling while creating new methods appropriate to both the print medium and the growing market of goods.

The manipulation of information in the affiches indicates a sophisticated understanding by retailers of the evolving market and growing consumer public. Advertisers aimed to please an increasing audience of both readers and buyers. They hoped to lure consumers by proposing better products, cheaper prices, or more evocative names within the framework of corporate quality and trust. These promises were repeated by advertisers to create a recognizable array of words and phrases associated with wearing cosmetics. Advertisers promoted themselves, their goods, and the properties of trust, pleasure, and usefulness as intrinsically tied together. Advertising melded with manufacturing, as a means of solidifying personal relations in an artisanal setting.

Yet just as important, advertisers promoted a dialogue with their targeted audience, emphasizing their own roles as creators and artists whose primary relationship was with their customers and the fulfillment of their desires for newness. Fashion and innovation, as much as tradition and trust, came to represent the ethos of the seller of beauty. The desires of potential buyers evoked in advertisements of all types helped lure buyers, educated by the discourses of consumerism. The spread of production techniques and the decline of home remedies encouraged shopping, but the development of publicity encouraged consumerism and, with it, the self-aware consumer.

Judging the effectiveness of advertisements, however, is difficult, even in the early twenty-first century. Innovative advertisers were hoping not to promote a lifestyle but to create the desire to buy. Compared with the prosaic powders and pomades listed in account books, these sellers aimed to stimulate a need for something slightly more exotic and novel. If their inserts, trade cards, and leaflets worked to make their products visible in an increasingly competitive market, then the minimal cost was worth it. Like advertisers today, shop owners probably asked their new customers where they had heard of their store or product, determining the effectiveness of publicity by word of mouth. Those who continued to place advertisements, it is assumed, found it useful to spreading their renown and increasing their sales. By the Revolution, the growth of repeat publicity increased name visibility for both the producers and their products. By the early nineteenth century, as the opportunities for advertising expanded, businesspeople certainly started realizing the usefulness and necessity of advertising. As one almanac put it, "commerce exists only by publicity."[82]

Advertising was not accepted by all as a viable means of bypassing traditional systems of sales. Early on, critics argued that publicity was based on empty symbols of quality, divorced from older forms of legitimacy. In this dangerous marketplace, selling beauty aids was particularly treacherous because in these matters the public was blinded by vanity. Because all wished to be beautiful "the public news-sheets were filled with promises from charlatans so seductive that many women, even without any confidence, succumbed to the temptation, almost despite themselves."[83] Yet the distrust of publicity, linked to the fear of charlatanism, could be transformed into a means of promotion. By the early nineteenth century, publicity had taken on a new form that intermixed critical awareness of fraud and deception with constant promotion of brand names in the guise of advice.[84] This was a commercial sphere that was at once treacherous and open. Pointing a finger at the false claims of others, retailers presented themselves as always honest and transparent in their use of publicity and promotion. They claimed to protect the consumer by this language of openness: "When consumerism is constant, the public can judge for itself the good or bad quality of items."[85] Buyers wanted to know what was being offered and at what prices to simplify choice and judgment. Clarity and simplicity were the ideal for economic exchanges.

Unlike England, where "puffing" was dissected and publicity had a well-articulated vocabulary, in France the culture of publicity and attacks on it were in their infancy in the late eighteenth century.[86] Attacks against cosmetics, however, spread widely through various means and most prominently in the journals that published advertisements. Just as the commerce of cosmetics placed them in the homes of the working classes, the voices of morality, reason, and taste pronounced makeup outmoded. A sharp contradiction took shape between the flowering of a cosmetics market, as identified in advertisements and the account books of perfumers, and the numerous attacks against makeup, which aimed to reformulate what it meant to be presentable in eighteenth-century France.

CHAPTER FOUR

Maligning Beauty
The Critics Take on Artifice

It is a quarrel about women (*querelle de femmes*). Men have entered the fray; it has become almost a civil war. The philosophers of the land make arguments for and against luxury. . . . The wits create catch-phrases, jokes, epigrams, songs; others say simply that reasonable women are the most amiable. Elegant women are not without worries . . . every day a few of them leave art to return to nature, and soon they will not be numerous or strong enough to fight against the Insurgents. We do not know when and how this large and small affair will finish.

—*Affiches de Toulouse*

This "large and small affair" was the debate over the uses and abuses of artifice at the end of the eighteenth century. Elegant women needed to worry because their makeup and extravagant frills were being replaced by more modest and simpler styles. Though the writer of this ridicule, a journalist for the *Affiches de Toulouse*, claimed not to know how this battle would end, he clearly favored the odds of the "insurgents" against artifice, and rightly so. By the 1780s, fashions had shifted radically for the elite and respectable citizens of France and their counterparts throughout Europe. Satirists and philosophers waged a war of words against women and men who masked their faces. At first playful and light, these criticisms grew more vehement as the century wore on, until few were willing to defend wearing makeup. Not only were the criticisms essentially unchallenged, but they came from all sections of intellectual society. As Daniel Roche points out, by the end of the century, "moral apologists for fashion were few."[1] The wig was toppled, the voluminous skirts shrank, and the painted face was scrubbed clean. Fashion is dead, long live fashion.

These attacks against fashion had as their enemies not just extravagant spending on frills but the aristocratic definition of selfhood. Criticisms of cosmetics were intrinsically tied to creating a public sphere for political discussion and dissent. Transparency of meaning in texts, behavior, and self-presentation was an essential aspect of the Enlightenment project and the physiognomist's science. The goal was to illuminate what had previously been hidden and to simplify what had previously been overdone. The word plays, innuendoes, and masked balls of the Old Regime elites were to be replaced by frank discussions, honest emotions, and polite soirées. Late eighteenth-century moralists were well aware that the luxurious clothing and artifice of the court was at the center of this redefinition of merit over birth and wealth. Because of the decline in sumptuary legislation and the consumer revolution, fear of emulation grew. Yet attacks against luxury were not principally to keep the lower orders in check but rather to distinguish a new elite from aristocratic excess and those who copied it. The aristocratic elite and their artifice no longer represented the ideals of honor and virtue, so a new, more acceptable system of fashion and luxury had to be created. A new group of elite, made up of both commoners and nobility, rallied around the concepts of virtuous luxury and natural beauty.[2]

Women and their roles in society were placed at the center of attempts at redefining fashion to fit notions of transparent and natural beauty. Femininity became a means of physically representing virtue. Women were to be treated with respect and reverence as long as they embodied the virtues of gentleness and sensibility that could be read on their faces.[3] Thus, to create an idealized world of republican fraternity, the spendthrift, sexually voracious, politically aware, and painted courtesan had to be replaced by the prudent, virtuous, domesticated, and natural mother.[4] Cosmetics were at the center of this redefinition not only because they created dissimulation but because "they *expose* the constructed qualities of masculinity and femininity." Women who wore cosmetics painted on their femininity, implying choice and control over their roles in society. Patricia Phillippy argues that the painted woman was threatening because she claimed "a creative and self-creative authority ordinarily reserved for men."[5] Though this was already a common concern of the Renaissance, it was essential to those critics who hoped to create a clear demarcation between the sexes in the eighteenth century.

In England, the turn against artifice began earlier and was in opposition to French fashions and practices. To wear French makeup was to be sexually and morally corrupt. Increasingly, French commentators adopted English values for both women's behavior and cosmetic use.[6] To save the women of France from corruption, many male critics felt they had to berate the practices of artifice while extolling the virtues of natural beauty. Adopting the language of physiognomists, commentators argued that if a woman was beautiful in her exterior traits, then she must embody purity within as well. This mix of interior and exterior beauty would allow her to function at the height of taste in the new social hierarchy. The new meaning of beauty by the end of the eighteenth century excluded masculine traits, emphasizing instead the physical and moral nature of femininity. Women represented beauty and thus embodied virtue, a quality that was to be prescribed to their faces by the rational male thinkers of the new elite.

Criticizing artifice was a fairly easy task with few detractors. Replacing it with a new aesthetic of beauty was altogether more complicated. Concretely defining "natural" fashion in either dress or makeup and then influencing the respectable feminine public to adopt these new styles was not an easy task. The newly naturalized and feminized body was an amorphous entity whose signs and meanings were much less easily pinned down than the regulated extravagance of court dress. The debate over cosmetics, essentially a war of words against those who continued to wear them, illustrates clearly the difficulty of presenting a workable alternative model of beauty. Aristocratic makeup, essentially rouge, white face paint, and powder, may have been discredited outside court, but the model of natural beauty that was meant to replace it left women (and men) with a confusing and ultimately highly malleable sphere in which to display and create their own sense of self.

Early Modern Toilette

The war of words against cosmetics in the eighteenth century was not new. The Greeks and Romans were ardent critics of cosmetics. The church fathers, from Tertullian to St. Jerome, also warned women away from the sins of makeup that disfigured their God-given beauty and encouraged vanity.[7] In the seventeenth century, most criticisms against finery and artifice were made in the name of God. For instance, in François De Grenaille's *L'honneste fille,* women were told that it was more important to be beautiful in the eyes of God than in the eyes of men.[8] M. de Fitelieu in *La contre-mode* of 1642 saw makeup as a tool for deception, invented by the devil, which was especially tempting to women, though no less dangerous for men.[9] Phillippy argues that early modern criticisms against cosmetics stressed feminine frailty and the need for male control. Her work indicates that cosmetic criticism was common throughout Europe.[10]

By the late seventeenth century and during the first half of the eighteenth century, wearing makeup was well established in the French court. The tone of criticism softened, and most comments were aimed at the misuses of makeup rather than its uses. Critics admonished women for wearing too much rouge if they were pretty or too little if they were ugly. One wag noted, "a Parisian woman would have less trouble staying two months locked up in her house than to appear one instant in public without being made-up."[11] English visitors, however, were especially shocked at the extent of French artifice, comparing it with the natural restraint of their own ladies in London. The *Gentleman's Magazine* commented that French women were "almost equally beautiful," but that the fashion for rouge meant that even those with naturally fair skin found "themselves obliged to lay on Red." Lady Mary Wortley Montagu was harsher on the overuse of makeup, calling French women "monstrously unnatural in their Paint."[12]

Before criticisms of makeup became ubiquitous in France, its application was an occasion for voyeurism as well as mockery. Elite women spent hours at their toilette, first in private to apply paint and rouge, a ritual to which "lovers were never admitted."[13] The second toilette was a public display of primping in the mirror before a table laden with pots and potions. As a reapplication of paint, this toilette became "a spectacle that magnifies the interplay between the hidden and the revealed body."[14] Men visited these provocateurs hoping for favors, intrigues, or glimpses of female flesh. The public toilette was a spectacle of coquetry in the first half of the century, meant to seduce and entertain one's guests by pretending to unveil one's hidden charms. At the toilette, women transformed themselves, and it was in this transformation from bedroom beauties to society ladies that the male gaze found its greatest pleasure. For the capable coquette, however, the spectacle of her toilette was carefully orchestrated so that the careless moments of undress were just as planned as the finishing touches on her wig and dress. The rouge women applied "painted lively freshness which love and the effects of the bath knew how to spread on the complexion, as well as tender and timorous modesty."[15] A true coquette could apply love's blushes at will.

Men who attended the toilette became the spectators of a seemingly private reversal of the strip show, portrayed in numerous pictorial and literary works. Writers and painters took playful jabs at women's vanity and frivolity while describing these traits as highly sensual. This female weakness was never seriously criticized because enhanced titillation for the male viewer was this vanity's ultimate outcome. Ensconced in the Rococo aesthetic of pleasure and illusion, the realm of feminine artifice became the realm of masculine desire.[16] A voyeur's fantasy, the coquette preened publicly out of a desire to be desired. Her sensuality was intrinsically wrapped up in "the art of dress" in which the dressing table and room were the entrance to the bedchamber. A woman's sensuality was detectable in her level of undress and her "lips of roses . . . burning and half-closed."[17] The morning toilette hinted at past misdeeds and sexual pleasures to come. As the libertine Casanova pointed out, rouge was not meant to look natural but to "please the eyes which see in it the marks of an intoxication heralding the most amorous fury."[18] Most early eighteenth-century descriptions and paintings evoked the feminine toilette not to sermonize but to titillate a masculine audience. Criticisms of women who wore paint in the early part of the century were often no more than flirtatious means of seduction, rather than serious attempts at changing women's habits.

The Dangers of Artifice: The Mask of Deceit

By the 1760s, the playful toilette was increasingly replaced by a much more moralizing and sinister vision of artifice; deception replaced seduction. Though often couched in humorous stories, such as the works of Louis Antoine de Caraccioli, Louis Mercier, and Nicolas-Edmé Restif de la Bretonne, commentary on vanity and artifice took on an almost universally proscriptive tone. Critics replaced sensual rouge, popular in the early part of the century, with a mask of unsightly paint. Instead of being socially cohesive and sexually titillating, this mask signified the dissolution of clear, distinct social relationships threatening to the male ego. The goal of critics was to tear off the disguise and reveal the authentic self underneath: a transparent, thus seemingly easily readable persona.

Wearing cosmetics became linked to two different types of corruption: aesthetic deception and moral degradation. Neither of these criticisms was new; they were commonly employed during the Renaissance.[19] What changed was the number and pervasiveness of these invectives and their relationship to the social and cultural context of the period. Critics called for an end to artifice because of its transformative powers and its link to the larger decay within society. They saw fard as artifice applied by women to deceive the viewer, most often innocent men. This deceit led to vanity in young women and falsity in older women attempting to conceal the effects of aging. For critics, attempts to turn old women into maidens and to improve beauty through paint were a complete failure (figure 3). Cosmetics did nothing to improve anyone's beauty, they argued, but instead led to revolting visages. Men who adopted cosmetics, however, turned into effeminate *petits maîtres* with blurred gender identities. Second, and more damaging, cosmetics use by both genders caused the degeneration and corruption of society. Paint represented moral decline, which led men and women not only to step outside their gender roles but to blur the social distinctions between noble and commoner, master and servant. Those who abused their faces with paint displayed personal decadence, as well as provided signs of a larger decline in the social hierarchy.

From its inception, the artifice of cosmetics was compared with the art of painting. In the late seventeenth century, those critical of the colorist school of painting adopted the term fard to describe these new artistic excesses.[20] Falsity in painting was termed fard and a "portrait without fard" came to mean a truthful description

Figure 3. L. Surugue, *La Folie pare la Décrépitude des ajustemens de la Jeunesse* (1745),
Bibliothèque nationale estampes

of character.[21] Though critics associated painting with makeup, the opposite was
also true. They described women's toilettes as "painter's studios," and the same pig-
ments were present in paint and makeup.[22] Though it may have been acceptable for
a portraitist to enhance the sitter's features and colors using pigment, the reproduc-
tion of this false veneer on a real face was seen as a futile attempt to enter the world
of art whose properties were incorporeal and static. The face functioned as a reusable
canvas, but, unlike a work of art, it would prove to be ephemeral and false.

    The made-up face was also related to the art of theater. Daniel Roche points out
that wearing actual masks was common in eighteenth-century high society, linking

the social practice of artificial appearance with the physical barriers of playacting. These faces of felt, like the application of makeup, were meant to create a social uniform, a regulation of fashion through artifice.[23] They also had the power to establish social distance and mystery, essential to the practices of sexual and political intrigue. Critics in the second half of the eighteenth century saw masks as a symbol of deception, rather than of social conformity or sexual foreplay. The literal face-paint mask was even more insidious than the felt mask or the oil painting. It functioned as a constant reminder that nothing in society was as it seemed, while also signifying society's conformity and order. It represented flesh and blood reproducing the expected norms of beauty—red cheeks and white skin—in women and for men who themselves were caught in the deception fard helped create.

Though the early practices of makeup created an artificial face prized for its falsity, by the later eighteenth century, makeup mimicked the natural, rather than supplanted it. Fard worn by women and men attempted to reproduce nature by enhancing or completely recreating the bloom of youth and beauty. What was once seen as artificial was now meant to be recognized as artificially natural. No eighteenth-century fashionable aristocrat would have failed to discern the application of paint and rouge, while still asserting that this mask was the recreation of the ideal beauty, a natural beauty that had to be artificial since it did not exist outside the boundaries of fashion. For its critics, the worst aspect of fard was its purported attempt to recreate norms of natural beauty while blatantly supporting the creation of further artifice. If makeup re-created nature, then the destruction of the mask was much more difficult.

Critics hoped to clarify the contradiction between the visually artificial exterior and the assumed natural model, which was at its most obvious in the relationship of the coquette to her physical beauty. The typically vain coquette "congratulates herself on her attractions which she owes to art and not nature . . . her lovers, duped by the paint and rouge, compliment her on her charms; and she, duped by this praise, which does not belong to her any more than her paint and her rouge, thinks herself truly beautiful."[24] Thus, the wearers of artifice were the first victims of its spell. Women believed themselves to be enhanced by the addition of paint. This false vanity not only obliterated any true beauty they might possess but helped establish a fashion that demanded wearing makeup by all women of the upper classes. If true beauty was defined through the use of artifice, then no scrubbed-clean beauty could compete. This was the first myth that critics wished to challenge. Artifice, they categorically stated, transformed women into unnatural creatures.

Critics accused women of consciously degrading their natural beauty in an attempt to outdo each other, since "the small number of [women] who have not yet

fully lost their beauty feel guilty and, in an admirable emulation, they make themselves as unsightly as possible to look fashionable."[25] Society, thus, dictated that
beauty and attractiveness be sacrificed to the whim of fashion. Cosmetics functioned
as a means of competition between women, causing the wearer to enter a world of
feminine rivalry and pettiness. Reasonable women were caught between "the desire
to please which custom contradicts and the desire to follow custom."[26] Frivolous
women could not stand the presence of prettier women who had no need for rouge,
so they constantly tried to coerce and humiliate others into applying as much artifice as themselves.[27] It was with peer pressure that the aging coquette corrupted
youth. A mother was jealous of her daughter whose presence "destroys everything as
soon she is near me, I feel uglier when I see her. And her youth and simple nature
do more than all my art, my attentions, and my attire."[28] To diminish the strength
of youth over age, older coquettes victimized those who had not yet learned the tricks
of flirtation.[29] Artifice was invented by "old age and ugliness" to confuse youth with
"the age of disgust."[30] Young, fresh-faced women who feared the loss of their beauty
were cunningly advised by their knowledgeable elders to apply makeup to fend off
the passage of time.

The end to youth came quickly in the eighteenth century. Marie-Antoinette was
said to invite only young women to her dinners since she did not conceive of how
"past thirty, a woman would dare appear in court."[31] The Comtesse de Genlis felt
old age started at thirty-five; Caraccioli identified twenty-five as his yardstick for the
loss of beauty.[32] Beauty was often compared to a flower that bloomed briefly and
spectacularly.[33] This loss of social status and attraction at an early age meant that all
women were at risk of becoming coquettes. Fearing the loss of their attractiveness,
women primped to keep their suitors. One fading beauty "in the past found it obvious that men would love her, now she is almost thankful."[34] Having reached old
age "a bitter anxiety broke her heart; in losing her charms, she felt she had lost her
being."[35]

Older women who wore cosmetics were not only to be pitied but also to be
laughed at as silly creatures unaware of their vanity. Pierre Jean Baptiste Nougaret
made fun of a fifty-year-old lady who "thought herself still pretty! Her skinny, dry
body was in striking contrast with the paint and rouge that covered her yellow
and livid complexion."[36] Casanova was disgusted when faced with a sixty-year-old
woman who still plastered her face.[37] Hardly ever portrayed in a sympathetic light,
older mothers and widows were left stranded when their daughters married, with no
place in society and no hope of further love affairs. The right behavior for a woman
over forty was to renounce coquettishness without regret.[38] Kept well away from the
sensitive eyes of intelligent men, these women should quietly live out their lives in

seclusion and charitable works, rather than dominate the salons of polite society. Women who reached old age were to mourn but accept their losses as "unfortunately everything changes in nature."[39]

Since artifice functioned as part of the social rituals of voyeurism and flirting, men too were implicated in its deceit. Though some men may have falsely complimented the wearer of makeup to ingratiate themselves with her, critics felt that the majority of men were unwitting dupes of manipulative women. Governments passed laws against wearing makeup to protect these men.[40] Innocent men were told to be on their guard against the false veneer of old or homely women. In one story, a young man learned the hard way of his lover's wrinkles and imperfections by handing her a bottle of ink in the dark rather than her usual rouge. Upon lighting a candle, he found himself face to face with a horrible hag covered in black spots. His first love affair ended in ridicule, teaching the young man not to trust the tender sex.[41] In another often-repeated story, a man followed a prostitute home only to find her attractions taken off one by one, to reveal a hideous shrew underneath.[42] The obvious moral was that in the dark streets of Paris or even in seductively lit boudoirs, there was no way of knowing what grotesque traits lay under the voluminous dresses, pounds of paint, and towering wigs. No man was safe from these harridans as long as the fashion of dissimulation held power over society. Men feared the unknown and naked self underneath the frills. Criticizing makeup meant criticizing a woman's attempt to hide from society her age, weight, skin blemishes, or social standing. Wearing paint implied unspoken faults. Visibility was the aim, but the critics warned that the woman underneath was as grotesque as her made-up counterpart.

It was not only the face underneath the paint that men feared but also the nature of the paint that they found offensive. The deceit of makeup made it unworthy of praise even though it might improve a woman's looks:

> The toilette has rendered their faces charming
> Not by natural graces and smiles
> But by the false art of applying polish.
> Oh, beauties! Who owe to paint alone
> The brilliant coloring of a skilful visage
> Far from attracting hearts, you make yourselves hated.[43]

Even if cosmetics managed to improve beauty or re-create it, its status as a form of trickery led to disgust of an otherwise attractive face. If cosmetics were aimed at enhancing natural beauty, then, most critics agreed, it was not succeeding because men certainly preferred the real thing to false hopes.

Though some critics admitted they were tricked by the falsity of fard and found it capable of re-creating beauty, most asserted that makeup did nothing to improve women's looks. Caraccioli believed that "the more she employs beauty aids, the more she makes herself ugly" and that a woman's application of rouge resembled bull's blood.[44] As one commentator righteously noted, "if they claim to please men by the help of the rouge and paint that they wear with so much profusion, they deceive themselves."[45] Women's beautification was the ultimate act of self-deception.

Because men found makeup intriguing, they were threatened by it and associated its use with guilt and deceit. Yet in a paradox, all rational men claimed the ability to see the true and often monstrous self beneath cosmetics. Caraccioli warned that "one thinks by using makeup to trick the masses and to attract a crowd of admirers; yet this makeup in the eyes of the wise is but a solemn and public confession of the annihilation of beauty."[46] The men who were tricked by cosmetics were under the spell of love and thus without their rational senses at the time.[47] This momentary loss of reason was as much a threat to the individual Romeo as to the fundamental functioning of society. If men could not judge their sexual surroundings, their ability to rule the state and economy was also in question. Critics uncovered the layers of paint to warn and educate less perceptive men to whom these truths were not so self-evident. Male commentators both feared the power of cosmetics to dissimulate ugliness or age while asserting that any reasonably astute male could see right through the disguises of artifice.

The aesthetic argument against cosmetics, though contradictory, was at its heart both an indictment of female deception and a practical means of redefining beauty as the domain of rational male thinkers. The makeup of the court and aristocratic circles of the early eighteenth century was meant to be a visible marker, openly deceiving the viewer while functioning as an intrinsic part of the game of seduction.[48] By the late eighteenth century, critics felt that it was necessary to point out and discredit makeup because its application had become subtler and more widespread. Not only could cosmetics create false veneers, but such masks were offensive themselves, having the opposite of the intended effect. There was little point, in these critics' eyes, to beauty products meant to hide flaws even if they were aesthetically pleasing. The erotic appeal of the mask was replaced by the vileness of any form of artifice.

The Dangers of Artifice: The Feminized Petits Maîtres

Men had to be taught to discern the falsity and ugliness of artifice, not only on their lovers but on themselves as well. Men's fashion, up until the eighteenth century, had often been more ornate and showy than women's. Most elite men wore powdered wigs, and by the early eighteenth century, it was also acceptable for them to wear rouge, face paint, and perfumes and creams. Men "spend much time and effort making themselves clean and well dressed."[49] These practices of beautification took place in male toilettes, where they could also entertain visitors and prepare for their outings.[50] As the century progressed, these spaces and practices were defined as feminine. Therefore, men were excluded from the vanity table and instead relegated to voyeur. What J. C. Flügel labels the "Great Masculine Renunciation" banned men from primping and left the male body with no obvious exhibitionary role. Despite evidence that men continued to purchase cosmetics, those who adopted artifice found themselves no longer in favor, and they could only continue to do so surreptitiously. A new version of masculinity privileged simplicity of dress and, more important, a retreat from notions of male beauty. The new man was a man because of his rough features, not despite them.

Fashionable men who wore beauty aids came under harsh scrutiny. The petits maîtres and their companions the *abbés poudrés,* both known for their frivolous pastimes and fashionable dress, became stock comic characters in plays, novels, and tracts. These men were depicted as even more concerned with their appearance than the women around them. Diderot's petit maître was highly self-conscious, "blowing on his sleeves, constantly readjusting his wig . . . and eyeing his rouge in the mirror."[51] This vision of male vanity caused Caraccioli to quip that petits maîtres were members of a secret "order of frivolity" who had to spend at least four hours at their toilettes every day.[52] Even the military, site of male power, was corrupted when "each officer procured himself a toilet-table and spent long hours there."[53] This loss of time seemed especially disgraceful for elderly statesmen and men of distinction, not to mention men of the church.[54]

Loss of productivity was not the greatest hazard of male vanity. Critics feared that men who wore cosmetics would eventually become undistinguishable from women. Men with toilettes were "as effeminate as women."[55] Young men were bewitched by "this seeming uniformity between the two sexes, that rouge . . . that air of coquettishness."[56] Men who had in the past sported masculine mustaches now wore "an effeminate face."[57] This ridiculous feminization of men, encouraged by social mores, led to their weakening and eventually to their loss of identity to the voracious women of society. The women who ran the popular salons controlled politics and power, since the fashionable men "have brains and almost faces and figures of women."[58] Aristocratic men who acted as women could not rule over society or expect their social inferiors to follow them. They upset the gender hierarchy and, in doing so, the hierarchy of social positions.

Feminized men were feared because they undermined the division between the sexes.[59] In one story, Restif de la Bretonne described a lovely boy whose "red mouth, garnished with the most beautiful teeth, resembled a rose bud; on his smooth complexion one can see the brilliance of youth and on his neck the whiteness of a lily." This description mimicked that of a pretty young women, and indeed, in this case, the feminized boy turned out to be a young woman in disguise. Restif de la Bretonne's criticism of society, however, was not only that girls dressed as boys but that such a feminine creature was an acceptable man to both the characters in his story and to contemporary readers.[60] The shift from a one-sex model, in which masculinity was the norm, to a two-sex model, in which men and women were seen as opposites, heightened concerns over gender identification.[61] Restif de La Bretonne stressed the importance of men and women's dress staying separate so that neither should slide into the realm of the other. He felt that "everything, about women must have a sex, the clothing, the hair, the shoes."[62] The young man who wore makeup may have done so to follow fashions but would unconsciously emulate the weaknesses of the opposite sex if he did not desist.

Cosmetics were not only a means of destroying gender identification but of destroying the link between age and respectability as well. Men, like women, were accused of attempting to dissimulate their age to make conquests. Nougaret told the story of a silly old man who hid his age by wearing an elegant wig and painting his eyebrows black. The older man in rouge and powder was no less "grotesquely ridiculous and ridiculously grotesque" than his female counterpart.[63] The moral of the story, as it had been for older coquettes, was that old, often impotent men were not made for love, which should be left to the younger generation. An older man should look on women only as friends from whom he wants conversation. For men, old age brought respectability and distinguished looks to even the ugliest facade.[64]

To point to the further inappropriateness of rouged men, critics turned to the opinions of women, whose desire for a more distinctly male partner was seen as the strongest argument for the banishment of all finery. The Countess of Getnon-Ville, in *L'épouse rare,* made this point explicitly. Her hero transformed himself from a selfish, priggish petit maître to an adoring, capable husband. In the story, a count married a good woman but soon returned to his mistress. When he developed smallpox, however, his mistress abandoned him to the disease. Only then did he think of his wife and realized that she too would no longer desire him because "I am no longer the Adonis to whom she gave her tenderness; I am only a monster who inspires horror and who merits only her disdain." His brother assured him that, on the contrary, pockmarks did not make men unsightly, "they even became advantageous by giving men a more masculine face and that [the count] who [currently] looked more like a woman than a man, would benefit more than any other" from this illness. The count's vanity, however, made him disregard both his brother's words and those of his wife, who swore she would love only her husband. Eventually, they were reunited, but not before he had drugged her, ravished her, and inundated her with presents to prove his love.[65] The husband, who had lived a lascivious and feminized lifestyle, reformed into a paragon of the new masculinity, complete with economic and physical power. His masculinity was reestablished by his wife's appropriately feminine humility and purity, rather than the mistress's coquettish behavior. The new man he became had to learn the value of masculine ruggedness as well as character. Harmony and domesticity were shown to be the rewards of this transformation, even though they were achieved through deception and violence.

Men who wore rouge had always been a minority, principally those at court. Thus, the criticism and eventual demise of makeup for men of the upper classes did not have the same social resonances as the criticism of women's toilettes. Yet these attacks also had another larger target in mind. They were aimed at discouraging women from adopting makeup. The male version of the coquette provided a mirror in which women could recognize the absurdity of their behavior. Women were to be the opposites of men by playing on their natural femininity without the need for the frivolity advocated in court life. The petit maître, even more than the coquette, pointed to the perils of artifice for both the women who frequented him and the men who admired his looks.

The Dangers of Artifice: The Immoral Coquette

Artifice was blamed for affectation, deception, vanity, and the creation of a race of feminized men. Yet the sin of vanity that led to the adoption of cosmetics by innocent young women and men was just the first step toward greater transgressions. Vanity led to an increasing need for attention, which in turn led to a desire for money and by default led women of the lower orders into prostitution or acting and tempted women of the upper echelons of society toward adultery and gambling. The coquette transformed herself from an innocent young woman to a treacherous courtesan by wearing makeup. Bad skin, which had to be masked with makeup, marked the wearer guilty of the sins of drink, sex, and gambling. Ultimately, in the imagery adopted by critics, artifice helped define and destroy the wearer's virtue, using makeup as a shorthand for immorality. The painted face was the equivalent of the tainted soul.[66] The powers of deception intrinsic in artifice, whether conscious or not on the part of the wearer, were as much a part of this immorality as gambling, loose morals, and drinking. The layers of paint were themselves the causes of corruption and not just its representation.

Though once praised for her seductive attributes, the coquette now under attack was by definition mannered and experienced, vain and self-centered, profligate and frivolous. Polite aristocratic society demanded that all women, at least temporarily, adopt the role of the coquette. For the critics of the court and aristocracy, she represented falsity and double dealings, which clashed with Enlightenment ideals. The *Encyclopédie* noted that false women and coquettes were "still more dangerous for the court and the spirit than were the courtiers."[67] Lynn Festa argues that the seductive role of coquettes had a political implication "since beauty allows non-aristocratic women like Louis XV's mistress, Mme de Pompadour, to gain dominion over the king." Cosmetics created a means of feminine power, a means of social elevation, and a means to "conceal the inner thoughts of the individual, creating a screen upon which other sentiments may be projected."[68] Affected manners not only stood in the way of enlightenment for the state and society but had deleterious effects on the women who adopted this fashion. Genlis believed that fashion "shrinks the spirit, renders it susceptible to the most ridiculous miseries, it extinguishes sensitivity and leads to the most awful mistakes." A true coquette had neither principals nor virtues; she was a complete moral outcast.[69]

To those who advocated a moral and simple lifestyle, the threat of the mannered and vain woman came from her ability to put on a persona that hid her true and evil nature. She was

> Sister of treachery
> She cherishes falsity and seductions. . . .
> Her modest glances offers to those who trust her
> Only softness, candor, virtue, severity
> But an enlightened eye. . . .
> Tearing off the imposter veil
> Soon penetrates the depths of her heart
> One sees then only false modesty. . . .
> More fard than virtue.[70]

The most maligned coquette was the one capable of seeming innocent and good. She could trick men into infamy and corrupt other women into immoral acts. The coquette stood for all that was false in the high society of Old Regime France.

Critics felt that coquettes were made from the inherent feminine failure of vanity rather than from social expectations of elite behavior. Vanity caused women to adopt fashionable clothing and makeup, leading to the sins of gambling, affairs, and worse. Eighteenth-century tales of feminine decadence, which described in pornographic detail the salacious elements of the coquette's life, ultimately ended badly for the protagonist.[71] In Nougaret's *Dangers de la seduction,* the heroine, Lucette, gave way to the barrage of attention by her suitors, blushing profusely as she recognized her own charms. Her adoption of rouge to cover her emotions marked the first step from innocent maid to coquette. Lucette soon gave in to the world of theater and gambling. After contracting syphilis, she finally lost her powers over men because "her charms evaporated, her eyes hollowed, her plumpness disappeared." Her descent into sin necessitated further application of rouge and other cosmetics to mask the marks of her lifestyle. The once naive Lucette ended up hanged after a life filled with sexual conquests, prostitution, and crime, all vividly detailed for the reader.[72] The moral of these tales was that young women should avoid the pitfalls of their vanity. The heroines of these novels abused their beauty for immoral ends and had either to learn from their mistakes through marriage to a good man or pay for them with death or, worse, the loss of their beauty. Young coquettes "imagine that they will never cease to be pretty and that the present will last forever; yet most of them die in the utmost misery."[73] Punished thoroughly, the coquette entertained male readers with her seductive figure and antics but had to be crushed and subdued in the end. Beauty was a major theme in eighteenth-century novels: it was necessary for success in society; yet, caused tragedy and loss when it was not protected.[74]

Thus, beauty was a curse for a young woman for whom modesty and constancy were more important values.[75] When these young beauties married, however, the danger remained. It was a well-known adage that a beautiful wife was a hazardous asset to a husband because she could evoke strong passions in other men. By the middle of the century, critics held that a wife who wore cosmetics was even more threatening. Restif de la Bretonne advised men choosing a wife that "a beauty is content to be so; she shows herself fully on the first day unlike those women to whom nature gave only partial charms [and] who use other means to supplement them."[76] The connection of artifice with adultery was simply the next step because these false women were made to seem beautiful and desirable to men. Caraccioli quipped that when a woman wore blanc "her husband never entirely held her in bed." He also believed that if women stopped spending so much time at their toilette they would stop gossiping, insulting men, and, most important, cheating on their husbands.[77] The toilette, thus, was a space of moral dissipation. Its public display of sexuality led to infidelity by allowing women to be admired by other men. Critics, with a nostalgic and fictive vision of the past, hoped that women would return to a simpler state, occupying themselves with feminine hobbies such as sewing, which would result in fidelity to their husbands.

The link between makeup and sexual debauchery was not new. Lichtenstein argues that throughout the Middle Ages and into the early modern period, artifice in art, in language, or in the face, was "immodest like adulterous desire, venal like prostituted pleasure."[78] From adultery, prostitution followed. Women who wore makeup shared this ritual with prostitutes who wore indecent amounts of rouge. The main perpetrators of this disgrace were aristocrats attempting to distinguish themselves from the rabble. Rousseau argued that since bourgeois women could now afford to buy luxuries, noble women had to find new ways of identifying their prominent social position. These aristocratic women "preferred their rank to their sex and imitated harlots."[79] In a failed attempt to remain in control of a world of growing consumerism, aristocrats debased themselves to the level of prostitutes.

Associated with prostitution were the actresses who were also believed to overindulge in the application of makeup on and offstage. Actresses who lost their lovers and thus their income were likely to fall into prostitution, as does Lucette. She finds herself forced into the hands of whores who provided her with "rouge, paint, fake hips, and breasts" to prepare her for her new line of work.[80] The excesses of cosmetics were clearly linked to this descent into sin and had a central role in the unnatural worlds of both the theater and the brothel. The theater, with its bright lights and costumes, necessitated an overuse of rouge and other artifice. Critics, however, bemoaned that respectable women adopted this fashion of wearing rouge in large dabs (*en placage*) for daily wear. A letter writer in the *Journal des Dames* was shocked that women might stoop to the level of base actresses to please a crowd of unknown spectators.[81] To be compared with an actress was as insulting as being likened to a prostitute. The Duchess de Berry was told that as first lady of the land, she ought to have "a little more gravity than to wear the beauty-marks of an actress in the theater."[82]

Cosmetics came to represent sexual deviance among the lower orders and their aristocratic betters and blurred the lines between these groups. Women who wore too much rouge could not be properly categorized. They might just as well be prostitutes as duchesses, and their morality was no different. The association of prostitutes and actresses with the comportment of France's elite was a clear sign of the growing instability in the system of rank. As early as the seventeenth century, commentators attacked the use of luxury due to its tendency to blur class lines.[83] By the eighteenth century, accusations of emulation were common. The poor of Paris "put no less art in masking misery, than in putting on their faces with the aid of a studied toilette."[84] Nothing was ever what it seemed and "each aspired to a rank above that which they should."[85] Philippe Perrot argues that in the "seventeenth century appearance still served to mark ranks, in the eighteenth century it starts to mask them."[86]

Though fear of emulation was likely unfounded, it represented the loss of respect for the social hierarchy, at the center of which had been the figure of the king.[87] No longer tied to a court system of rank, the adoption of excessive jewels, frills, and powder by individual members of the aristocracy undermined the respect due to the elite. Critics felt as threatened by the elites who debased themselves to the level of prostitutes, than by prostitutes who copied their betters. Mercier's telling description of prostitutes dressed as bourgeois women indicates how far the standards of the aristocracy had fallen.[88] Rather than lead the lower classes toward virtue and honor, elite women were blamed for providing corrupted models of aristocratic femininity. Women of the upper classes disfigured "nature, making themselves hideous with the help of an art more showy than educational."[89] The consequence of vanity and paint was a sinful lifestyle passed on from mother to daughter, from waning coquette to newly arrived beauty, from naive youth to blasé petit maître, from prostitute to aristocrat, and finally from bourgeois to servant. This spread of immorality through paint, which at least symbolically reached all aspects of French society, came to be much more than a personal concern. As Caraccioli so graphically put it, "we live in infection, carrying with us always an unbearable odor. The worms are in our midst and the rot never leaves us."[90]

Je ne sais quoi: Natural Beauty Triumphant

"I want women to have the courage to be ugly if they are; that old women have the majesty of their age, the air of goodness and compassion which goes with their white hair; that the young, without any other finery than cloth on which they have drawn the prettiest flowers, without any other hairdo than their beautiful hair, allow themselves all honest pleasures."[91]

During the late Enlightenment the aristocratic hold over fashion was replaced by a consumer culture that promoted individualism rather than corporate or elite standing.[92] Fashion choices, including what to wear on the face, were part of defining the individual alongside the social actor, "and that individual identity was now perceived to be shaped by nature and gender as much as by class and rank."[93] In the democratization of fashion described by Jennifer Jones and others, individual aristocratic extravagance faded as the autocratic monarchical system of style, best exemplified by Louis XIV, lost its power. Those who wished to overthrow the reign of artifice did so in the name of transparent social relations and a new definition of an ideal natural beauty based in *moeurs* that valued rural and family life.[94]

Intrinsically tied to the pseudoscience of physiognomy, the concept of the pure face was at its heart a rendition of the soul and its emotional representations on a physical surface. Artificiality was the bane of a trained physiognomist because it stood in the way of a legible reading. Though not all commentators agreed with the scientific claims of physiognomy, the belief in the legibility of a natural face was popular and highly practical in a society whose own legibility was in crisis.[95] Unable to pinpoint social rank through exterior dress and behavior, late eighteenth-century commentators turned to categorizing individuals by their innate characteristics, principally the naked and highly expressive face. This scrubbed-clean visage had to be already pure to truly represent the new taste. The expectation of natural and even moral beauty put women into untenable positions: those who had adopted makeup in the past for reasons of fashion were now associated with its sinful taint; older women who attempted to hide their age were to be relegated to private spaces; and even those perceived to be young and beautiful were burdened with the task of being and acting natural at all times, and thus readable to their male companions. The paradox of this prescription was that to be "natural," women had consciously to alter their way of dressing and primping to fit fashion expectations.

Once scrubbed free of makeup, women were to display their beauty simply and without help. Yet what were the accepted norms of beauty by the end of the century? The definition of beauty varied from those who believed that all beauty was subjective to those who felt that true beauty was definable through a series of proportions.[96] These proportions, however, had to be interpreted by viewers, whose reason and knowledge of science determined their ability to judge.[97] Pernety felt he knew exactly what beauty was, listing a small forehead, white teeth and skin, vivacious lips, and a shapely nose among other desirable traits for women, while men were simply to be well proportioned and tall.[98] A more subjective view of beauty held that personal taste, cultural, and even racial differences implied multiple forms of perfection. For many, such as Rousseau, taste was personal, based on a certain *je ne sais quoi* that only the viewer could pinpoint.[99] Yet even in this subjective view, the point of *je ne sais quoi* was not that it was indefinable and illusive, but that most male critics knew exactly what it was when they saw it. More important, physical beauty was not enough to capture the love of men. Though most critics of cosmetics believed in the natural proportions of beauty, this perfect harmony was nothing without grace and character. A young man may have wanted a pretty woman for a mistress, but he would marry one with "that vivacity of spirit which was so natural to her."[100] Though the coquette of the earlier part of the century also had a *je ne sais quoi* that elevated her exterior beauty through character and wit, her main attraction was in her sensuality. The eyes of the natural woman had to reflect innocence and not provocation, her smile sweetness and not desire. The roses of chastity were much more important than the red cheeks of artifice.

Yet defining innocence and sweetness was as difficult as pinpointing beauty itself. To facilitate identification of purity, those who were covered in flounces and rouge were labeled corrupt, while those who relied on their natural hue and simple accouterments were defined as the new ideal.[101] Men wrote poems to immortalize this new ideal of beauty: "Worthy student of nature / Your game, your charm owe nothing to art / You draw your pure expression from your heart / These sentiments without study and without artifice."[102] In the character and traits of this perfect woman, moral and aesthetic arguments against cosmetics were justified. Her goodness was indicated by her lack of artifice; her beauty was made clear and certain to the viewer without obfuscation. The ideal specimen could wake up in the morning "without art, without ornaments, without borrowed charms, she was beautiful by her own beauty. . . . I saw her dressed without affectation or mystery."[103] Though still attractive, the natural woman's sensuality was not meant to be threatening or aggressive.

The simple charm of the new natural woman belonged above all in the countryside, in opposition to the urban debaucheries of the salons or prostitutes: "a few ribbons and the crook of a country shepherdess forms the complete dress."[104] The solution to the rampant luxury and artifice of the Old Regime was a return to rural values, which included hard work, healthful living, and Rousseau's promotion of breastfeeding. L'abbé de Favre, who described in detail the urban toilette, ultimately felt that women should adopt "the dress of a shepherdess . . . [they] will see that only nature should dress [them]."[105] Caraccioli also preferred the rosy natural hue of the peasant maid to that of her urban counterpart.[106] Marie-Antoinette's simple dresses and interaction with real farmers at her *hameau* at Versailles represents the most extreme example of pastoral seduction.

Yet critics did not tout the ruddy complexion of a milkmaid, but the same creamy skin and red cheeks that had been the desired effect of rouge and paint. In this rural setting, tender beauties were supposed to be "adorned with all the graces which nature can embellish its masterpiece . . . this tender red which colors the open rose is no more vivid, more splendid than that which is spread on her cheeks."[107] Red cheeks should come from innocent blushing; white skin from naturally pale skin well protected from the elements and nocturnal activities. Thus, the turn to natural beauty was an attempt to free young beauties from the tyranny of artifice, while nonetheless reinforcing the same expectations.

In demanding a strict avoidance of worldly practices of beauty, critics of fashion hoped for an unconscious beauty: "unlike the spirit and the heart, beauty does not need culture."[108] Young women were asked to be unaware of their own beauty, seemingly unconscious of their own innocent seduction; conscious only of having left behind all masks. Rousseau described women as being "more beautiful since they no longer try to be . . . to please, they only needed not to disguise themselves."[109] Thus true beauty must create for the viewer a perception of natural grace. Yet even

Rousseau admitted that this pure beauty and bearing had to be learned. In *Emile,* Rousseau described Sophie as being the epitome of purity. In her dress she was "simplicity joined with elegance. . . . There is no other young person who seems dressed with less affectation and whose attire is more studied; not an item of hers is chosen haphazardly, and art appears in none of them." Rousseau contrasted choices and care to the visible art of the past. He believed in educating young women to be naturally charming and innocent as long as their beauty lasted.[110] Genlis also advocated teaching girls to distrust the lure of fashion and frivolity. She advised mothers to tell their daughters they were pretty without laying undue stress on this attribute. She believed young women should be told "that if she saves her figure until the age of twenty-five, which is very uncertain, she will see one hundred women successively preferred to her who do not have her regularity nor her beauty, but who fashion and fantasy have made charming."[111] Thus, young women should be prepared to face a world of vanity and deception, so as not to succumb to the temptations of coquetry. They should repeatedly be reminded of their own faults and defects, with the goal of making them impervious to vanity.

Emphasis on training and lessons in correct and natural fashion implied that a good deal of work went into creating the perfect woman. Yet men such as Rousseau did not want to be able to discern this construction of natural beauty. Women were to aspire to a childlike innocence, hiding from the viewer its artificial constructs. Once achieved, this state of artificial nature became the apotheosis of femininity. The new aesthetic of beauty stressed transparency; yet, it expected these ideals to be expressed through the traditional means of deception. The new woman had to perform the "natural" so that the act would become indistinguishable from "reality." The young ingénue, Julie, like her coquettish elder, played a game of seduction whose rules were laid out by cultural conceptions of beauty and fashion.

The expectation of having to look natural can be seen at its most contradictory in the work of P. A. F. Choderlos de Laclos. In *De l'éducation des femmes,* Laclos argued for a return to a natural state in which women would overcome their inferiority to men and bask in their maternal duties. Laclos stressed that natural woman "has neither white nor delicate skin . . . she has, above all, none of the resources of attire which women of all climates know so well how to utilize." Though he eulogized natural beauty, Laclos also gave his female readers advice on how best to benefit from their natural traits through the application of cosmetics and perfumes. His list of reprimands to women included not drinking, since it made the skin unhealthy; not screaming, since the face would be contorted; and not being moody, since it made the face ungracious.[112] Though Laclos wanted to construct the social world in accord with the natural one, he still felt that women's concern with appearances had an important role in contemporary society. For Laclos, the philosophes lent their attention to fashion because "it pertains to men's happiness by contributing to their pleasures."[113]

Similarly, Mercier, Rousseau, and others expressed their satisfaction at seeing a beautiful and well-dressed woman. Since it was obvious to these critics that women's ultimate goal should be to please men, it was not out of line for them to "give them advice and pronounce on the manner by which we wish they would offer themselves."[114] Employing the terms *natural, artificial,* and *coquette* became means by which men could control and define women, both as a sex and as individuals. For example, when a woman he was pursuing rejected Rousseau, he called her a coquette, hoping to ruin her reputation in society.[115] Beauty in the eye of the beholder created love, but when that love was rebuffed, the object of desire became "every day . . . uglier."[116] As is evident in the sexual exploits of Rousseau, Restif de la Bretonne, or Nougaret, a real beauty was one who acquiesced to men's attentions. These critics' definitions of beauty erased women who did not fit in and objectified those who did.

If the new woman was a natural beauty ready to please those around her, then the new man was the one who could appreciate her charms. The new man did not follow the regulations of fashion, purging from his wardrobe all aspects of femininity and artifice. Men needed to adopt a new version of masculinity that stressed simplicity, subtlety, and quality. He should grow a beard and mustache (unpopular during most of the eighteenth century) to stress the distance between men and women. "A handsome man" had not "the least bit of vanity. The innocence and simplicity of his soul kept his physical qualities from prevailing."[117] The ideal man could have the petits maîtres' sensitivity and politeness, but he should have "no more red high-heels, no more perfume, no more borrowed complexion" and importantly he no longer cheated on his wife.[118] Like his female partner, the main criteria was transparency, which the philosophes believed would show men to be creatures immune to vanity. In 1783, Mercier was happy to note that men wore simpler and more becoming clothing than fifteen years previously, apparel that gave them a dignified appearance.[119] Young men could still hope to be charming, but their moral fiber and public endeavors were more important than their pretty faces. Rousseau most clearly laid out the fundamental traits of the natural man in *Emile,* whose education was meant to distance him from effeminate urban men.[120]

Conclusion

In the late eighteenth century, the model of aristocratic fashion and artifice was firmly replaced by a moral model that stressed natural beauty and simplicity. All discussions of cosmetics were couched in ethical or aesthetic reprimands. The quantity of criticisms was so overwhelming that it would have been a wonder to see anyone at all walk the streets of Paris wearing rouge and blanc by the late 1780s, though it was still acceptable at court. Alongside the spread of Enlightenment ideals of transparency, the virtuous elite's fear of confusion with their corrupt superiors and inferiors helped cause this shift in fashion. The criticism of the high aristocracy for their debauchery and the destruction of a visible social hierarchy due to the availability of consumer fashions increased the elite's support for a society based on merit, virtue, and transparency, a shift that had occurred much earlier in Britain.

The philosophes' redefinition of the public polity altered fashion's place within civil society. Simplicity and visibility were powerful concepts because they allowed the new order to justify its ascendancy over the old aristocratic heritage without overthrowing the members of that coterie. Social relationships were meant to become transparent, allowing for merit to shine through just like true beauty would appear beneath layers of rouge. In this new world, critics hoped that aristocrats would no longer rule with excess over social mannerisms and prostitutes could no longer pass themselves off as decent citizens. Fashion would no longer represent the unnatural hierarchy of the aristocracy (including the newly ennobled wealthy) but would become the monopoly of women, albeit with a different model of femininity. The new woman, pure and moral, replaced the coquette.[121]

Natural beauty was no less complex than previous fashions. The subjective reading of the face made it difficult for both those who chose to judge good taste and those who represented it to know where they stood. The *je ne sais quoi* of the farm girl was to be the ideal of the newly reformed coquette, but only after it was adapted to the world of fashionable Parisians and to the sexual desires of male voyeurs. A visual representation of the shift in beauty and its complexity can be seen in René Nicolas Jollain's duo *La toilette* (figure 4) and *Le bain* painted in the late 1770s. Both paintings, in the Cognacq-Jay Museum, depict a fully naked woman being ministered to by a maid. The surroundings are typical of late eighteenth-century boudoir scenes. The maid wears a *robe à panier* along with copious rouge. In *La toilette,* a portrait of a wigged gentleman looks upon the scene, while luxuries decorate the mantel and toilette table. The nude in both paintings, however, has a small head, which does not seem to correspond either to her body or to the aesthetic of beauty of the 1770s when they were most likely painted. The head has little face color and dark pulled-back hair. When looked at carefully, a rather large halo of lighter paint around her head indicates that at some point it was considerably larger. In his 1781 engravings of both paintings, Louis Marin Bonnet added a large *pouf* covering a blond towering hairdo as well as giving the nude a sly coquettish gaze and rouged

Figure 4. René Nicolas Jollain, *La toilette,* Musée Cognacq-Jay, Roger-Viollet

cheeks (figure 5). The museum's catalogue assumes that Bonnet inserted the hat as his own original touch, calling it "ridiculous."[122]

I would argue, instead, that rather than being ridiculous, this larger head and pouf may have initially graced the Jollain original and were likely to have been painted over at some point after 1781. Thus, Jollain's altered paintings literally erased the Old Regime aesthetic of beauty to redefine the figure of the nude, not in her body but in her face and hair while the maid and surroundings were left untouched. The current paintings reflect a mixing of old and new, allowing the elite to evolve into a new aesthetic of beauty while anchoring their inferiors and material luxuries to the old world. The contrast between the mistress's nudity and the maid's elaborate (and old-fashioned) clothing further highlights the seductive availability of the flesh to the male viewer. The nude is prepared and presented as an appetizing meal, coyly turning her head away. The originals' pouf and makeup (as well as coquettish

La Toilette

Figure 5. Louis Marin Bonnet, *La toilette, d'après Jollain* (1781), Bibliothèque nationale estampes

gaze) impeded direct access to the nude. The hat and the artifice of hairpiece and rouge negated the purity of the body, reminding the viewer of the constant playacting, intrigue, and deceit involved in Old Regime seduction. The hat, makeup, and wig's disappearance erased potentially difficult, and more equal, games of *badinage,* leaving the new woman and her passive beauty immediately accessible to the men who gazed upon her.

CHAPTER FIVE

Domesticating Beauty
The Medical Supervision of Women's Toilette

On September 4, 1818, the *Gazette de France* reported on the tumultuous scenes occurring outside Parisian booksellers. The journalist was surprised to find crowds of people all demanding one book: "I noticed many women in their carriages, who waited impatiently for the return of their husbands . . . they had their eyes fixed on the store, their necks craned, their arms outstretched; they grabbed rather than received the book, they devoured it rather than perused it."[1] The sought-after tome was the *Alliance d'hygie et de la beauté*, newly arrived in stores. The *Alliance* was a history of beauty and a complete guide for female behavior written by Dr. J. B. Mège, a member of the medical faculty of Paris. The scenes of chaos that it caused indicate the huge popularity by the early nineteenth century of works that proposed to divulge beauty secrets. This popularity had its roots in the eighteenth century when the genre of beauty manuals provided an alternative to calls for a ban on all cosmetics found in tracts, novels, and newspapers. Educated women of the middle and upper classes found solace in the pages of advice manuals.[2] This genre not only provided women with recipes but also set the boundaries for the practices of beautification. Increasingly, it was the practitioners of medical science who dictated these boundaries. By defining what was acceptable and saleable, medical doctors could make sure that consumers were not duped by charlatans or endangered by noxious chemicals present in makeup. The life-threatening use of arsenic, mercury, lead, and other poisonous chemicals in cosmetics alarmed doctors and the public. The growing number of diseases and even deaths blamed on artifice increased concern for regulating both home and commercial production of noxious goods.[3] Doctors could do so by marshaling twin weapons: they authored advice manuals, and they regulated the invention of new cosmetics.

The growing medical authority over women's fashions was part of a larger shift toward creating healthier subjects through science. Michel Foucault argued that medical practitioners gained power in the late eighteenth century as a result of the political importance of hygiene and health for social control. Doctors infiltrated elite family units as advisers and controllers of personal habits.[4] The new bourgeois body was to be created through practices of hygiene and healthful behavior, instituted by science and policed by the self. Philippe Perrot believes that doctors' advice in the name of "rationality and a well assured technical prowess . . . acquired a legitimacy and a new pertinence" in the context of a hygienic revolution.[5] This legitimacy helped doctors create a professional ethos with which to attack charlatans, faith healers, and midwives. At the center of this struggle was the metaphorical and physical control of women's bodies. Lindsay Wilson asserts that women were the primary targets or clients for enlightened medicine because of their increasingly central position within the household economy. The patronage of upper- and middle-class women could lead to lucrative medical contracts.[6]

As Foucault himself stated, power is a productive as well as a repressive force.[7] The medicalization of the female body was not a one-sided story of oppression by the masculine gaze. Women were not the passive pawns of a contest for professional legitimacy but actively involved in shaping the definition of their health and hygiene. Wilson shows that the medical control of women's bodies was inconclusive and tenuous in the late eighteenth century. Medical practitioners' authority was constantly under attack because of a lack of medical progress in feminine diseases.[8] Women's voices continued to play a part in the creation of knowledge, helping to discredit certain theories while giving credence to others. Male doctors may have carved a specific niche for themselves, but it was one that necessitated compromise rather than guaranteeing tyrannical control.

Central to this struggle for medical supervision in cooperation with women of the elite was the promotion of hygienic habits that were meant to replace the artificial and complex grooming of the aristocracy. George Vigarello has convincingly showed that by the end of the century hygiene had become the new, fashionable means of achieving both health and beauty. Until then, physicians feared that water would enter the body through the pores and contaminate the internal organs, affecting the humeral balance. Increasingly, medical practitioners tried to encourage their readers to bathe more frequently and use water instead of oils to wash their faces and bodies. Public baths opened on the Seine in 1761, heartily supported by new medical findings. Though private bathtubs remained infrequent, by the end of the century, basins were a common sight in the *cabinets de toilette* of the middle and upper classes. Doctors advised women to wash with water and soap, exercise, and wear less-constricting clothing to help strengthen the body and stave off illness.[9] Washing also helped repair the ravages caused by makeup. The well-known physician S. A. D. Tissot recommended "water as the only valuable cosmetic."[10] If doctors now encouraged bathing, they discouraged the use of strong scents to mask bodily smells. Alain Corbin argues that the hygienic revolution was matched by a trans-formation in scents, shifting from animal perfumes to lighter vegetable scents. The fashion for fresh smells emphasized the natural over the artificial as both more at-tractive and more beneficial for health.[11]

Cosmetics were central to the wider redefinition of a healthy toilette. By focus-ing on makeup and other cosmetics, doctors tapped into a productive and profitable position as beauty advisers, which allowed their entrée into women's private lives. Half of the beauty advice manuals published between 1750 and 1818 were written by doctors, and most of the rest referred to medical opinion. By the end of the eigh-teenth century, the physician became the main purveyor of beauty advice, over-shadowing the professional perfumer, the hairdresser, and the apothecary. Physicians had the professional knowledge to counsel female users, without the fear of com-mercial self-interest. Stressing scientific rationality and truth, they disassociated cos-metics from aristocratic decadence and immoral coquettes. Instead, physicians cre-ated a vision of healthy and hygienic beauty that placed female vanity within the domestic sphere, always under the strict eye of a trained professional. By stressing safety, doctors could influence women's product choices. Doctors promoted women's feminine desire to please, a necessary part of a happy marriage. They advocated a vi-sion of femininity that integrated the "new natural woman" with the medicalized practices of the toilette.

The increased visibility of doctors in beautification practices (through advice lit-erature or counseling) correlated with the growing concern over potentially life-threatening ingredients included in many cosmetics' recipes. Using medical experi-mentation, doctors asserted that the ingredients commonly used in cosmetics would damage the skin as well as the overall health of the wearer. A plethora of scientific knowledge was marshaled to prove that the ingredients in cosmetics were lethal to the French public's health. The power of this argument against cosmetics, in oppo-sition to those postulated by Rousseau, Nougaret, or Caraccioli, lay in its use of sci-entific proof. Critics' highly subjective aesthetic and moral judgments against arti-fice paled in significance to empirical truths. Medical opinions, it was hoped, could inspire fear and awe in the hearts of fashion-conscious women, and, to a lesser de-gree, men.

Yet, by choosing to advise women and to judge cosmetic products empirically, doctors placed themselves at the center of the growing debates on fashion and arti-fice. Instead of adopting prescriptive and threatening tones, these physicians oper-ated within the boundaries of the genre they worked in. The advice manual, by definition, provided readers with practical solutions to problems. Advice manuals advocated beauty aids as long as these products fit models of hygiene, health, and, most important, safety as judged by science. Similarly, when testing products, they could find no reason to ban those they found perfectly safe despite their opposition to them. The process by which medical doctors entered the toilettes of their female patients and readers was one of compromise. By relying on their self-imposed method of examination, medical professionals unwittingly authenticated and perpetuated cosmetic consumption in the name of science.

Deadly Artifice: Medical Science Judges Cosmetics

Scientific opinion condemned the use of chemical ingredients such as camphor and lead in beauty aids since the sixteenth century. Early Modern invectives against cosmetics often linked them to the decay of the body, as well as the soul.[12] Yet most doctors who wrote about cosmetics before the eighteenth century did so to promote their own recipes.[13] For example, one of the *médecins du roi* published a recipe book on cosmetics in 1661, following the tradition of the notorious doctor Michel de Nostredame in the 1550s.[14] These works and others that followed offered various well-known recipes and said little about the actual dangers of cosmetics. In many treatises on health published during the seventeenth century, cosmetics were considered medicines for the face and skin.[15] By the late seventeenth and early eighteenth centuries, medical manuals started to correct the mistakes of earlier books of secrets. Doctors focused on teaching patients how to keep clean, prevent illness, and avoid the "dangers of quacks and popular errors."[16] A main thrust of these works was to promote forms of hygiene that would further health, but none directly addressed the problem of cosmetics.

Only in the mid-eighteenth century did doctors begin to write serious tomes about beauty and cosmetic use. Physicians marshaled chemical and medical knowledge to comment on the effects of beauty aids. Empiricism became the main criterion for determining the worth of ingredients and products.[17] Chemists, doctors, and scientists tested and analyzed the qualities of each ingredient, not on actual subjects, but in laboratory experiments. They singled out minerals such as white lead (*céruse*), mercury, and sulfur as damaging to the skin because of their chemical properties. Though scientists did not concur as to the extent of the possible harm, they agreed that these noxious ingredients were not suited for beauty products. These warnings escalated as new discoveries were made in science. The updated 1756 version of the seventeenth-century *Cours de chymie* still encouraged including bismuth and white lead in skin whiteners.[18] In 1804, the physician P. J. Marie de Saint-Ursin in his *L'ami des femmes* cautioned that these same chemicals induced skin eruptions and would eventually lead to grave maladies.[19] The medical community increasingly identified ingredients that were truly hazardous and potentially deadly.

When doctors analyzed a cosmetic, they were most concerned with "mineral, metallic, or saline" ingredients rather than vegetable and animal ones.[20] Marie de Saint-Ursin listed nitric acid and mercury as unwholesome additions, unlike cucumbers, almond paste, milk, honey, and egg yolks.[21] Rouge recipes from plants such as red sandalwood or saffron were acceptable, whereas minium (lead oxide) and cinnabar (red mercury sulfur) were to be avoided.[22] By the end of the century, rouge made of minerals (mostly vermillion/cinnabar and lead) and those made of vinegar were condemned, but rouge made with vegetable and animal substances were typically seen as safe. One of Louis XVI's doctors was one of the few to point out the potential dangers of vegetable rouge.[23] Remedies containing strawberry juice, melon seeds, hazelnuts, and distilled beef bile could replace cosmetics made out of lead and other minerals.[24] Playing on images of natural beauty, doctors categorized mineral elements as less pure than vegetable matter.

Doctors focused their attention first on the corruption of the skin's outer layers. The imagery in medical texts was of rotting, diseased flesh. This corruption of the flesh was the ironic outcome of products intended to mask already present flaws. Creams made with white lead or bismuth promised to "whiten the skin, soften wrinkles," but the chemical properties of these concoctions meant that their effects presented "a much more disagreeable picture than the natural blemishes which women were so obsessed with correcting."[25] One physician felt that all skin creams and paint plugged the skin's pores, impeding natural sweat, causing dryness as well as "skin diseases, pimples, scabs, redness."[26] Products meant to invigorate the skin and diminish wrinkles had the opposite effect and even scented waters or simple creams dried and hardened the face.

Cosmetics also threatened the integrity of the mouth. Medical men terrified readers with pictures of rotting, crumbling teeth attacked inside and out by vile products. The doctor Antoine Le Camus warned women that the mercury in rouge would cause them to "lose their teeth, acquire bad breath, or to have abundant discharges of saliva."[27] Healthy teeth were essential to the face's overall beauty since the mouth was a symbol of potency and sexuality in the eighteenth century.[28] Yet the frequency of bad teeth and stinking breath led to a culture in which the smile was a rare practice in polite company.[29] Cosmetics were all the more insidious if they undermined the wearer's smile, leading to the desperate use of false teeth. Attempts to fix the ravages of cosmetics with other chemical products led to further destruction. Doctors warned that opiates or teeth whiteners would strip the teeth of their enamel.

Advice manuals suggested that instead of using harsh chemicals, teeth should be washed with alcohol, brushed with a sponge, and once in a while scrubbed with coffee, burnt bread, tobacco, or wine to eliminate tartar. Dentists' promises were also not to be trusted. Naive clients would find themselves with even less to laugh about.[30]

The loss of beauty was not the only consequence of adopting artifice. Disease and death were the inevitable followers of fading looks. Once the skin was exposed and damaged, the chemicals in cosmetics affected the functioning of the senses and even the internal organs. Eighteenth-century humeral theory postulated that any foreign element in contact with the body forced normally expelled fluids into key organs or blood vessels, destabilizing the body's balance. Thickly applied cosmetics blocked transpiration.[31] Creams adopted to remove stains and acne might "transfer dangerous materials to internal organs."[32] Certain cosmetics were especially hazardous. In 1760, the physician Deshais-Gendron believed that the high rate of pulmonary disease among rich women was brought on by the white paint they applied on their face, neck, and chest, which attacked "the porous substances of the lungs."[33] Deshais-Gendron, using highly scientific terminology, laid out precise, convincing reasons for rejecting face paint, hoping to scare his readers away from practicing artifice. Rouge was also attacked for its deleterious effect on both the skin and the rest of the body's health. Diseases linked to rouge included skin diseases, such as itching, acne, and eruptions, as well as excoriations of the pituitary membrane, and sore throats.[34]

The growing concern with dangerous makeup led doctors to advise women to keep both their faces and their bodies clean and natural. Only the practices of the toilette aimed at cleanliness should be continued.[35] In practical terms, this meant products to cleanse and soften the skin naturally. Since the skin was highly porous, its treatments had to be gentle. The goal was to "imbibe, nourish, moisturize, polish with cosmetic creams . . . these methods are simple; they are the real saviors of health."[36] Doctors touted simple creams, oils, and lotions made of vegetable matter to save the skin from aging and the misuse of cosmetics.

Medical science also alleviated a primary reason for adopting makeup. Many women justified wearing paint as a means to cover the scars of disease, especially smallpox. The threat of scars was so strong that in *Les liaisons dangereuses,* Choderlos de Laclos chose to punish Madame de Merteuil for her immoral behavior by having her horrendously disfigured by the disease.[37] Patients were warned "if you dare scratch yourself, you will become so hideous that no one will love you thereafter," a most effective injunction.[38] By the late eighteenth century, however, incidents of smallpox declined because inoculation and then vaccination were popularized.[39] Mercier entreated fathers of the lower classes to take advantage of this new discovery, asking, "why does the Parisian obstinately wish to see the nose and cheeks of his daughters eaten and scarred . . . when they could conserve the polish . . . which would make them the most charming creatures of Europe?"[40] The popularization of inoculation gave women one fewer reason to feel insecure about their looks, rendering medical arguments against cosmetics even more persuasive.

To the medical profession, adopting chemical cosmetics was antithetical to beauty. Doctors hoped that women would realize it was in their interest "not to let themselves be fooled on the effects which are normally attributed to rouge and white paint; they see by the experience of others that the best makeup cannot repair the injuries of time, nor reestablish lost beauty, that on the contrary cosmetics are only capable of ruining the skin, wrinkling it, altering it, and fading natural colors."[41] It was also imperative that doctors' influence young women before they turned to the addictive habit of wearing makeup, since "their complexion will conserve its freshness longer."[42] Cosmetics, not sin and debauchery, were the ultimate destroyers of young girls' bodies. Yet many doctors believed that their admonitions would have little effect because "health, beauty and the desire to live can do nothing against a servile, absurd, expensive, dirty and unbecoming imitation" of fashion.[43] After Tissot laid out the dangers of cosmetic use in his treatise, he concluded that "unfortunately these examples are not frightening enough" since most women simply ignored his advice.[44]

Doctors were not the only ones who felt strongly about the health and hygiene of women. Fears of harmful medicines increased the policing of recipe books written by perfumers and other artisans. In 1761, *Le parfumeur royal* could only be published after Jean-Etienne Guettard, the naturalist and geologist who had been asked to inspect its content by the censors, omitted all recipes that included oxidized lead, carbonated lead, corrosive mercury chloride, alum, or nitrate.[45] Though government censorship may not have caught all injurious chemicals, writers made sure to announce their own purging of noxious ingredients. The distiller Hornot wrote in his introduction: "I would reproach myself even more, if, among recipes for the maintenance of beauty, I had inserted a few whose nature was to alter health, this blessing a thousand times more precious."[46] Two popular early nineteenth-century perfumers made good use of the doctor Le Camus' earlier recipes, but criticized his lack of real medical knowledge, calling on modern chemistry to correct his mistakes.[47]

The strength of medical arguments influenced not only perfumers' manuals but also encyclopedias and journals. Many articles on cosmetics in Diderot's *Encyclopédie* commented openly about their dangers. The article on blanc by Louis de Jaucourt warned that those containing lead, vinegar, and bismuth "which make in truth the most beautiful white paints in the world" were also "due to their salivary, poisonous, arsenic, indelible properties" the most harmful.[48] Abbé Jaubert's *Dictionnaire raisonné,* which, for the most part, provided definitions and descriptions of trades without comment, was harshly critical of the ingredients employed by perfumers. The dictionary concluded that "it is thus dangerous to use all cosmetics which block the skin, dry it, and wear it down," allowing that only "rouge . . . does not have this inconvenience."[49] The popular press also warned the public about cosmetic dangers. In 1777, *La feuille sans titre* published a doctor's findings from *La gazette de santé.* The article emphasized that women had to take extra precautions to ensure the safety of the products they bought and wore.[50]

Male doctors emphasized feminine weaknesses that necessitated the costly attentions of a personal physician. Women who did not have the ability to discern a good doctor from a charlatan or a good product from a bad one had to be supervised in the toilette. A letter written to the *Journal des dames* hoped that the works of medical doctors "could enter into the toilettes of women who would then realize the multitude of accidents that are produced by makeup."[51] Le Camus, in his oriental tale *Abdeker,* had his fictional doctor become the teacher to his odalisque lover, assuring her that "it was the same mouth proffering the oracles of health that will dictate which precepts belong to the conservation of beauty."[52] Literate women could acquire medical information from these books or a diversity of other sources without direct access to a physician. Because readers shared books and newspapers, these ideas were likely to be disseminated quickly through conversation as well. Once women were warned of possible dangers, they could arm themselves with further knowledge, no longer trusting the promises of their perfumer or the corner charlatan, instead turning to a respectable physician.

By specifying the need for a masculine, medical presence at a woman's daily toilette, doctors also eliminated its association with sexual and theatrical intrigue. Under the supervision of a doctor, the *cabinet de toilette* was rehabilitated into a functional and practical space. Home remedies based on doctors' recipes or goods purchased based on their advice were essential to a young girl's upbringing. By imposing a teacher on their readers, they emphasized masculine learning and knowledge over female ingenuity. The tradition of oral recipes passed down from mother to daughter was to be replaced by properly vetted published recipes or store-bought concoctions. The male medical knowledge needed to transmit beauty distanced women from their own beautification processes, inserting doctors in their midst. Medical advice allowed male professionals to enter private spaces, not as lovers or servants but as all-knowing supervisors who firmly closed the door of the now domesticated *cabinet de toilette* behind them.

Scientific Vanity: The Educated Woman at Her Toilette

Medical and professional experts sought to shape the creation and purchase of cosmetics. Yet beauty manuals gave the assumed audience of female readers the final say in the content of these works. Doctors could rail against cosmetics, but, by publishing advice, they would ultimately have to provide solutions to beauty problems. The dual purposes of manuals coexisted: doctors hoped to limit and control the use of cosmetics, while readers expected advice for beauty enhancement. Authors who published their advice were distinctly aware of the importance of public opinion, specifically of their readership. Jean Goulin bent to the demands of his female patients. These women, confused by the multitude of books on cosmetics, asked him to "extract from these different authors what you judge best suits us." Though he found such a task belittling, he assured his readers that he gave it "all [his] attention."[53] Despite their dislike of such works, doctors realized that popular advice books helped to establish their names outside their clientele and discredit the work of those they saw as charlatans.

The doctors' awareness of their audience's needs led them to omit discussions of moral behavior. Instead of linking cosmetics directly with corruption and sin, as many other critics did, they instructed women in the conduct most suitable for enhancing their looks. They adopted the arguments of moral physiologists that behavior and emotions had physical and often dangerous effects on the body.[54] For instance, they pointed out that too much dancing, drinking, and sun led to unhealthy skin. Though such comments might be viewed as moral judgments of women's lifestyles, other less questionable emotional states and physical activities were also blamed for causing bad skin: sadness, fear, remorse, overwork, lack of exercise, and bad digestion.[55] This list makes assumptions about women's lifestyles and physical capabilities: women had softer bodies and more sensitive nerves. Yet similar lists can be found in medical advice manuals aimed at men. Ultimately, doctors viewed excess of any kind as potentially dangerous for healthy living, and by stressing the threat to women's beauty, they hoped to induce more moderate habits. Though Wilson argues that the medical regulation of women's bodies was played out in moral terms, advice manuals for the most part stressed physical rather than spiritual repercussions.[56]

Advice literature was practical and straightforward, discrediting those who tried to use morality as a means for regulating fashion and beauty. For example, Marie de Saint-Ursin argued that a pure girl's position in society could not be harmed by her application of makeup, as long as this practice did not endanger her health or inherent beauty. He stated plainly that "honest young women will stay thus despite the resources which we present to them." He blamed men who seduced girls into lives of sin, and not cosmetics, for any immoralities present in French society. Criticism of cosmetics for medical reasons was one thing, but Marie de Saint-Ursin was not willing to assume a correlation between beauty and sin. He only condemned "artificial compositions . . . because of the harm they do to women and not because of the harm that they could do to their happy dupes." His goal was to educate women in the utility and safety of beauty products while encouraging exercise, baths, and proper daily hygiene.[57]

Advice manuals and recipe books advocated cosmetics, though the range and utility of listed products differed. Makeup that was not artificial (and thus chemical) was acceptable for attracting men's stares or jealous rivals. Not all doctors advocated layers of paint; yet, most found ways to advise women to maintain a youthful glow and reduce the onslaught of time. Despite his reluctance to include cosmetics, Goulin listed a number of traditional recipes at the end of his *Médecin des dames,* even a face paint made with silver litharge (the residue of lead oxide) and white vinegar, two very questionable ingredients.[58] Deshais-Gendron, one of the harshest critics of cosmetics, proposed replacing chemical face paints with alcohol-based astringents meant to whiten the skin.[59]

Instead of writers of advice manuals lecturing women about their moral duties, they stated that vanity and pride were necessary social traits rather than sinful failings. These doctors felt that "it would be missing out on what one deserves to refuse oneself simple and well-known ways of gaining the satisfaction of pleasing oneself and others."[60] Thus, basic knowledge of beauty should not be suppressed if it allowed society to be more pleasant, healthier, and happier. It was natural for women to want to please both themselves and the men around them. Pride in one's looks created visual and sensory pleasures that benefited men and women alike and was essential to a happy marriage.[61] Men were warned that young girls who at fifteen did not seek to please would turn into very disagreeable wives at twenty-five.[62] Personal satisfaction and a healthy dose of vanity were the keys to happiness. The ambition to primp and please was "the soul of society and we can state that both sexes obey equally this law of nature."[63] The soul, which had been labeled tainted because of the presence of makeup by numerous critics of cosmetics, could be saved through a simpler version of pleasurable vanity.

Science validated the notion that beauty and vanity were part of the laws of nature, but only for women. Pierre Roussel's influential *Système physique et moral de la femme* defined a vision of women's health that was firmly linked to their physical traits.[64] Roussel was one of the first doctors to stress that the form and function of a woman's organism was different, and ultimately weaker, than a man's, thus she needed male protection.[65] Women could achieve these ends through their beauty, since men would be biologically attracted to women whose looks represented their health and fertility. The biological explanation for beauty focused on women's roles as wives and, more important, as mothers. Once childbearing was finished, beauty and its alter ego vanity were no longer necessary and most often faded away.[66] The scientific validation of vanity in premenopausal women allowed doctors to advocate the continued use of beauty aids. Letting the face deteriorate naturally was not a practical means of ensuring a husband's love. It was the wife's job to keep her husband desiring her, thus increasing her need for valid medical counsel. In a humorous version of such counsel, the *Dentiste des dames* argued that if a husband left his wife it was because she did not take good care of her teeth.[67]

Vanity as an ultimately feminine and necessary trait was part of a traditional emphasis on female reproductive functions that dates back to the Renaissance. Yet vanity also demarcated a new role for beauty as a social necessity for respectable families. According to Thorstein Veblen, women's beauty practices were essential to "conspicuous consumption," in which women stood in for their husband's or father's ability to afford leisure.[68] When it came to the use of makeup, however, this was not an extravagant display of luxury but a subtle form of tasteful and literally inconspicuous consumption. By the end of the century, women hoped to wear rouge and powder undetected, highlighting their natural beauty and health and reinforcing the biological justifications for the toilette. Unlike the early eighteenth-century artifice, invisible beauty aids were meant to underline the individual's taste and worth in the enlightened family unit. Private, and thus hidden, makeup was necessary for public presentation; yet, it was not to be openly discussed or noticed.

In this newly privatized *cabinet de toilette,* the doctor was to be the trusted adviser and the confidant who would protect the secret uses of artifice under a different name. In 1804, Marie de Saint-Ursin tried to deny this role of confidant, wanting women to be more honest with themselves and their entourage about their makeup. Though these women had given up wearing the thick layers of paint of the Old Regime aristocracy, they justified wearing light rouge and white powder because it was worn "without artifice, in truth, and only to seem less frighteningly ugly." He goaded these women by proclaiming them "vain and lying" and asked sarcastically "is this carmine not makeup?"[69] What Marie de Saint-Ursin wanted was an open dialogue about the social importance of vanity and artifice, something that was unlikely to happen in the context of naturalized, transparent beauty. Though the rouge wearers of the new elite would not confess publicly, his recipes allowed them, safely and without guilt, to continue their private ablutions. The doctor and his findings were being used to justify a continued use of paint, legitimating the practice of primping in the name of science.

Distancing themselves from the severe criticisms of philosophes, playwrights, and poets, doctors gained a tenable middle position in which they could decry cosmetics for medical reasons while still proposing to make women's lives more pleasant through their application. Rather than simply scaring or scolding their audience, doctors wooed female readers by offering them real solutions to everyday problems within a domestic setting. Beauty manuals provided rational, scientific arguments for and against beauty products, justified by social expectations and biological urges. They also did not underestimate their audience. In his introduction, Le Camus stated that intelligent, cultured women "will not be frightened of a few scientific term which they will come across. They are so enlightened at present, that one has the right to count on their understanding."[70] The information available in scientific dictionaries and medical tracts allowed women to make increasingly sophisticated judgments when it came to the products they wore on their faces and bodies. In the midst of public disapproval, this specialist knowledge gave women a means to reclaim beauty practices for themselves.

Acceptable Artifice: The Medical Academy's Patents

By allying themselves with the practices of beautification, doctors also tied themselves to the growing consumer market. Their advice manuals were aimed at controlling the stores of perfumers, as much as the purchases of women. The discourses on charlatanism, publicity, and legitimacy permeated both the worlds of commerce and science. To be the successful guides for increasingly savvy female consumers, doctors had to transform themselves into objects of consumption, wrapped up in the market of all things medical and cosmetic. Doctors entered the cosmetics market most obviously when they took on the responsibility of issuing patents to commercial products. It was in this approval of inventions that the medical profession saw the greatest clash between its concerns with health and hygiene and its ideals of professionalism and empiricism. Physicians who defined their work as a serious scientific pursuit, far removed from the daily concerns of the toilette, found themselves caught up in the debates about cosmetics safety and commercial viability. The intersection of commercial promotion and medical supervision led doctors to attempt to control cosmetics both in ladies' boudoirs and on street corners of French cities.

The first system of patents in France was formalized in 1762 for industrial innovation and invention.[71] This patent system did not cover medicinal or beauty products, though some gained recognition from the Academy of Sciences and the Medical Faculty. In 1772, increased fears over harmful medicines led the government to delegate the *Commission royale de médecine,* made up of the king's physicians, to judge and issue privileges for medical inventions. Though this commission was not meant to examine cosmetics, it nonetheless granted twenty-six permissions to a variety of cosmetics.[72] In 1778, the Royal Commission's work was taken over by the newly formed *Société royale de médecine.* Using experimental evaluations, the society tried to rein in the profitable market of medicines. They were more concerned with controlling the definition of medicines than in ending the practice of secret remedies, because many owned their own medical patents.[73] In 1781, the society decreed that potentially harmful cosmetics could also be examined but would only be given tacit approvals.[74]

From 1778 to 1790, 115 cosmetics were examined of which 71 were given tacit permissions and one a full approval.[75] Overall, these figures represent a 62 percent acceptance rate compared with the 6 percent acceptance rate of medicinal goods.[76] The society, thus, was strict in its medicine authorizations but more liberal with cosmetics. These figures seem in blatant contradiction to the medical warnings against hazardous rouges and creams. While one group of doctors decried the dangers of cosmetic products in advice books aimed at women, a group of elite physicians freely authorized selling such goods. To understand this discrepancy, we need to know on what grounds physicians approved these remedies.

The medical commission and society had safety in mind when they set out to approve a product. They demanded lists of ingredients so they could compare them to other known products. In a few cases, they actually tested the product, though no more than with their eyes, nose, and mouth. They took seriously their role as judges, not wishing to slight a useful product, yet wary of approving a harmful one. The society refused to give a tacit permission for *Crème anglaise* because it was made of lead, vinegar, and salt, inadmissible ingredients. They deemed another request for *Eau de Circe* dangerous because of its caustic ingredients, which were likely to make hair fall out. Surprisingly, this concern for ingredients was rare. The society mostly ignored the chemicals involved, even judging goods made of sulfur to be safe. For instance, they approved a hair dye made up of "white lead, lead, litharge, quicklime, [and] lemon" because it included no dangerous ingredients.[77] Out of thirty-eight rejected cosmetics, only eight were turned down as health hazards. Though fully aware of the debate over the dangers of cosmetics, the medical examiners either ignored or were unconvinced of the real dangers of the most commonly used ingredients.

The main rejection criterion the committee used was not so much dangerous ingredients as false claims. The doctors felt that many of the products presented to them were unoriginal and widely available. The society denied a 1786 request because the recipe had been available to the public for twenty years and was in no way a new discovery. In some cases, doctors in charge gave their approval for a well-known product, but the larger committee reversed their decision. The committee was often exasperated by petitioners' attempts to pass themselves off as inventors. In the case of a request for seven different permissions, the doctors found nothing wrong with the cosmetics but found the petitioner "too entrepreneurial," deciding "the company can not permit itself to approve any of his recipes." The doctors who wrote this judgment believed they had a say in setting the limits of commerce and defining invention, a task that was never part of their purpose. Yet, mostly, banality or theft did not necessarily lead to a rejection. Many products received tacit permissions even though they were common and derivative. Though most doctors studying the ingredients of a cream felt that "this object does not directly concern the Royal Society" because of its common nature, they also believed that "nothing impedes us from giving a tacit permission."[78] Overall, the society did not have a strict policy when it came to associating permissions with invention. In the eyes of most physicians, permissions were not validating inventors but simply providing a scientific evaluation of harm.

In this definition of the patent system, those rejected for being derivative could still sell their wares as long as they did not trespass on the regulations of the guilds and the lieutenant of police. Some decisions stated openly that the inventor had to "conform to the rules of the perfumers."[79] In 1783, the society felt that it needed to be more careful in its approvals because charlatans could usurp perfumers' rights. Despite the police's work, the society felt that it was impossible to apprehend all culprits.[80] In a 1785 rejection for Mme Jalifier, the notes from the society complain about the patent system's laxity toward charlatans who bypass guild regulations. Despite these concerns, the same doctors felt that their system's goal should be to try to prohibit perfumers from selling dangerous products, rather than wasting time on "a multitude of little sellers" who "sell drugs under false pretexts that are not harmful."[81] They believed in guild rights, but they did not feel that it was their role to police them; they saw themselves as protectors of consumer safety. It is telling that the majority of tacit approvals were given to nonguild members.

Much more threatening than encroachments on guilds' monopolies was the seller's appropriation of medical qualities. Doctors felt that sellers of cosmetics should not claim that their goods could produce any miraculous transformations of the face or body since these claims were false and infringed on the properties of medical cures. While reviewing the products of vinegar makers, the society doctors found that Maille's products to cure skin diseases were infringing on the rights of apothe-caries and dangerous to the buying public.[82] Doctors also critiqued Mlle Guérin's *Eau pour le teint* for being made "in a ridiculous container and without principles" as well as for not living up to its claims of removing freckles and blemishes.[83] These physicians' main concern was the medical inefficiency of certain products, which led them to stipulate, in certain cases, that even though they would allow a tacit per-mission they would protect the public by denying the right to "print the name and permission of the society [of medicine]."[84] In certain cases, doctors censored the lan-guage of publicity, making sure it contained no claims of medical qualities. For in-stance, the maker of the *Pommade de Venus* was told to omit the claims that her prod-uct "fed," "firmed," and was "very useful after smallpox." She was only allowed to describe her cream as refreshing and softening to the skin, neutral and nonscientific terms applicable only to cosmetics.[85]

Unlike creams that asserted they could alter the wearer's face and implicitly their health, fards made no such claims. The members of the society were aware that most rouges sold on the market were made with innocuous ingredients (a mixture of saffron, lemon, and talc), and thus each request was derivative of the previous ones and could be given a permission. For instance, the Academy of Sciences, which also gave out approvals, found through examinations of Collin's recipe and ingredients that his rouge "contained nothing that could harm one's health or destroy one's skin, an advantage that not all such products have . . . We think M. Collin's rouge is worth more than all of these, and that the author should be praised for having sought to compose a rouge to which nothing hazardous is added."[86]

The Academy of Science defended the rights of the public while upholding an inventor's rights to sell safe products openly. Mme Quesnel, however, wrote to the Society of Medicine to complain that the majority of petitioners lied, leaving out the essential addition of potash, which was necessary to create rouge made with saffron. She specifically accused the most famous rouge makers of hiding this ingre-dient. Surprisingly, her request for a patent was accepted after she gave her explana-tion of its use.[87] Because rouge was a mask, did not impinge on the medical world, and belonged to no guild outright, it was less controversial than other products.

Though the medical society saw no reason to complain about the onslaught of similar rouge demands, the Academy of Sciences was less patient. In 1775, after hav-ing issued Collin's approval, the chemist Antoine Lavoisier, tired of being "constantly interrupted for such a trivial subject," wished to prove once and for all that the rouges sold in Paris were safe to wear. After testing a dozen different cheap rouges of inferior quality, Lavoisier proclaimed, "these rouges are not the only ones deserving approval . . . in the future [the Academy of Sciences] will no longer pronounce on the different rouges presented to it, unless there is something new in their composition or in their fabrication methods." As a distinguished member of the Academy of Sciences, Lavoisier hoped to minimize the time he spent testing unimportant and ultimately unthreatening products. Yet Lavoisier was also a consummate Enlightenment scientist, taking care to back up his claims with empirical tests that he thought would be credible in the eyes of his colleagues and of the Parisian public.[88] Doctor Lefebvre also performed chemical tests on rouge at the request of the Comtesse de Carbon, reassuring her in a sixteen-page letter that he had found only innocuous vegetable ingredients in the rouges of Collin and his competitor Dubost.[89] Lavoisier's and Lefebvre's findings confirmed that due to its vegetable ingredients the rouge currently sold on the Parisian market was not the direct cause of illness.

Lefebvre published his letter to the Comtesse and Lavoisier's results were published in the *Journal de politique et de littérature*.[90] Publicizing these experiments was part of a push to inform the growing consumer public of scientific findings to ensure their safety as buyers. The Academy of Medicine periodically published lists of products for which patents had been denied. Their intention was to try to stop unscrupulous producers from "distributing their remedies in the provinces [where] a few have even had the nerve to say that they were approved by [the Academy]." The academy thus hoped to warn the public ahead of time so that "all educated persons can and should have recourse to this work to defend the health of their fellow citizens against the enterprises of charlatans."[91] One rejected inventor advertised his failed product as safe and useful, confirming the academy's worst fears.[92] Despite being more liberal than most advice writers, these scientists' findings also reinforced their control over both women's toilettes and the commerce of cosmetics. By reassuring buyers and validating specific sellers, doctors hoped to make the market of cosmetics safe.

The Revolution, however, impeded these institutions' ability to supervise the dissemination of cures. In 1791, the guilds were abolished and the medical profession lost what little control it had over producing and selling *remèdes secrets,* including cosmetics. By 1793, the Society of Medicine and the Medical Faculty were abolished. The early years of the Revolution created an institutional vacuum and a free market for producers of illicit goods. The creation of an official government patent on March 25, 1791, attempted to fill this gap and control the growing competition for industrial inventions. The most important difference between the revolutionary system of granting patents and the Old Regime medical approval procedure was that no demand could be turned down if all the paperwork had been correctly filed and the fee paid. For revolutionaries, the law of 1791 was a means to free the French from the tyranny of favors and corruption and to allow the great minds of France to finally overcome their English rivals. As property, patents needed to be protected and honored.[93]

This revolutionary promotion of private property did not in practice give free reign to inventors.[94] Responding to the fears of pernicious ingredients and the growing power of the medical profession, an extra step was added for all medicinal and cosmetic products. All requests for patents first had to pass the test of the *Commission de santé,* set up in 1797, and later of the Commission of *remèdes secrets* of the *Faculté de médecine.* If doctors ruled their invention as unoriginal or detrimental to health, the Ministry of the Interior strongly advised the inventor to withdraw the demand. There was, however, no official way to enforce the medical faculty's will. If inventors insisted on patents, even if their product was hazardous or useless, the ministry would be forced to do so. In one case, the medical professional in charge of the tests refused to sign the patent, forcing a two-year struggle for the recognition of a highly dubious invention.[95] In the case of intransigent producers of potentially dangerous cosmetics or medicines, the ministry's last resort was to alert the local police so that they could prevent inventors from selling their goods publicly.[96]

Scientists and doctors who spent time reviewing the files of inventors felt frustrated by this state of affairs. As with the Old Regime Society of Medicine, the new commission despaired that they had to give seemingly repetitive rouges patents. Unlike their predecessors, they were more concerned with defining invention, but felt powerless because all they could do was judge safety and even that without much muscle.[97] This frustration with the system led to a high degree of sarcasm. When a chemist from Rouen proposed a banal eau de Cologne, the commission jokingly proposed replacing the chemist's absinthe with another ingredient, thus earning them a patent from the government.[98] To slow down the onslaught of useless inventions, the committee asked petitioners for extra explanations and missing details of ingredients. They complained if files were not properly submitted, knowing full well that if the inventor persisted they would eventually have to give in.[99]

As the medical community professionalized, they hoped to gain greater control over the sphere of medicine and, with it, beauty products. Old Regime doctors were concerned with medical language but did not see themselves as authorizing invention, only safety. By the early nineteenth century, doctors felt that they should have more power to police not just the ingredients of products but their status as inventions. Revolutionary ideals of private property and invention, however, limited their real power, frustrating those who now saw themselves as a professional corps. Despite this lack of actual control, the medical elite symbolically controlled the official stamp of legitimacy over medicines and cosmetics. For this position to have any power, it had to be constantly reaffirmed through the publication of patent lists and advice manuals and even through police force. Doctors, like those who sold makeup, had to place themselves in the public sphere to keep control of the thriving cosmetics market and the practices of women in their toilettes. When Lavoisier made his (real or fictional) shopping trip to the rouge sellers of Paris, he performed the role of both consumer and advisor. Though less bombastic than doctors who published advice and less frustrated than those who issued patents, the great chemist also proposed to regulate and control the practices of the toilette. Doctors who felt their true calling was in science found themselves caught up in the fight for control of the consumer market for beauty aids.

Conclusion

The growing importance of the medical profession on the feminine toilette and its repercussions for the sale of cosmetics can be illustrated by three examples. In 1778, the *Affiches de Provence* published a letter from a young woman asking a doctor's advice about wearing makeup. Her mother had employed moral and aesthetic arguments against its use, believing that only vain girls trying to deceive men and snatch a husband dyed their hair and powdered their faces. The young woman, hoping for a second opinion, asked the doctor to "make me capable of proving to my mother that this drug does not harm the skin and that my application of it is not incompatible with modesty and virtue." She put herself into his hands as "you are the doctor, I must hide nothing from you."[100] The doctor's reply was that even though there were neither moral nor aesthetic reasons against wearing makeup, there were medical ones. He warned her that, "it is absolutely impossible for me to prove that makeup will not harm the skin." But, not wishing her to think he was mollifying her mother, he included recipes for cosmetics by a medical colleague that were sure to be safe.[101] This dialogue indicates the ascendancy of medical discourses in matters of beauty: the young girl trusted medical advice and the doctor based his judgments on scientific reasoning. With neither moral nor aesthetic reasons to deny the use of makeup, this representative of science had to agree, however unwillingly, that safe cosmetics were socially acceptable.

In doing his research for *César Birotteau,* Balzac too contacted a doctor, a family friend Nacquart, about how to protect the skin. Nacquart replied that on the question of cosmetics, "the Hippocratic sciences and the art of the perfumer express opposing doctrines." He advised that pure water was the best option, except in circumstances when the skin was damaged by use of makeup or weather, when other potions were needed such as eau de cologne, almond oils, and cucumber paste.[102] Nacquart's advice was to use the most simple vegetable products, considering the harms done by makeup. In the novel, Balzac chose to have scientific advice offered by Nicolas Vauquelin, the illustrious chemist and member of the Academy of Sciences. Vauquelin advised Birotteau that he should not ask for a patent since "quacks have taken the name of the Academy in vain so often, that it would not help you at all."[103] Despite these discouraging words, the fictional Vauquelin gave Birotteau his approval because his product to grow hair was no worse or better than others on the market. A maker of eau de cologne accused the real Vauquelin of only smelling concoctions before approving them.[104] Both Vauquelins were thus cynical about the academy's motives when it came to commercial products. In the novel, Birotteau bribed Vauquelin with a painting. A feeling of frustration, similar to that expressed by Lavoisier, may have led the real Vauquelin to be less than professional in his inspections.

The *Alliance d'hygie et de la beauté,* which had attracted such a crowd at the time of its publication in 1818, provides a different and final version of scientific supervision. The same journalist who noted the chaos it produced critiqued the contents of the book. Dr. Mège's work was compared to Le Camus' still popular *Abdeker* published in 1753. Unlike the old favorite, the *Alliance* was found to be a much harsher model for women to follow. Mège insisted that women "throw out the window all [their] bottles, all their pretty porcelain jars; he condemns without pity their marvelous washes, admirable creams, miraculous elixirs." If women replied that their products were approved by the Society of Medicine, Mège would retort that this approval had no real meaning, being undermined by the committee's low standards. The intrepid journalist, who rightly pointed out that Mège himself owned a patent for a cosmetic creation, advised female consumers to adhere to a minimum standard when purchasing cosmetics. Though they might not be any better than others on the market, cosmetics with a patent were at least "approved by the Faculty." Despite harsh words by a fellow doctor, the journalist felt that the medical stamp of approval still had some worth in the complex market of goods.[105]

The anonymous doctor of the *Affiches* and Vauquelin represented men of science who were willing to allow for the wearing of rouge and powder as long as these cosmetics were safe. Mège and Nacquart both represented a stricter type of doctor who emphasized hygiene and medical safety over all fantasy and vanity and who criticized their colleagues who did not uphold such high standards. Medical science could attempt to prescribe the uses of cosmetics; yet as long as it issued patents to rouge and offered recipes for safe face whiteners, it would continue to support their wear. The biological and social arguments in favor of feminine vanity helped give legitimacy to these options, which were supported by scientific experiments. Purported knowledge about ingredients and their effects was a means of controlling the toilette. It gave physicians well-defined boundaries (created and often expanded by themselves) with which they could justify their presence in a world of feminine frivolity. Though his book stirred up a frenzy among buyers, because he advocated the end of all beauty products, Mège would surely not remain popular for long.

The medical profession's solution was a mix of health lessons, practical advice, and attempted control over products sold in stores. As markers of commercial and consumer respectability, the patent and the advice manual became the medical profession's main justification for the continued supervision of increasingly knowledgeable and demanding female consumers. Though it is harder to find evidence of consumer attitudes, women who bought cosmetics had access to medical language and justifications to shape their practices. The information provided by scientific dictionaries, medical advice manuals, and even advertisements, allowed women to make increasingly more sophisticated judgments when it came to the products they used on their faces and bodies. Amid public disapproval, this specialist knowledge gave female users a means to reclaim beauty practices for themselves. The doctor in the *cabinet de toilette* was an ally rather than an enemy, a qualitative addition to books of endless and undifferentiated recipes by perfumers. He set the limits on products, while leaving the practice up to the user's discretion and personal definitions of attractiveness, allowing for flexibility in the use of makeup. Even though medical manuals were overshadowed in the second half of the nineteenth century by brand-name cosmetics and recipe books written by actresses and noble women, medical language continued to be used to justify ingredients and recipes.[106] And the legacy of medical beauty in France today can be found in the prominent pseudoscientific names of popular cosmetics, cosmetics companies' use of *laboratoire* and *docteur,* and the pharmaceutical monopoly of prominent cosmetic brands.

CHAPTER SIX

Selling Natural Artifice

Entrepreneurs Redefine the Commerce of Cosmetics

The flurry of concern over cosmetics for aesthetic, moral, or medical reasons reinforced an ideal of beauty that mimicked nature through the use of only safe, healthy products for women and men, to a lesser extent. In this atmosphere, the attempts by cosmetics advertisers to market their products aggressively could be construed as an act of desperation, the last breaths of a soon to be defunct sector of the economy. Those who made a living selling cosmetics had to be the most adventurous entrepreneurs precisely because their products were under fire. The criticisms of cosmetics led to an all-out war, which retailers fought both on their own territory—in commerce and marketing—and in the spaces of their attackers. With marketing, they had the upper hand, as they were able to formulate the language of advertising and the representation of beauty to fit their interests. Like the doctors in advice manuals, *philosophes* in tracts, and social commentators in newspapers, cosmetics retailers in the pages of the *affiches* and other journals hoped to control the meaning of consumption and with it feminine beauty practices. These retailers, having created a structure and language of publicity, further supported the sale of their specific products by adopting and reformulating the arguments of their critics. The arguments against cosmetics were turned around and applied to prove their products' worth. Rather than deny or ignore attacks against them, advertisers and promoters publicly used them to rehabilitate the tarnished reputation of artifice, asserting their position as the key taste masters of beauty.

Cosmetics were not the only luxuries to come under fire at the end of the eighteenth century. Changing fashions meant that many artisanal products lost their power over the hearts of Parisian coquettes as these women transformed themselves into respectable ladies. These luxury goods either disappeared from view or adapted to the changing circumstances of the market. Silk producers and merchants lost clientele when cotton became popular, never regaining the same hold over French fashions they had during the Old Regime. Wigmakers declined in number during the Revolution as their function became outdated. These trades were unable to fully adapt to changing fashions and were soon replaced by others, such as *marchandes de mode* and hairdressers.

The criticisms of artifice in advice manuals, journal articles, and tracts transformed the commerce of cosmetics as well. Rouge was to be replaced by vegetable coloring, white face paint by lotions, and chemical potions by scented waters. Women were to be the sole wearers of makeup. Sellers adopted these new definitions of beauty and, in some limited way, gender to remake the image of their old products, rather than actually create new ones. To do so, they reconstructed the representation and cultural function of these aristocratic luxuries. Cosmetics underwent an image conversion from suspect, unsafe goods that transformed women into immoral coquettes and men into petits maîtres, to pure, hygienic products that naturally enhanced beauty. Cosmetics advertisers based their marketing on the same ideals of science and aesthetic purity evoked by the critics of artifice, while ignoring the accusations of immorality.

Yet when these new discourses entered the marketplace, commerce altered their meaning. When sellers adopted Enlightenment discourses of transparency and nature, they helped rehabilitate their own trade while also linking femininity and beauty to the consumer market. Inventors applied for medical patents that promoted the sale of safe goods, allowing them to harness the power of scientific language and to distance themselves from accusations of charlatanism. Building on the new fashion of purity, advertisers manipulated the language of the natural to establish their products as aesthetically pleasing within the framework of Rousseau's pastoral idyll. In the specific case of rouge, numerous entrepreneurs attempted to harness the language of the Enlightenment as well as the feminization of beauty and consumerism to gain a monopoly over the production of this highly profitable product, while also hoping to reinstate an aristocratic, hierarchical model of buying. In these three cases, sellers were acutely aware of the criticisms leveled at their goods. Their responses showed an ability to adapt quickly to changes in the world of fashion as well as an attempt (not always successful) to slow or even stop these changes.

Safe and Tested: Advertising Medical Legitimacy

Although medical patents were meant to protect the public from dangerous goods, they were fundamental in redefining cosmetics as acceptable consumer products. A patent's inherent scientific declaration of safety allowed cosmetics sellers to use the language of science to market their goods. Savvy sellers of cosmetics featured their patents in advertisements, catering to both the public's belief in science and, as one seller so rightly noted, the "capable doctors" who had analyzed the goods and honored them with "their approbation."[1] Upon reading the affiches, an educated public of buyers could thus identify the signs of respectability and safety that they had been taught to recognize by male medical professionals.

Sellers petitioned for patents for interconnected reasons. First, they needed a patent from the Société royale de médecine to get the approval of the Lieutenant de police to post advertisements. Although for most products the signature of the lieutenant was enough, goods that infringed on the medical world were referred to the physicians. In their letters of request, inventors made it clear that they wanted this permission to be able to spread their renown. Once acquired, the tacit permission allowed manufacturers to print publicity sheets and posters that could be legally distributed throughout Paris and the provinces. For instance, one seller of hair dye from Strasbourg printed four thousand leaflets describing his product, before he had been given legal approval.[2] Others wanted an official copy of their permission to compete with neighboring stores that already posted publicity prominently on their storefronts.[3] Still others used their permission to advertise in the many journals that contained announcements, such as the *Affiches* or the *Mercure de France,* though permissions were unnecessary for this form of free promotion. More than half of those who received patents used them in print advertisements before the Revolution.[4] A considerable number of sellers quoted the text and date of the patent.[5] Second, the right to publicize their wares had the added bonus of legitimating cosmetic products as medically safe in the public market. Those who petitioned for patents were savvy entrepreneurs who understood the cachet of an official stamp of approval. One petitioning couple stated that their secret recipe for rouge was useless without a patent because it was thus "deprived of the confidence of those who use it."[6] Sellers did not see the patent as a means of protecting their inventions (since few were original) but as a way of making quite common cosmetics seem safe, approved, and innovative.

The presentation of official patents in print helped legitimate and perpetuate a system of production that had broken away from the guilds.[7] Despite their emphasis on the rights of guilds, neither the society nor the police made any formal checks into their petitioners' backgrounds. Many owners of permissions were either not guild members or were overstepping corporate guidelines. Mercers asked for the right to make rouge, silk merchants the right to sell creams, and servants the right to sell hair powders of their own invention. Perfumers who advertised patents were just as likely to be selling medicines as cosmetics. The largest subgroup (31%) represented among these nonofficial producers were women, either widowed, single, or married, who based their demands on their respectability and family responsibilities.[8] One daughter of a respectable bourgeois family of nine begged the commission for a patent for her father's sake. Others used their status as the daughters or wives of the original inventors to make their petitions.[9]

For outsiders patents were a sign of acceptance, safety, and reliability. Even though the doctors who examined their recipes never claimed to judge effectiveness, patentees asserted that they had passed rigorous tests. Advertisers who had been given only tacit permissions claimed to have the "approbation" of the committee. M. Neuman stated that his eau de cologne was "approved for its superior quality." Mme Josse claimed that doctors had analyzed her rouge before they gave their approval. Durochereau's eau de cologne had "undergone the examination of the *commission consultative des arts*" to get its patent.[10] By claiming approval, advertisers linked their claims of whitening, nourishing, and purifying to the medical professionals' guarantee. A myth of efficiency as well as safety was created around their products.

Collin used his letter of patent from the Academy of Sciences as a means to combat attacks against rouge. His patent text was inserted at the back of Deshais-Gendron's virulent attack on the injurious fards sold in Paris. Pasting an advertisement in this tract outlining the most gruesome diseases caused by rouge indicates savvy marketing by either a crafty publisher or by Collin.[11] The same journals that publicized Lavoisier and the doctor Lefebvre's tests of safe vegetable rouge also visibly advertised Collin's rouge, implying that Collin may have had a role in spreading these studies.[12] Collin cleverly associated his name with scientists' concerns for women's health. Mimicking medical articles on the dangers of artifice, he assured his readers that he "could not be more concerned with women's health." He acknowledged "censors, without doubt too severe, have risen up from all sides against the abuses of rouge." Collin, however, felt that "women today know how to make good use of" his rouge in a way that would guarantee their safety.[13] Science had proved that his buyers could ignore the critics of artifice.

The association of science and cosmetics was most blatant in the *Avant coureur* and the *Journal de politique et de littérature,* both edited by the conservative journalist lawyer Simon-Nicolas-Henri Linguet. Separated into categories such as science, commerce, arts, and literature, the *Avant coureur* included under science the subcategory "médecine-cosmétique," coexisting with such prestigious titles as chemistry, physics, and geography. The *Avant coureur* solicited articles on new discoveries, "which can be an object of commerce or utility. This desire on our part should engage all those who would communicate their observations and their experiences."[14] Yet these claims were not investigated, allowing multiple "real" vegetable rouges to jostle one another for the attention of the public. Understandably, Linguet's journals were popular spaces for manufacturers of cosmetics to publicize their patents and reinforce their uniqueness.[15]

Their presence alongside scientific discoveries enabled cosmetic advertisers not only to tout their approbation by the medical or scientific academies but also to give their products medical qualities. Maille asserted that the Royal Commission of Medicine applauded his Roman vinegar "for the conservation of the mouth and teeth . . . this vinegar is spirituous, penetrating, dehydrating, balsamic, and will fight against scurvy."[16] Another owner of a patent proclaimed that his product, a cosmetic cream, was aimed "for the healing of pockmarks and acne" among other diseases of the skin.[17] Nonmedical practitioners employed scientific and medical language to ascribe to their goods veritable healing qualities, the very thing that physicians of the Society of Medicine tried to dissuade through censorship.[18]

Advertisers also used fear of charlatans, so present in the medical criticisms of cosmetics, to justify selling safer makeup. A revolutionary retailer assured his readers that "there is no lead monoxide (*litharge*), no iron in [his cream] by which charlatans trick women, destroying their health and yellowing their skin; on the contrary, it eradicates all these pernicious cosmetics in an instant." Thus, this fard was not a fard at all but a healing product that worked against the dangers of real makeup. The advertisement finished by saying, "the only merit of the person who presents it is to have rendered it incorruptible and at a price all can afford."[19] For a reasonable price, one could purchase a safe cosmetic with the same properties but without the inconveniences as the artifice of previous years. A *médecin chimiste* promised that his "natural rouge" was colored water made with *simples* and flowers rather than vinegar or other noxious ingredients. The new cosmetics contained "no suspect or dangerous drugs."[20] Advertisers of cosmetics heartily acknowledged medical dangers and charlatanry, placing their goods in opposition to the chemical products sold secretively by others.

Advertisers who publicized patents or adopted medical language were acutely aware of the benefits of scientific approval and, more important, of the criticisms that their products attracted. They addressed directly the medical criticisms put to them and found useful support in the medical professionals' faith in proof and verification. Producers used scientific discourses as the main criteria for judging their inventions in a market system based less on corporate standing than on marketing prowess. Cosmetics advertisers presented their patents as an assurance to the public that attacks against rouge and other cosmetics were not based on fact or, if they were, did not apply to their products. As science had been mobilized to prove that cosmetics were harmful, it was now employed to prove the innocuous nature of cosmetics sold on the market. The possibility of owning and advertising medical patents pushed the discussion of health and safety firmly into the sphere of marketing.

Rousseau's Rouge: Advertising Natural Beauty

In adopting the language of medicine and promoting their patents, advertisers sought to discount not only fears of harmful products but also concerns with the aesthetic properties of makeup. By associating cosmetics with health, nature, and hygiene, advertisers adopted the pastoral image of femininity preached by Rousseau and other critics. Healthy cosmetics increased natural beauty rather than masking or destroying it. By adopting the aesthetic of the natural, those who sold cosmetics discredited accusations that their art was capable only of deceit, hideousness, and immorality. These advertisers asserted that their products were not part of the frenzied system of emulation and aristocratic debauchery but rather capable of transforming any woman into a pure, respectable beauty. The new style of makeup became representative of the transparency of the woman who chose to wear it.

Even as advertisers stressed the agreeable properties of their goods, evoking aristocratic luxury, they also stressed utility, a combination of values also espoused by the affiches. Utility could counter accusations of immorality, though no advertiser openly took on these criticisms. Instead, sellers focused on the need to improve oneself with products that were practical and ultimately highly effective in respectable social spheres. Maille's rouge remained faithful through the heat of Parisian balls. He promised that his creation would not run throughout the evening and night. A 1768 article in the *Avant coureur* asked, "to how many different conditions are Maille's vinegars applicable? It suffices to give the list to realize that he has made the best use of an already useful product."[21] Rouges, vinegars, creams, and powders were utilitarian and necessary tools for the social integration of all who wished to become respectable citizens.

To underline this sense of utility, advertisers stressed the hygienic value of their products and their distance from previous forms of makeup. One of the most desired effects for new cosmetics was salvaging damages done by paint. "Eau for the complexion" was meant to whiten the skin, soften it, and "to remove rouge and dissipate the noxious effect that it has on the skin." As early as 1761, advertisers stated that their eau was safer than white face paint, making its use unnecessary. These eaux promised to restore the skin to its previous health and beauty, one seller calling his "of the virgin." Advertisers also promoted pastes (usually made with almonds) that could wash away any traces of makeup. When used with water, these could promote healthier skin and one seller even sold a pink variety meant to stimulate color. A few sellers touted the ability of their soap to help men shave as well as assist women in washing away the effects of other cosmetics.[22]

White face paint was the most suspect cosmetic of all due to its noxious ingredients and ability to mask the wearer's true self and had to be either redefined or, more profitably, replaced. Mme Josse sold a "white . . . that nourishes and conserves the skin" rather than harming it. One seller of a "baume blanc" promised that it was "not makeup, but a simple and natural remedy" while another's contained "only vegetable matter." Mlle Pissonet's secret recipe for whitening cream did not contain "any type of white." And, whitening creams could mimic nature: the rightly named *Crème de beauté* was "so perfect for the skin that is it impossible to notice that the beauty it gives comes from art."[23] Everything but actual face paint was touted in advertisements: vinegars, waters, oils, and spirits meant to whiten the face without the inconvenience of actual makeup. One inventor came up with a base to apply to the face before women of society put on their face paint. She assured her buyers that she had improved its consistency, making it easier to spread on the face.[24] These sorts of products, associated with rejuvenating and whitening the skin, were the most common inventions advertised in the eighteenth century. There are very few actual advertisements for blanc (only seven found), not because women no longer wore it but because it was both too banal and too suspect to advertise aggressively. Instead, the substitute whiteners that saved women from the dangers of real makeup were touted as much more reasonable and attractive purchases.

Rouge also needed to be redefined, but, unlike face paint, its role as artifice remained central to its sale. To sell rouge in the second half of the eighteenth century was to market vegetable coloring that was safe but also beneficial for the skin. Rouge increasingly shifted away from powders and vinegars to *rouge en pot,* which used oils as their base and vegetable coloring as their tone. Verbs such as "nourish," "appease," and "conserve" referred to products that had previously been assumed to function only as masks. One seller advertised having not just different hues of rouge but different levels of hydration for those with oily or dry skin. Another advertiser admitted that women would be better off not wearing rouge at all since it was potentially harmful and unappealing. But because fashion dictated rosy cheeks, women should adopt "rouge water . . . made of natural ingredients, which, instead of altering the skin, nourishes and softens it . . . [giving it the] same tone that blood produces in people who have coloring." And rouge helped "contribute to the upkeep of women's complexions and conserve the freshness of youth."[25]

Though they would alter the wearer's color, these new forms of rouge were meant to enhance or create natural beauty rather than mask it. Josse advertised her rouge as more "agreeable to the eye than natural colors." Maille assured women that his rouge conserved the skin and could also give it "colors more beautiful than those which blood can produce to trick the eye." Grimod de la Reynière, the famous food critic, reinforced this claim by stating that only Maille's red vinegar produced color like flesh, while his competitors' vinegars left a purple tint that destroyed skin tissue.[26] The presumptuous assertion that makeup could be more authentic than the real thing reinforced the importance of natural fashions.

One seller touted his rouge as a means of slowly giving up the habit. He argued that since his rouge could be wiped for subtle gradations of color; women who wished to stop using rouge but did not want to change their tone overnight could slowly habituate themselves and their viewers to this shift. This insert was one of the few to consider the problem of lack of natural color in women who, listening to critics, wished to do without makeup. It does not, however, imply that women should stop using rouge forever but only temporarily.[27] By the 1790s, women who did not wish to break the color habit but wished to look natural could turn to newly invented liquid rouge, which was easier to apply than the thick pastes and powders, allowing for lighter color. Instructions for how to apply it stressed gentle brush strokes.[28] This rouge could "soften the skin, give vivacity to the eye, the freshness of the first bloom of youth, without anyone being able to guess that one uses" it.[29] Even more discrete *rouge-vert,* a precipitate of vegetable rouge that went from green to red, could be carried on small sheets of paper.[30] Women should have fresh faces, but there was no harm in applying light colors if they did not come naturally. Tasteful and feminine, this style of wearing fard fit the new aesthetics.

Advertisements for rouge, more than any other, reinforced the newly defined feminine toilette. They openly acknowledged that women should care about their looks in the interest of the larger society. It was "contributing to the good of society in which women are the principal ornament . . . to discover the means of rendering them more agreeable in our eyes."[31] This was not the deceit of courtesans in the salons but the simple desire of women no longer in the bloom of youth to please their husbands and reaffirm their looks. Sellers of cosmetics, like scientists and doctors, believed in the biological imperative of vanity. All women, no matter their class or rank, had private and personal reasons for wanting to appear youthful, beautiful, and natural. Rouge and other cosmetics were the cheapest, easiest, and most reliable means of ensuring private and public successes.

Yet rehabilitating makeup did not simply limit women's roles to passive wives dressed and made up to please their husbands. Advertisers asserted that their products could mimic nature and create true beauty, but, like doctors, they did not take on the issue of morality. They very rarely placed their products in a specific context, and, when they did, they were the public balls of respectable society. When dangerous behavior was mentioned, it was not gambling and prostitution, but too much sun and disease. Women were encouraged in their search for youth and beauty but not admonished for their spending or teased for their frivolous pastimes. Instead, advertisers implied that their goods were necessary for all women. Rouge was to be worn for nourishing color both in private and in public; it had a purpose in almost any home. By adopting the model of a natural and thus pure beauty, advertisers may have evoked the moral roles associated with these fashions, but they never articulated the social expectations of appropriate femininity.

It was the fashion press, which blossomed in the late 1790s, which made the association of natural cosmetics with respectable readers more obvious. The *Journal des dames* made clear that its readership was not the old and ugly (for whom the products mentioned were not appropriate) but the young and potentially pretty, if not naturally so.[32] Despite acknowledging in other parts of the journal that makeup was out of fashion, the journal still promoted using rouge and other cosmetics. The *Petit magasin des modes* felt that their female readers had the knowledge to use beauty products without detection, thus allowing them to follow contemporary natural fashions described elsewhere in the journal.[33]

What was key to achieving respectable, youthful natural beauty was following the advice of the journal as to where and what to buy. The *Journal des dames* made fun of the growing number of advertisements in the affiches that lured buyers with false promises of new shipments and cheap prices.[34] In contrast, it promoted its own consumer information as unbiased and representing safer, more effective and fashionable options. By 1815, the journal was selling a list of vetted cosmetics and perfumes.[35] However, these promotions were likely paid for by gifts to the editor, Pierre de La Mésangère, who had a considerable stock of luxury clothing items upon his death. Since most readers did not know of this arrangement, they would have assumed that the stores mentioned in the journal stood for proper values and fashions.[36] Other journals followed suit. The *Observateur des modes* announced new products, judging them by their medical approval and their utility to women.[37] Overall, journals aimed at women promised readers (of the upper classes) natural beauty and safe havens from the fraud of the market. As providers of concrete beauty advice, early nineteenth-century women's journals promoted makeup when bought from well-connected sellers.

These early nineteenth-century promotions of both natural beauty and respectable cosmetics occurred alongside the advent of the cult of paleness associated with the Romantics.[38] An 1802 article in the *Journal des dames* argued that rouge's demise was near. Women wanted to be pale, a style that would soon mean that, "a made-up woman will no longer be able to enter public gatherings."[39] The writer blamed rouge's decline on the Revolution and concerns for health. And yet advertisements and articles in fashion journals continued to promote natural vegetable rouges.[40] In 1811, a journalist compared the plastered paint of the Old Regime to the present when "rouge is liquid and one uses it with moderation."[41] By 1821, one commentator stated that the new use of rouge by "opulent classes" meant that it was no longer as ostentatiously displayed at court but hidden from view.[42] Whether the fashion was pale faces or naturally ruddy complexions, the fashion press encouraged private makeup and other forms of cosmetics for women without fear of aesthetic or moral failing.

As Jennifer Jones has shown, late eighteenth- and early nineteenth-century fashion magazines adopted the new naturalized taste and transformed it into a purely feminized and thus trivial fashion, no less expensive and changing as the previous aristocratic model.[43] What articles in women's journals postulated was the continued acceptance of cosmetics within a new framework: youthful natural beauty accentuated with rouge was a necessary part of social integration but attempts to cover the lines of aging were self-deceiving and frivolous and thus linked to the aesthetics of the Old Regime court. These journals were widely disseminated in Paris, and the provinces and were highly influential in determining feminine purchases.[44] Advertisers knew that overt cosmetics were being critiqued in fashion journals, so they worded and positioned their texts to adopt the language of the new fashion. By paying for special mention or simply advertising in the journals, sellers connected themselves to the journals' goal of enlightening female shoppers.

The rehabilitation of makeup was made possible by the buyers' continued belief in daily miracles. A woman who felt the need for extra color, whether to please a husband, a lover, or herself, could turn to the less proscriptive tone of advertisements. They promised the ideals of safety, utility, and natural beauty. They provided an alternative but also complimented the other widely available discourses on cosmetics: the moralistic stances of philosophes, the all-knowing gaze of advice writers, and the paternalistic tone of medical practitioners. Women's journals added to this alternative sphere by combining practical advice with consumer tips. They encouraged wearing makeup by respectable women, allowing their readers to set limits found elsewhere in the journal. The literature of the boudoir, whether fashion journal or even medical treatise, left enough leeway for the application of almost any cosmetic, leaving the moral lessons to other spaces.

Selling Femininity: Dreams of a National Rouge Industry

Though advertisers did not often deal with morality, social class, and even gender, another group of sellers hoping to profit from the popularity of rouge were less circumspect. Entrepreneurs who made requests to create monopolies for rouge very clearly hoped to associate with both the concerns for health and beauty and feminine respectability. The transformation of rouge from aristocratic color to "vegetable rouge" meant that numerous small-time producers, especially women, could profit from this uncontrolled product. This freedom frustrated traditional male entrepreneurs who advocated conservative policies: commercial monopolies and elite privilege. They hoped to profit from the popularity of rouge while slowing the boom in consumerism, asserting the right of the aristocracy or the elite to set the tone and control fashion. Though they failed to stop the widespread adoption of natural fashions or to interest the government in their protectionist policies, their attempts reinforced the use of rouge as a feminine necessity and underlined the market's importance at the end of the eighteenth century.

The growing concerns with corrosive ingredients and the feminization of men who continued to wear rouge were used to justify entrepreneurial producers' need for greater economic control. Because rouge was a highly profitable industry, these men hoped to harness its economic potential by appealing to the ideal of "natural" domestic femininity that could be protected by a monopoly. The widespread fears of artifice were evoked to argue for establishing official manufactures, which would regulate quality and price as well as produce a profit for the state. From 1778 to 1796, entrepreneurs hoping to gain control of rouge manufacturing made nine official petitions to the government.

The government was the first to call for curtailing rouge production due to concerns about dangerous products. In 1778, an edict outlined the means of suppressing the use of noxious ingredients, especially those found in rouge: "The large consumption of rouge and the profits which are made by it have spurred a number of individuals to produce it, but these makers not having the proper knowledge necessary to distinguish between the drugs and ingredients that have to be included, having tried too hard to find the least expensive methods, [they] produce many harmful rouges, so that those who wear them are victims of the deceitfulness and stinginess of their makers." The edict set guidelines for the formation of a royal rouge factory to be run by four select families of producers picked for the quality and safety of their goods. It also set the size of jars and the price of four different varieties, ranging from three to thirty livres, prices that limited sales to the wealthy. Current retailers and rouge makers were given four months to rid themselves of all stock. This plan attempted to establish monopoly control over a product that lay outside corporate privileges, and the four manufacturers involved were quite likely the instigators.[45]

The edict was never implemented, and, in 1780, the debate was reopened in the press and in pamphlets. In its public presentation, a monopoly over rouge sales became not only a means of ensuring safety and regulating production but also a profitable means of regulating womanhood. The chevalier d'Elbée proposed a plan to create a national industry of rouge whose profits would go to the needy sisters of rich consumers: poor noble women and war widows.[46] He estimated that France consumed two million jars of rouge a year and could count on respectable ladies to continue to wear cosmetics. He also proposed that the newly created corporation would set up warehouses in all the large cities of France and send out traveling salesmen throughout the countryside to promote rouge consumption.[47] Elbée's plan attempted to sway the government into giving him the monopoly because of his charitable impulses. In effect, the libertines, actresses, and aristocrats of Paris would subsidize their more unfortunate sisters; the practices of high society would pay for the ideals of domestic sufficiency represented by the respectable but impoverished rural nobility. Elbée did not condemn wearing rouge, but rather he hoped to increase it. Consumption, in whatever form it took, could be harnessed for positive results. From a feminine and potentially dangerous practice, shopping could be transformed into a productive, reformative act that linked together all women of France.

Elbée's proposal for what was essentially a new guild was unpopular because of the increasing acceptance of greater market freedoms and opportunities for the talented. Under attack by the rouge makers of Paris, Elbée stoutly denied that he was interested in profit and maintained that the best rouge makers would find a place in his association, forcing the worst to look elsewhere for work. He accused other rouge makers of being principally "hairdressers, toilette sellers, hawkers, clerks, etc. As they have acquaintances in all the houses, it is easy for them to sway the servants in their favor; they have lawyers everywhere; and here is the pack that barks against my project. They say 'An exclusive privilege! Goodbye liberty, goodbye industry.' But should all be permitted to sell poison? That is what comes of the liberty to make rouge; should we let this situation continue?"[48] Elbée portrayed the struggle as one pitting himself, upholder of helpless women, against the encroaching free market whose intimacy with the consumer unfairly skewed the outcome. To Elbée, servants and hairdressers were uncouth, profit-hungry charlatans, not concerned with the health and happiness of the ladies they served. In reality, as we have seen, most small rouge sellers were women who were kept out of other professions. By forming a national monopoly, Elbée hoped to enhance quality and ensure the safety of respectable female wearers, while cutting out working-class women from its profits.

Elbée's proposal was much discussed in the press. Despite poking fun at Elbée's serious tone, Linguet backed the plan in his *Journal de politique*. Even though Linguet had earlier published Lavoisier's findings about the safety of rouge, by 1780, he had adopted the well-worn opinion that there were hidden perils in the free market of cosmetics. Not typically a supporter of monopolies, he backed Elbée's plan because it concerned nonessential, frivolous goods that could prove harmful. He argued that rouge would no more lose its hold over women than tobacco and card playing would over men, making a monopoly highly profitable in the long run. Because of the popularity of rouge, the government needed to protect innocent women from the dangers lurking in street commerce.[49]

The feminization of the consumer made it easier for male entrepreneurs to propose a monopoly but did not bring them success. In 1780, the Sieur Montclav et compagnie offered the state 1,200,000 livres and a percentage of their sales for the exclusive privilege of making innocuous vegetable rouge. These artisans justified their demand by asserting that they were the true inventors of vegetable rouge, "which today is at the highest degree of perfection due to their studies of procedures." Though this company promised to "reassure the public of all fears," government bureaucrats ignored their request.[50] In response, Montclav offered two million livres payment, and, when this enormous sum was turned down, made a last attempt to gain recognition by proposing to open a royal manufacture of rouge whose profits would be shared with the state.[51] The company continued to make proposals for the next two years, never with any concrete results. In 1787, another group of rouge makers, arguing that they were the first and oldest makers of vegetable rouge approved by the Academy of Sciences, proposed a royal manufacture whose profits would also go to the state. They endorsed doctors' findings who warned of hazardous chemical ingredients and criticized the mass proliferation of rouge sellers on every street corner. This group of four artisans hoped to destroy the present system of rouge sales that made possible both the fortunes of charlatans and the availability of luxuries meant for the elite to all but the poorest residents of Paris and other cities.[52] The wealthy were to reclaim luxury from the prostitutes and charlatans who now controlled it.

Another player in the contest to control rouge was the highly visible Collin. Having gone bankrupt in 1786, Collin restarted his career as a rouge manufacturer. As an owner of a rouge patent and a supposedly thriving factory, he felt it was his right to participate in the government's potential regulation, making at least four attempts to get the government's ear. Collin's plan, however, was not a monopoly for himself but rather control over other makers. He asked for the position of "rouge inspector," which gave him the power to supervise other manufacturers and more important collect a tax. If his request was not granted, he threatened to move his factories to Germany and England, thus causing France to lose substantial export tariffs and jobs. Citing as his patrons the Marquis de Rubel and an archbishop, he also asked that his "laboratory" be named the Royal Manufacture of Rouge, a title that Catherine the Great had allegedly given him. Yet Collin swore that his own proposal supported free trade, unlike others who wished to monopolize the market. His belief in laissez-faire tied to a strong sense of French nationalism and mercantilism, made Collin a savvy manipulator of contemporary economic discourses. Unfortunately, he too was unsuccessful in persuading the government that rouge was a worthwhile concern, and his letters went unanswered.[53]

Requests for control over rouge production continued throughout the Revolution. Like other entrepreneurs of the period, the perfumer Guérin proposed to employ orphans (twenty or thirty of both sexes) to run his rouge factory, providing them with a pension when they reached adulthood. He argued that his rouge production "could only be advantageous to the Republic since it would reinvigorate a considerable branch of commerce which in the last few years has diminished abroad due to lack of means."[54] He wished to do all he could to help France stabilize its economy. The Ministry of the Interior, however, replied that it was too preoccupied with "objects linked to the prosperity of commerce . . . to stop and examine an industry which only profits luxury." The state solely assisted industries that were beneficial to the larger well being of the nation and which could give to "the Republic the degree of splendor to which it aspires and that it will inevitably attain." Nonetheless, Guérin was congratulated for his enthusiasm and encouraged to continue his good works.[55]

Other proposals were sent to the ministry, but all failed to elicit results. Forced to answer oft-repeated demands, government officials expressed their exasperation and annoyance. Though aristocrats and members of the royal family supported many of these proposals, none was seen as a potential solution for the financial woes of the Old Regime or the Republic. Hilton Root argues that the crown encouraged corporatism to stifle unregulated luxury trades.[56] Steven Kaplan, however, shows that after August 1776, the crown promoted more competition within commerce while increasing government oversight and policing over the guilds for its own benefit.[57] These proposals' lack of success indicates that the market for rouge was not seen as a threat to the government, thus not necessitating more regulation. And, as the revolutionary government moved to abolish the guilds in April 1791, any projects for monopolies would have been frowned on.[58]

Though rouge was profitable, its critics and supporters alike defined it as an unimportant luxury product associated with feminine fashion. Ultimately, both those for and against regulation agreed that its manufacture and sale invoked mere frivolity. Elbée and others linked their proposals to fashion and feminine needs, hoping that this consumption could be seen as capable of providing charity for "young ladies of quality, orphans, and poor."[59] Though they failed to woo the government, the entrepreneurs' portrayal of rouge as a beneficial, though feminine, luxury product that might elevate the standing of the poor and protect the health of the rich was a strong justification for its continued sale. The link of fashion goods and feminine frivolity was a widespread concern for those involved in their production. Jennifer Jones argues "male and female artisans resisted the feminization of 'the agreeable art of clothing'" and tried unsuccessfully to associate themselves with *beaux art* rather than *art utile*.[60] Yet in this case, most proposals by cosmetic producers immediately accepted the frivolity (and thus feminine nature) of their products, finding commercial clout in precisely this association.

What concerned these entrepreneurs more was the association of their luxury product with the wrong women and with the wrong producers. These inventors and entrepreneurs felt uncomfortable with the changes brought by the consumer revolution. Rouge was to be sold, as Elbée stated, not in bedrooms but in an open marketplace where it could be watched and controlled. As a necessary and increasingly important commodity, rouge had to be secured by the government for its feminine population, a group thought to consist of the middle and upper classes. Rouge was to be repackaged so that it might regain its position as a luxury item, outside the reach of prostitutes but within grasp of the respectable classes. Much like the doctors who hoped to control the toilette, these manufacturers hoped to gain an even more powerful position in regulating production and sales. To do so, entrepreneurs readily transformed the fear of deceit into a distrust of the working classes, represented by both the immoral women who wore rouge and the questionable female artisans who sold it.

These ideals, had they been implemented fully, would have circumscribed the market for rouge, reinforcing a hierarchy based on social standing and corporate manufacture. They would have tied the buying of rouge to elite and respectable women and erased the possibility for a larger customer base. The failure to implement monopoly plans allowed the already booming market to continue to grow unabated. Those who sold a hodgepodge of beauty products to the Paris working classes benefited from the lack of government interference, while larger enterprises strengthened their hold over an elite clientele by assuring them of their quality and prestige. Though the proposals for monopolies were triggered by conservative impulses, they upheld the concerns of health, reliability, and proper femininity common to Enlightenment critics and medical professionals alike, as well as the open market of cosmetics advertisers. By taking these arguments into the realm of the market, they asserted that commerce was essential to the definition of femininity as well as beauty.

Conclusion

Artisans and producers involved in the commerce of cosmetics had two choices at the end of the eighteenth century. Either they could go about their business as usual or they could adapt to changing times by placing advertisements, applying for medical patents, ensuring their clientele of the safety and naturalness of their "new" products, and promoting monopolies. Though many cosmetics retailers chose the first option, a growing number saw the profitability of altering their business practices to counter and answer the attacks of their numerous critics. These entrepreneurs were conscious of the debates occurring in the texts of journals, philosophical tracts, and medical advice manuals.[61] Furthermore, they quickly learned how to adapt these debates to market their products as the smart consumer's first choice.

The state's institutionalization of a patent system for medicines in the 1770s, the ongoing dissolution of the guilds' power, and the official view that cosmetics were unimportant and trivial commodities further spurred the counterattack by cosmetics retailers. The government's promotion of laissez-faire policies meant that this battle for legitimacy was fought almost solely in the public arena of the market, putting all retailers on an even keel when it came to promotion and publicity. Many perfumers or retailers of cosmetics were able to benefit from this freedom and to adapt their goods to changing times. Savvy use of contemporary discourses complemented the free market. Advertisers who adopted medical language assuaged consumer fears. Those who adopted the language of the natural evoked pastoral beauties rather than artificial aristocratic ones. Entrepreneurs failed to establish rouge monopolies but did reinforce the representation of cosmetics as safe, domestic, and feminine products. Ultimately, those who marketed cosmetics created a sphere in which values of health, nature, and beauty went hand in hand with buying consumer goods. The aesthetics of nature became one with the aesthetics of natural art.

What advertisers did not address were the moral aspects of this new beauty, leaving women's roles unspecified. When put alongside women's fashion journals, their publicity took on a more specific, though never very strict, definition of femininity. Only when attempting to sway government bureaucrats did entrepreneurs openly take on the issue of appropriate female behavior. And many did so by associating cosmetics with the worlds of prostitutes and aristocrats, in opposition to a purer respectable womanhood that did not wear rouge. In this way and by attempting to gain privileges in a period of laxer economic control, they were out of step with changes in the larger market. Advertisers knew well that they could not ignore the changing ideals in their reconceptualization of the marketplace, but they did not want to limit or cordon off their customer base. References to natural beauty and medical safety were successful because of the association of luxury with the concerns of the French populous at large. At the end of the century, commercial success meant welcoming any buyer with money or credit, thus achieving the very mixing of classes so feared by Elbée. The small rouge pot, labeled as safe and natural, could now give the neighborhood laundress natural color as well as mark her entry into the paired worlds of consumerism and fashion.

By appropriating the very criticisms directed at their much-maligned products, advertisers were able irrevocably to alter the terms of the debate. They legitimated selling and purchasing cosmetics, as well as fixing beauty practices firmly in the sphere of commerce. Concerns about women's behavior, looks, and toilettes revolved around commercial availability, pricing, reliability, scientific legitimacy, and consumer know-how. Women, taught to be good consumers, were to worry about which cosmetics to buy and from whom, rather than about their moral or aesthetic failings. By the end of the eighteenth century and well into the nineteenth century, the conversation had shifted from the salons to the stores, from private toilettes to public displays of consumption, and from the texts of moralists to those of doctors, perfumers, and fashion magazines.

CHAPTER SEVEN

Selling the Orient

From the Exotic Harem to Napoleon's Colonial Enterprise

In the French popular imagination, the Eastern harem was populated with sensuous white beauties captured by fearsome Ottomans. Travel writers filled their works with anecdotes depicting these captives as the perfect representations of femininity, guarded fearlessly by sadistic eunuchs.[1] The paintings of Carle and Amadée Van Loo for Madame de Pompadour and Madame du Barry, respectively, inserted the favorites into their own idealized harems.[2] From the court, the fashion for *turquerie* spread to all aspects of the fashionable interior and dress.[3] French women adopted the style *à la sultane,* imitating what they thought of as Eastern customs.[4] The commerce of cosmetics also adopted imagery of the orient to sell its products. To separate itself from aristocratic spheres, it redefined literary and artistic exoticism to fit the needs of a wider audience. This change in context gave new meanings to both cosmetics and the European depictions of the "other," which evolved from these purchases.

There was one essential reason for which the Orient became a primary means of selling cosmetics. This was the direct implication that harem women, chosen by the sultan for his pleasure, represented true beauty. These were women whose only goal in life was to please their master and whose beautification rituals thus had to be highly effective. Unlike their French counterparts, their rituals were not attempts to cover sins or deformities because they were unquestionably beautiful. Cosmetics used by harem women were exotic and effective, not masks of false paint. And in conjunction, they were also linked to awakening the senses—the scents, hot baths, and artful ministrations. Buying Oriental cosmetics was a means of reproducing at home the harem ambiance for personal pleasure.

Yet, this association of harem women and beauty implied sexual desire and possible depravity. By the 1770s, art critics attacked harem scenes as examples of corrupt, shallow, and debased lifestyles.[5] These paintings of luxurious toilettes evoked aristocratic primping that had already come under attack. The cosmetics used by odalisques were no less sexual in their goal than the toiletries of coquettes. This association tainted beauty products labeled as coming from the harem. How could they be any purer and less immoral than those used by French women, if their effects were the same, if not worse? Second, despite the myth that the harem's inmates were kidnapped white (and thus often Christian) women, the location invoked both dark skins and a despotic culture. Even if the odalisques were European, they were still foreign in their dress, speech, and tastes. They were asked to mix with black eunuchs and to be at the beck and call of their master. If it was acceptable for the aristocracy to dress up as *Orientales* in their portraits and balls, did these practices apply to the artisan's wife or provincial noblewoman?

The commercial possibilities of the exotic were both powerful and problematic. The harem could invoke foreignness and sensuality, promising effects that no French product could. It had true unadulterated beauty and personal pleasure on its side, but with it came issues of race and sexuality not so easily dismissed. The Orient had to appeal to a desire for novelty without associating with the artifice and debauchery of the upper classes. Treading this fine line, sellers of cosmetics created a long-lived and profitable relationship between their goods and the East. They did so by modifying the tone and vision of the harem, eliminating all traces of racial difference and overt sexual encounter. Instead, they left women with a vision of effective beautification, gratification, and sensuality appropriate for the homes of the bourgeoisie. By the early nineteenth century, redefining the harem had gone one step further, erasing almost completely the odalisques as actors in the exchange of goods and beauty. Cosmetics sellers successfully manipulated the image of the Orient to fit their marketing needs, justifying the purchase of artifice with foreign associations and cajoling buyers with a safe version of Eastern sensuality.

A Harem of Beauties: The Literary Orient

From the translation of *A Thousand and One Nights* in 1704 to the depictions of harems by Carle Van Loo, Eastern women were associated with sexuality, desirability, and unquestionable beauty. The image of an erotic Orient appeared first in seventeenth-century French travel literature.[6] Travelers to foreign lands had no access to the harem; yet, their works were filled with conjectures and anecdotes bought from guards or inspired by visits to the slave market.[7] They described the women on the inside as captives of the Ottoman's enemies. Of these, the Circassians and Georgians, having the whitest skins, were the most beautiful and desirable.[8] One storyteller described Georgian slave girls sold in India as having traditional French traits: "What beauties! And what pretty little faces! Big eyes, fresh complexion, such small mouths."[9]

Seventeenth-century tales soon spawned a vast literature of Orientalist texts that, according to Edward Said, essentialized the East and allowed European political domination based on mastery of knowledge about the "other."[10] Even as it was Europeanized, this literature also marked a transition in relationships between Christianity and Islam. Because of embassy visits, trade, and colonization, Europeans no longer felt threatened by the Muslim world in the eighteenth century. European powers were more confident and thus emphasized a weakened, feminized, and secretive East, best represented by the odalisques.[11] Yet, even though the recounting of the harem was the creation of European tellers, it did not always represent European superiority and imperialism.[12] For many writers, the harem became a literary trope just as notions of individuality and liberty were growing in importance in European political thought.[13] The harem could stand in for more familiar spaces of despotism: the monastic life or the king's court. It could also serve as a setting for the critique of the subordination of women in European society.

A second genre used the harem to create romantic tales that glorified French/European customs while humanizing and reforming Eastern ones. Ultimately, these stories were about the possibility of romantic love and individual fulfillment, ending in the triumph of heterosexual marriage. These stories domesticated and venerated one special woman of the harem, giving her moral means to escape her fate. Two basic formulas applied: in one the sultan bought a kidnapped foreign woman (often French) who resisted his advances due to her strong sense of self, and eventually, she reunited with her true love.[14] In the second formula, the foreign woman succeeded in reforming the sultan's ways by her arguments for true love and respect for the individual woman. The best and most copied example of this story is that of Roxelane, the Polish concubine who became the wife of Suleiman the Magnificent.[15] Possibly the most popular genre, harem pornography, undermined these stories of domestic bliss by focusing on both the sultan's inordinate lust and the odalisques' deviant sexuality.

All three genres, political, romantic, and pornographic, assumed the connection between harem women and beauty, mediated through the use of cosmetics. Montesquieu's *Persian Letters* and its many imitations are the best examples of the politicization of the harem.[16] Though Montesquieu's text was not bereft of titillating sexuality, a more fully pornographic example, *L'odalisque,* points to the impossibility of separating Eastern beauty practices from sexual laxity. The most important reflection on the relationship between cosmetics and the harem comes in the form of a romantic tale, Antoine Le Camus' *Abdeker.* All three genres affected European perceptions of Eastern beauty practices, though only the romantic tale managed to glorify and justify the use of makeup for moral purposes.

The *Persian Letters* contrast what Usbek, a Persian nobleman, experienced in

Parisian society with the closed world of the harem described by himself and his concubines. Usbek enjoyed the openness of French society and its women. Yet the thick
layers of paint they wore to attract gullible men shocked him. These women primped
well into old age, their vanity making them believe that rouge and paint could hide
their wrinkles. For Usbek, French women's ability to manipulate makeup and "the
desire to be attractive which continually preoccupies them, detract from their virtue
and are an affront to their husbands."[17] In contrast, harem women's beauty practices were discrete and pure. Usbek's favorite brought "out the beauty of [her] complexion with the finest shades of color" and applied "the most precious lotions," taking advantage of secret Oriental cosmetics to enhance her natural traits even when
he was not there.[18] Montesquieu's harem beauties improved their natural colors
rather than pasting on artificial ones. Instead of paint, the harem reeked of perfume
and oils, part of the frequent rituals of bathing.

   Though Montesquieu critiqued the despotic realm of the harem and promoted
the freer treatment of women in France, he nonetheless accused his countrywomen
of vanity and falsity by positing a true Oriental beauty redolent with Eastern essences
and charms. The sensuality of Eastern beauty practices made them both more natural but also more dangerous to men than the telltale masks of French women. These
naturally beautiful women of all races (yellow-skinned women were present) par-
took in lascivious sexual acts and rebelled against their master because of his lack of
attention as much as his despotism.[19] Usbek believed that increasing the number of
pretty women and keeping them in constant competition for his attentions was a
means of ensuring obedience to the master and his guards.[20] Yet, this expectation of
competition between the women backfired. Promises of constant beautification during his absence turned out to be motivated by new lovers, breaking the rules of the
seraglio.[21] Ultimately, Usbek was deceived not by the false faces of his wives and mistresses, but by their false claims to faithfulness in a prison environment. He may
have seen through the artifice of French society and its women, but he failed to see
the irony of his situation. Rather than simply highlight their beauty, harem women
used beautification practices as a means to fool their master into believing their pretenses of love.

   Similarly to most eighteenth-century commentators, Montesquieu used the application of cosmetics, whether for artifice or amplification, as a metaphor for the
corruption of French high society as well as a lighthearted attack on the frivolous
pastimes of women in general. Men's constant desires for youth and newness imposed these pastimes on them. When the courtesans of the harem aged, the master
simply replaced them. When the French man's wife wrinkled, he took a younger mistress.[22] Usbek's harem mirrored the French society that he so carefully studied. Men

did not trust women and had to control them because of "their natural tendency to-ward sexual excess, duplicity, and irrational behavior."[23] Montesquieu recognized that beauty could sway despots and simple men alike, warning of the deception inherent in any process of feminine self-beautification. Yet he understood that both Persian and French women had few other weapons to use in the cages imposed on them by tradition and social norms.

Like Montesquieu, most literary Orientalist genres, whether moral, political, or pornographic, presented the kidnapped women of the harem as ideal beauties who had nothing else to do but primp, bathe, and learn tricks to please their master. Often, the woman who rejected these daily rituals as demeaning (thus rejecting the culture of the French toilette as well) was the most authentic in her charms and most likely to escape the confines of the harem or rise in stature within it. In the play *Le sérail à l'encan,* by Sedaine de Sarcy, a vizier must sell his odalisques, most of whom he did not care about because of their grating obsequiousness. The only one he hoped to buy back was the simply dressed *péruvienne* Nadine, whose naturalness seemed fresh and original. In contrast, the women for sale, covered in paint and fancy dress, looked like "Bayonne hams," each interchangeable and sellable by men. Tellingly, Sedaine de Sarcy described the representative French slave as being so perfumed and painted that potential buyers could not see her real face. An even more painted slave sold for cheap to a stereotypical Jew because no one else wanted her. The judges of beauty felt that "well placed rouge . . . does not count for much here." In the end, Nadine succeeded, through her own cunning, to buy her freedom and ultimately to marry the vizier as an equal.[24]

The average odalisque was not cunning and rebellious but uninteresting and self-centered. Even though the harem represented the ideal space for beauty, the types of activities (all sensual or sexual in nature) it nurtured were suspect. If critics of cosmetics deemed the coquette at her toilette egotistical and frivolous, the unending beautification available in the harem made the odalisques even more so. That these ministrations were practiced without legions of admirers and with little chance of notice made them all the more dangerous and easily corrupted into deviant sexuality. Tellingly, when the vizier put his harem up for sale, he had never seen the faces of his slaves, underlining the grotesqueness of most of their paint. That the only true beauty was a *péruvienne,* and thus from the New World, emphasized her separation from the corruption of both Europe and the East.[25]

The association of harems with beauty, thus, did not necessarily mean that French women should copy their practices because they might lead to sexual deviance and self-indulgence. It was an association, both assumed and fraught with tensions, inherent in women's relationship with their own self-beautification. Just like the coquette at her toilette, the odalisque threatened men by her ministrations and her powers. In literary Orients, the relationship between beauty products and the East reinforced the criticisms of cosmetics aimed at French women. Yet, in 1754, Antoine Le Camus, a well-respected doctor, redefined the relationship between harem and beauty. He gave the practices of primping meaning and justification when practiced in the exact space that had previously implied lascivious pampering. By doing so, he justified French women using Eastern cosmetics for personal pleasure and enhancement of true love, separating them from accusations of vanity and falsity. He also placed the discovery of makeup in the harem setting, defined as an invention of love and a weapon against despotism. His harem beauty, like many of her counterparts, turned out to be European and escaped her prison for the enlightened shores of Italy with the help of her rouge.

In the two volumes of *Abdeker ou l'art de conserver la beauté,* Le Camus laid out cosmetic recipes culled from previous sources and an elaborate Oriental tale in which to contextualize this beauty advice. Le Camus claimed that his book was an authentic fifteenth-century Arab manuscript brought to Paris in 1740 by Diamentes Ulasto, doctor to the Turkish ambassador. Le Camus informed his female readers of the uses and hazards of cosmetics in the guise of lessons by Abdeker, the harem's doctor, to Fatmé, the most beautiful woman of the harem. Abdeker used his skills to invent both creams and makeup as tools for the captive beauty. While the doctor spent hours teaching Fatmé the secrets of beauty and health, they inevitably fell in love. Luckily for the young couple, Fatmé was revealed to be the daughter of a Christian woman and the long-lost half-sister of the Sultan, Mohamet the Great. Now morally barred from her bed, the enraged sultan plotted to poison her. Crafty and loyal Abdeker, however, marshaled his medical skills to fake her death, allowing the lovers to flee to Italy where they converted to Christianity, married, and lived happily ever after. Artifice, in all senses of the word, had triumphed over evil. Le Camus filled the second half of the book with recipes and instructions necessary for securing Fatmé's lasting beauty.

Le Camus' story was for entertaining his female readership. But he also repositioned the invention of cosmetics in the harem, a move that turned artifice into a tool for both true beautification (in opposition to Parisian salons) and resistance against despotism (literally within Eastern cultures, but figuratively in European households as well). Fatmé's lessons were not meant to create beauty where there was none, but rather to enhance and sustain the natural beauty she already possessed. Unlike the women of the French salons, Fatmé did not aim to trick the viewer into believing she was beautiful. Instead, much like Montesquieu's harem women, she used beautification to resist her captor and guards. As she fell in love, Fatmé lost her natural coloring and blushed at the most inopportune moments. Abdeker "wanted to spread artificial colors that could serve as a mask for the natural colors which shone on the Sultana's skin."[26] Thus, he invented makeup to mask Fatmé's moods: the application of rouge hid her true feelings from pesky eunuchs. Despotism was tricked and ultimately won over by the use of artifice. As Tassie Gwilliam, working from the slightly different 1754 English translation, has argued "by presenting the stabilization of a woman's complexion as a hedge against unjust sexual surveillance, *Abdeker* justifies feminine disguise, removing the woman from the prying eyes of patriarchal authority."[27]

Yet this liberation from the sultan and all other oppressive gazes through makeup also denied Fatmé any physical revolt from her condition as captive, giving Abdeker ultimate control over her fate. Unlike Usbek's wives who took over the harem, Fatmé's love for Abdeker and willingness to let him cover her natural beauty forced her to remain passive. Her desire to be taught coquetry led her to promise docility, for she did not "think that a woman could be a rebel when her vanity is flattered and when she is given the means of seduction." She installed a shrine to beauty in her bedroom decorated with bottles and perfumes to which she offered daily vows, having dutifully turned Abdeker's lessons into her one and only true faith. Moreover, Abdeker threatened that "staying up too late, hard work, as well as too much sleep, ruins one's colors." Sorrow, fear, a guilty conscience, and excessive physical pleasure were also sure methods of destroying beauty.[28] In exchange for the knowledge of paint, Fatmé had to become a model citizen of the harem. It was only after she was found to be the sultan's sister that, with the help of Abdeker's continued artifice, she could escape despotism. Until then she could only deceive it.

Artifice, as taught by Abdeker and related by Le Camus, became both a powerful beauty tool and a solution for female rebellion. Le Camus argued that the practices of beautification would cause women to become self-involved and passive, unwilling to act aggressively. Unlike Montesquieu, for Le Camus beauty represented faithfulness and sexual innocence. In most eighteenth-century texts, the artificial blush (meant to create a constant modesty) threatened men's ability to judge and chose among women. For Le Camus, however, the use of rouge denoted privacy, privileged love, and "a positive defense against illegitimate penetration."[29] Le Camus created a world of the toilette in opposition to its predecessor; the adulterous and vain coquette depicted in the *Persian Letters* became the passive wife whose true beauty shone only for her husband or her doctor. Unlike Montesquieu's women, Fatmé was moral, the perfect partner for Abdeker. These traits for an exotic heroine, as Julia Douthwaite argues, were mostly present in novels written by women in the eighteenth century, making Le Camus unusual.[30]

Fatmé was not only the perfect wife, but she also could provide a template for French women to follow in their toilettes. The standard of beauty upheld in his harem was the same as that in the Parisian boudoir: "a very white skin on which is found a veneer of rose."[31] Le Camus gave examples of Arab women trying to whiten their olive and brown skin. Their successes or even failures reemphasized the primacy of this aesthetic. His stress on smooth, light skin created for European readers a harem filled with women like themselves. It was no surprise that the heroine turned out to be a Christian all along, in her heart if not in her practices. Le Camus' harem was both a mysterious and strangely familiar space. Creating the perfect white woman was the goal, and an Eastern princess such as Fatmé was easily transformed into a domesticated European wife.

Though Le Camus' redefinition of the harem as a space for respectable yet pleasurable beautification practices proved popular and longlasting, the underlying subtext to most male-authored harem stories was unbridled desire and deviant sexuality. It was easy to transform Abdeker's innocent beauty lessons into European male fantasies of sexual fulfillment. A 1796 story purported to be by Voltaire (and undoubtedly not), *L'odalisque,* mimicked the tone of advice manuals to teach its readers sexual techniques. Contrary to the innocent and justified motives of the lessons taught by Le Camus, the lessons taught in this story by a eunuch to a thirteen-year-old slave focused on beauty and adornment as a means for sexual pleasure for himself and the sultan. The message of this tale was not that harem women can become domesticated European wives but that French women should learn to be more submissive and more aware of their lover's needs because they too were "sultanas in this agreeable moment." The eunuch's contradictory goal for training new odalisques was both to rein in their sexual desires (for each other) and to teach them to please the sultan as much as possible. His special protégée was a Georgian girl, Zeni, who he hoped would become the sultan's favorite if he protected her and cultivated her beauty. Zeni's lessons were sexually graphic descriptions of how she could stop pain during intercourse and keep her private parts clean. As with Abdeker, the eunuch fell in love with his charge. When he attempted to have sex with her, she fainted from the pain, and he only felt frustrated. Because the Sultan's ultimate goal was sex (and not the subtler pleasures emphasized by the eunuch), he nonetheless took Zeni as his favorite and exiled the eunuch for falling in love.[32] As the antithesis of Abdeker, the eunuch was now alone and a foreigner in a strange land.

This story made obvious the implications of a harem story, even one as tame as *Abdeker.* Because European commentators defined the harem as a space filled with natural beauties taught to please men, sexual practices were implied. Amid the story's pornography, the author gave lessons to French women about their duty and their beauty practices. Though the readership was undoubtedly male, the author mimicked popular advice literature to women. What women were to learn (or what the male reader's wished them to) was the real goal of better cosmetic aids: sexuality unbound for the pleasure of men. The thirteen-year-old Zeni, who washed with the famous *baume de mecque* perfume and whose cheeks naturally blushed, had important lessons to teach her French elders, even if they had to apply rouge to sustain their lover's passion.[33]

The lascivious harem, thus, was not much different from the debauched boudoir of a French coquette. A popular caricature from the early nineteenth century transferred the sensual harem to a Western setting. *Le sultan parisien* shows an overweight aesthete making his choice among a gaggle of women, both black and white, from many different nationalities. Lolling in his chair, unable to hold the flowers he will present to his beauty of choice, he is an indolent, depraved sultan. Neither are his choices as pure as Fatmé. They wear the diaphanous see-through Empire style popular at the time, breasts about to tumble out of their bodices, posing so that his majesty might pick them (figure 6). Despite Le Camus' whitewashing (literally) of the harem, in contemporary minds the Orient still referred to the corruption of mores and mixing the races. And since cosmetics were also suspect, they fit perfectly into the harem space, whether put there by their supporters or their detractors.

Commercializing the Harem

If the harem could be both domestic and pure as well as corrupt and sexual, while always indicative of beauty, then it had potential as a marketing tool for cosmetic sellers. Artisans who hoped to market their goods as Oriental in provenance and spirit appealed overtly to popular conceptions of the exotic East found in stories and images. Women who wore these Oriental goods could achieve the mysterious allure of true exoticism not offered by French-made goods. Yet, by incorporating the harem into publicity, advertisers transformed its meaning. The harem was not sold as a sphere of threatening sexual passion and despotism, but as a safe yet exotic warehouse full of useful and pleasurable products. By using the Orient as a marketing tool to sell populuxe goods, advertisers, following Le Camus' lead, distanced themselves from accusations that makeup was a sign of falsity and vanity. By transferring the site of beautification to the harem, they rehabilitated the French practices of beauty, at the same time making the sensual East palatable to their buyers.

Abdeker and other literary references to the beauty of odalisques concretized the French buyer's perception that beauty products originated in the Orient. This per-

Figure 6. Le sultan parisien, Bibliothèque nationale estampes

ception was not completely false because many of the key ingredients to cosmetics were originally imported from the Near East. The French had long prized the perfumes and minerals that originated in the Ottoman Empire, though the shift in trade away from the Mediterranean and toward Asia in the late seventeenth and eighteenth centuries diminished these imports. Whether from the Ottoman Empire or further afield, exotic goods used for beauty—such as cochineal (from Goa), vermillion (from China) cinnabar, tartar, musk, rose water (from Persia), grey amber, and carmine, as well as countless spices—were shipped to French ports to be disseminated throughout the country and then packaged for consumption by apothecaries and grocers.[34] The ingredients' rareness led to the creation of populuxe copies that could be sold more cheaply and widely. Though French critics accused unscrupulous Muslim merchants of adulterating their goods to dupe naive French buyers, local artisans probably did most of the falsifying.[35] Affordable goods from Turkey or Egypt, whether or not fully authentic, entered the homes of consumers through the ingenuity of peddlers or local retailers who sold promises of beauty alongside cheap Oriental tales.

As César Birotteau asserted in Balzac's novel, the foreign sounding names "were humbug; they had been invented to amuse the French nation, who cannot abide anything that is made in France." Despite this marketing savvy, Birotteau himself did not know where his products came from and assumed that "aloes and opium were only to be found in the rue des Lombards."[36]

Birotteau, playing on the credulity of the French public, invented a product called *Pâte des sultanes* after reading *Abdeker* because these words were like magic in a "country where every man has a natural turn for the part of a sultan, and every woman is no less minded to become a sultana."[37] Eighteenth-century advertisers, much like Balzac's fictional perfumer, depended on their readers' association of their goods with literary and artistic Orientalism, bereft of any actual threat. Readers of advertisements were meant to link goods called *Pommade de la sultane* and *Eau du sérail* with the overt eroticism found in paintings and novels. Advertisements for *l'Eau Georgienne* and *Pommade Circassienne* referred to the locations from which the most beautiful concubines were captured, according to travelers and libertine poets. The *Essence Roxelanne* alluded to the famous sultana.[38] One advertiser claimed that his invention could make real the miraculous potions described by Le Camus.[39] Advertisers evoked the East to make their customers' dreams come true.

Like Le Camus, advertisers also promised to share the secrets of the harem with their readers but without the hassle of home production. French women were offered an irrefutable deal: at a reasonable price they could purchase all the proven advantages of Oriental beauty without the disadvantages of the harem. For instance, one beauty cream gave "Circassian and Asian women in general . . . that brilliance, that freshness, and that whiteness of skin for which they are renowned."[40] The seller of the *Crème Ekmecq* reprimanded French women for taking less care of their beauty than did Oriental women: "it is not enough to wash: whitening, softening, firming, and perfuming the skin . . . are important cares which are dangerous to neglect."[41] In a marketing tactic meant to disassociate cosmetics from criticisms of artifice and aristocracy, sellers advised French women to abandon their old products and learn from their more beautiful sisters of the East. Since these products had already been proved effective for the odalisques, it was "now up to French women to procure this advantage."[42]

The sellers' use of an unquestionable exotic "other" to market cosmetics helped create a sphere of artifice outside the traditional Parisian and provincial markets. Most of the advertisers who adopted images of the Orient were nonguild members. By turning to the mythical "other" of the Orient, these advertisers could refashion both their products and themselves as part of a foreign world of goods. The ad for *Essence Roxelanne* claimed that an Arab philosopher invented it.[43] Publicity for the

Figure 7. Serkis du sérail, Dissey et Piver, Bibliothèque nationale estampes

Eau de sultane asserted that its recipe was stolen from the harem by an officer of the seraglio, presumably a eunuch, and sold to a French sailor in Constantinople.[44]

Though for Montesquieu and other earlier travel writers, racial difference appealed to a sense of danger and eroticism, late eighteenth-century images of the harem showed it as a playground for European women dressed up in exotic finery. Similarly, advertisements inserted French women into a safe sphere of personal pampering and grooming. On a label for the famous *Serkis du sérail,* by Dissey and Piver, a powder to whiten the skin (and replace more artificial face paint), an Eastern harem is recreated yet its emphasis is fully European (figure 7). In this image, a sultan smilingly offers gifts to his sultana, surrounded by benign servants. The tone of the advertisement is lightly flirtatious. The sultana is a European dressed up in fancy clothes, receiving harmless luxuries, and not sexual propositions.

In a much more sensual advertisement for the *Oléine du Louqsor* (a hair oil) from the early nineteenth century, a similarly Europeanized sultana is coiffed by her black slave. Covered only in revealing white drapery, the beauty gazes demurely away and protects her breast with her hand. The Orientalist image of a harem garden is surrounded by Egyptian symbols, the fruits of Napoleon's adventures in Empire building. The black slave and white mistress mimic the popular trope of harem paintings, as can be seen in Amédee Van Loo's *La toilette d'une sultane,* depicting Madame du Barry. A contemporary critic of the painting pointed out that "the sultana resembles perhaps a little too much our Parisian coquettes," making it impossible, as another wrote, for these women to be "Greek, Georgian, Circassian, etc."[45] Critics of Van Loo did not want the sultana to be black, as was her maid, but they wanted the white captives of the harem to be less familiar. Advertisers, however, did not wish to alienate their audience, portraying the representative of their cosmetics as Western and French in her beauty, despite her dress, surroundings, or, in this case, nudity. Buyers wanted not actual exoticism but its trappings in either their purchases or their fantasies.

Works such as Abdeker and advertisements for Oriental goods helped counter the accusations that makeup was a deceitful and unflattering pastime. In doing so, they also provided a definition of the "other," which was no longer simply related to aristocratic taste. Unlike the secretive and titillating descriptions of the harem in earlier literary works, the cosmetics advertised were commodities whose mystery had been completely revealed for the good of French women. Any wearer of cosmetics could now buy or make a piece of the Orient. Advertisements revealed that the secrets of the harem were as much fruitful and pleasurable beauty practices as corrupt sexual intrigue. Entrepreneurs tied beauty not only to the mythical women of the harem but directly to the Eastern products that they sold. They created a desirable commodity out of a commodity of desire.

Napoleon's Empire and the Commercialization of Eastern Beauty

Napoleon's adventure in Egypt amplified French ideals of the Eastern exotic, bringing to France artifacts and images of the ancient civilization. Though the imagery may have increased in visibility, the Napoleonic wars and rise of British influence led to a sharp decline in trade with the Levant. By 1815, France controlled only onefourth of Levantine commerce to Europe, from a high of one-half in the 1780s.[46] This decline in French commercial might did not, however, disassociate the growing French cosmetic industry from the East. Because of the growing popularity of imported goods such as tea, sugar, and porcelain, merchants and sellers heralded a new age of prosperity and respectability. In this expanding new world of goods, luxuries and necessities functioned together.[47] Commerce created this interlinking world in which Eastern cosmetics could mix with European ideals of beauty. During the Napoleonic Empire and the Restoration, the exotic East continued to be one of the main means of selling dreams of beauty. At the height of the Napoleonic Empire, French commercial acumen, Turkish masculine ingenuity, and the emperor sold beauty goods, not the now almost invisible participants of the harem.

In the world of cosmetics, commercial globalization was highly profitable yet dangerous. A rising number of critics encouraged women to look locally for their solutions and to give up on the false promises of the Orient. Because of the ultimate sexual perversion that the harem represented, commentators questioned the validity of odalisques as models for Western beauty. By the early nineteenth century, commentators in popular newspapers or advice manuals clearly linked harem women and suspect primping. French women should not copy Turkish harem women because these odalisques knew nothing other than the practices of beautification. This made them lazy and boring. Even if these women remained the prettiest (if they were Georgian or Circassian, of course), harem practices degraded their morality and destroyed their self-esteem.[48] Openly associating harem mores with the habits of the French leisured class was not new, but criticizing Oriental models of beauty was new. In 1810, the *Journal des dames et des modes* stated that Turkish women lost their beauty earlier than European women because of their lack of masculine company. Similarly, they had not yet evolved from "sumptuosity" to "elegance" in style, an oversight fed by their loose morals and lack of domestic virtues.[49] This lack of domestic virtues could be seen in Turkish women's use of abortions to maintain their beauty longer.[50]

The newly aggressive stance toward women of the East, which would only become more sexualized and graphic as the century went on, caused advertisers to shift their campaign focus. The solution for advertisers was not to give up their exotic bestsellers but to distance themselves from the harem and its inhabitants. Instead, they stressed the role of both French and foreign male creators. The Napoleonic wars and blockade made it more difficult for French ships to trade, so traders from the Levant increased in number and visibility.[51] M. Ghalib, a Turkish chemist associated with "one of the most knowledgeable chemists in Paris," set up his own manufacture of liquid soap for shaving and perfuming the body, though he sold his product through a French-owned shop.[52] A doctor from Constantinople imported a cosmetic cream, which was sold by a female reseller.[53] ABDAG (his capitals) emphasized his authenticity and ties to the elite of Constantinople when he opened a depot of perfumes.[54] Though most of these Turks sold their goods in Parisian-owned shops, their names (fictitious or not) helped bolster the links between French and Ottoman markets and between French and Eastern beauty.

Fashion journals emphasized the legitimacy and authenticity of Oriental goods sold by Turks. In a mock fashion trial, published in the journal *Paris et ses modes,* cosmetics were judged and categorized. Though the men complained that this was a trivial topic, they were quieted by the mention of Ghalib el Tadgir's *Savon turc* for the beard. Such a marvelous concoction was sold at numerous French-owned businesses, as was the "rouge of sultanas . . . veritable extract of Oriental roses and balm of Mecca." When a doubter questioned the origin of these goods, the mediator of the trial, Whim, replied "nothing is more certain. The inventor of these perfumes is named Ismael; he resides in Constantinople, and I myself have seen him recently in Paris."[55] The trial was not about the authenticity of these goods as harem potions but as inventions and concoctions of Turkish chemists.

French men were also touted as savvy adventurers with connections in the East. In a long letter to the editor, which reads much like an advertisement, a subscriber assured consumers that the perfumes and creams sold by the Parisian merchant Hebert did truly originate in Constantinople. He was sure of this because of his own voyages to the Near East, where he had studied and examined the products of each country. He found the perfumes of Constantinople of high quality and was amazed to find this same quality available in Paris on his return.[56] A seasoned traveler, thus, legitimized Hebert. Hebert had a competitor, however, M. E. Gabriel, who called himself a Turkish merchant with a direct contact to Constantinople. Both Gabriel and Hebert advertised voraciously, placing the same advertisement on alternative days for a nine-year period.[57]

These sellers and others stressed the cooperation of Eastern inventors with Western markets. Though Napoleon's empire and excursion into Egypt helped reinforce the power of Westerners to control and harness Eastern art, science, and literature, the imagery of cosmetic commerce was still one of exchange.[58] Following the much earlier tradition of travel narratives, either French or foreign commercial entrepreneurs promoted themselves as adventurers who had gone to great risks to make their new and exciting discoveries available to the French public. Unlike travel writers, however, these men did not claim to have secret information about the harem beauties themselves but instead bragged about commercial connections in Eastern cities. They brought cosmetics to France that could work wonders due as much to their astute understanding of ingredients as to Eastern harem traditions.

A telling case of the ingenious French traveler and Eastern inventor can be found in the tale of a beleaguered *chevalier de la legion d'honneur*. The captain Bacheville fled France in danger of his life and honor, looking for safety abroad and hoping to prove his innocence. In the three years he wandered the globe, he quickly spent his meager savings from a glorious eighteen-year military career. At an all-time low, he entered Constantinople, little thinking that these strangers would be "sensible to bad luck and generous in their succor." However, a friendly Turk with a good reputation felt pity for this poor beleaguered French man. The aid that this generous Turk provided was the well-guarded recipe for an *Eau merveilleuse* made by the women of the harem. This exchange of information, as important to the people of France as political or military secrets, allowed the captain to regain his fortune and, by 1819, his good name as well. His was a global product, invented in Turkey and made only with pure vegetable substances found in India's benign climates. Bacheville assured the female readers of his advertisements that his intentions were noble and that they could use it advantageously "no matter their social position."[59] In this story, multiple marketing ploys combined to win over the reader: the trustworthy voyager, the kindly foreigner, and the authentic creation. The odalisques, purported to be the inventors, were not emphasized as central to the relationship between the seller and the buyer.

An even more obvious attempt at linking male inventors and adventurers with commercial possibilities comes in the updated advertisement for *Serkis du sérail* from the Napoleonic period. Dissey and Piver no longer felt the need to represent the harem or its women to evoke the link between beauty and the East (figure 8). Instead, the picture focuses on the male go-betweens who purchased and marketed the goods harem women wore to enhance their looks. French power, represented both by the boats and the Napoleonic columns anchoring the picture, has come to haul away the fruits of Eastern knowledge, repackaging and relabeling them for their own respectable customers' tastes and needs. Local men meet them, ready to trade their secrets for a fair price, equal participants in this man's world. The only places the actual harem and the sultana (whose favorite product this is) appear are in the text in the middle. The text is the same that Dissey and Piver used in newspaper advertisements, though the addition of imagery has shifted the focus away from the activity and subjectivity of the harem women to the work of the male traders who collected and discovered their secrets.

Though foreign men were often present when information and goods were transferred (giving them control over their use), some advertisements relied entirely on French commercial dominance. A bizarre advertisement for Lagoutte Parfumeur for a variety of goods, most prominently *Eau de Cologne nationale*, features Napoleon's disembodied head, encircled with rays of light, hovering over a scene of French industry, represented by distillation equipment (figure 9). French perfumery is legitimated by his presence and his domination of Europe. It too can conquer and appropriate for itself the cultures and profits of other nations and peoples. Tellingly, two Egyptian obelisks, possibly pilfered by Napoleon, surround this extreme image of national commercial might. On the left-hand column above the banner, the company advertises one of its many products: *Épilatoire du serial,* a depilatory cream used by the harem women. On the top of the other column, the *Crème de Perse* is touted

Figure 8. Serkis du sérail, Dissey et Piver, Bibliothèque nationale estampes

Figure 9. Lagoutte parfumeur, Bibliothèque nationale estampes

as used throughout Asia by women who appreciate beautiful skin tone. Here the line between the sublime and the ridiculous seems mighty thin. Though invisible, the women of the harem continued to give away for free their exotic beauty secrets, now brought to French women thanks for the Imperial projects of their Emperor.

Conclusion

In 1841, the *Mercure galant* told a story about the intrinsic and European fickleness of fashion. Aisha was a young, pretty *bayadère*, defined in this story as a sacred virgin raised amid the "great pagodas" of Asia but literally meaning a temple dancer from India. A rich French traveler spotted her in her native element dressed in European clothes. The traveler fell madly in love with her Asiatic physiognomy, not least of which was the diamond tattoo on her forehead and the stars on her cheeks. He found these gave her majesty and sparkle, attributes he was certain French women would want to copy. Upon his return to Paris, however, he soon got bored with her permanent signs and wished to have them hidden. He complained that "it is rather monotonous to always see stars on your cheeks! . . . It is ridiculously pretentious." In an attempt to rid her of these offending marks, he consulted chemists and perfumers, buying countless jars and vials of miraculous whitening cosmetics. Poor Aisha was the passive victim of these attempts, rubbing her cheeks so hard that they turned as red as a lobster. In desperation, her benefactor tried to burn the marks off. The result was so gruesome, that her lover fled in disgust, forcing her to become a miserable washerwoman in the rue St Denis.[60]

This story, occurring as it did fifty years after the demise of beauty spots, many of which were shaped like stars and diamonds, reflected on the ridiculousness of a long-gone European fashion. Yet, its hero does not seem to be familiar with this fashion, finding Aisha's tattoos new and exciting. Unlike Western ideals of ever-changing beauty, her marks were permanent: she cannot be read as anything other than an Asian, despite wearing European clothing at all times. Her lover's attempts to transform her into a white woman failed miserably, as he literally tried to obliterate her racial markings. The whitening potions he purchased offered hope, but no results. One of these potions may well have been the *Eau de bayadère*, a well-known skin whitener.[61] The name of this beauty aid was rife with Oriental connotations, but its application was not. It and others were the perfect successors of *Abdeker's* recipes, offering the possibility of creating pure whiteness in a mythical harem setting and thus fulfilling the desires of European women and their male lovers. When applied to the "other," these extravagant luxuries led only to disappointment and social denigration, a further sign that race could not be overcome.[62] Aisha, whose attraction to her lover came both from her exotic position (as dancer) and the sensuality of her physical markings, could not sustain it for long or ever belong to Parisian society, so her lover repudiated and rejected her.

The folly of fashion and men's inherent fickleness in this story contrasted with the rational, adventurous male who brought exotic products to the women of France, rather than actual Eastern women like Aisha. Yet both point to the uneasy relationship between cosmetics and Eastern beauties. Eighteenth-century images reveled in the seduction and promises of the East for bringing pleasure and fulfillment in love. The goods that harem women could provide to the West were adapted for white audiences and skins and thus could not be retransferred to the dark skins of the East. In selling the Orient, the sexually perverted universe of the harem had to be sanitized and focused on the exchange of knowledge for domestic heterosexual seduction. Instead of a direct relationship (real or imagined) between European and Eastern women, the goods for sale mediated their interactions. The knowledge French women could gain from the Orient was always enveloped in the familiarity of white and European odalisques and more important in the product. The ultimate seduction of consumerism created a safe haven for *affiches* readers and cosmetics buyers. By the early nineteenth century, a strong return to a sexualized male-fantasy harem (in both stories and images), caused the publicity for cosmetics to filter out the active presence of odalisques. The new hero was the astute entrepreneur who had ferreted the secret goods out of the East and into the arms of French women. The ultimate seduction, consumerism, was meant to placate any fears of corruption by foreign goods.

Though cosmetic advertisements no longer pictured the odalisques, they could not sell cosmetics without evoking her name. The attraction of these goods over beauty products linked to Canada (as bear grease was) or England (as toilette soaps were) was the promise of authentic beauty and sensual pleasure. Only the East could make that promise, though even this was questioned. French woman bought these goods in hopes of maintaining their whiteness in a period when face paint was no longer popular. They hoped to appropriate products that could be separated from French aristocratic decadence, while at the same time mimicking the fictional pampered, secluded lifestyle of the harem. French advertisers recreated the harem as a European, passive space for beautification, meant to lend an air of foreign trustworthiness to cosmetic goods. And yet, the products they created to distinguish themselves from traditional French artifice were appealing precisely because of their association with the sexuality that made the harem so titillating to readers of Oriental tales. The commodity fetish of Oriental cosmetics was sustained not just by the hoped-for miracles but also by their names, ingredients, and provenance. Despite a pretense to erase and to subsume the odalisques, advertisers needed their products to feed the fantasy of the sexualized exotic. A fine line was drawn between creating safe, domesticated, useable products and titillating the senses. This marketing ploy must have been successful, as indicated by the pervasive use of Oriental cosmetics in the stores and homes of France.

CHAPTER EIGHT

Selling Masculinity

The Commercial Competition over Men's Hair

Women now only wear blanc, leaving rouge to the men. This young Titus who feigns the greatest simplicity, who had banished powder, scents, and silk clothing, has kept precisely from the old costume what had belonged primarily to women; that vermillion tone, which contrasts so admirably with his black wig, is borrowed.

—Auguste Kotzebue, *Souvenir de Paris*

By 1790, despite a change in aesthetics, women created their pale faces as before with artifice. Men were meant to be even more natural in practice, but, as the playwright and visitor to Paris Kotzebue suggests, some men wore discernable rouge to go along with new hair fashions. Evidence from the revolutionary years and the Napoleonic period indicate that the so-called Great Masculine Renunciation was nowhere near complete. Though male fashions certainly moved away from thick makeup and primping, men continued to take part in exhibitionism. Men were very much part of the consumer market created in the eighteenth century and very much part of the marketing campaigns of sellers of cosmetics. Though Kotzebue implicates men in the wearing of rouge, his comment on black-haired wigs is telling. Hair was the aspect of the toilette that men would continue to participate in most actively, though in completely new ways than in the eighteenth century. Since the wig was associated with the Old Regime, men had to face a new future without cover for their biological weaknesses. Hair loss (and to a lesser extent unfashionable hair color) forced men to enter into the commercial world of cosmetic practices in a period when most forms of male vanity were suspect.

Not surprisingly, by the early nineteenth century, the most prominent and profitable cosmetics were those for hair. Unlike rouge and Oriental creams, however, hair products had to be fully revised and reinvented to fit the new trends. The great cosmetic casualty was hair powder, replaced by new hair products such as dyes and growth potions. Men gave up their protective covers and needed to be reassured of their redefined masculinity. The accessories that came with the new styles were aimed at assuaging masculine egos: hair extensions, small and imperceptible toupees, and miraculous hair creams. That women might also need these was simply an additional benefit for the sellers. Despite being ousted from public practices of the toilette (both as actors and voyeurs), men without wig and powder remained vulnerable to the publicity ploys of inventive entrepreneurs. Men's heads, natural and uncovered, were the sites for marketing campaigns that helped male consumers to survive the transition from wig to hair.

Masculine and Fashionable in Postrevolutionary France

Following the lead of sociologists, historians of fashion and masculinity until recently assumed that the shift toward a more functional and staid form of male dress occurred in the late eighteenth century. J. C. Flügel uses the term "Great Masculine Renunciation" in *The Psychology of Clothes* to indicate men's begrudging rejection of exhibitionism. This Great Masculine Renunciation, which Flügel blames on the Revolution, solidified the roles of men and women, making men into unwilling voyeurs and women into objects.[1] Men were to give up all pretensions of fashion and makeup, adopting more subtle lines and colors. The new male's worth was not based on blood, leisure, and artifice, but on respectability, hard work, and capital accumulation. Revolutionaries promoted the adoption of a male uniform, linking men across class lines.[2] Though the uniform did not become popular, the three-piece suit emerged as the ideal, muted wrapping of homogeneity and respectability. A virile, active, often military male became an archetype of revolutionary and Napoleonic France, auguring the triumph of bourgeois respectability over aristocratic sociability.[3]

Yet, as much as his Old Regime predecessor, this was a figure dependent on fashion and style and, because of it, caught up in the growing consumer market. David Kuchta, writing on English fashion, finds the new simpler masculinity "no less performative, and no more authentic, than luxury and effeminacy."[4] Flügel's renunciation was neither straightforward nor complete. The cult of youth dominated revolutionary and Napoleonic France. For the classical heroes of the Revolution, the romantics of the Napoleonic era or the dandies of the Restoration, self-presentation and fashion were essential to their social and sexual personas. Outside these iconic masculinities, the ubiquitous soldier and the rapidly rising entrepreneur needed to represent martial or financial success in their physical appearance. The imposition of a draft, the extreme militarism of Napoleon's court, and the wars themselves focused attention on the courage of youthful male citizens.[5] As with the military, new commercial possibilities after the Revolution allowed sons of artisans to join the ranks of the wealthy, creating a new generation of entrepreneurs and merchants. The uniforms and suits of these new elite stressed the inherent physicality of both economic and social success.

Art historians stress the highly charged presence of homosocial desire in early nineteenth-century imagery. Corporeal, virile masculine beauty evoked ancient Greece, endorsed by both male and female voyeurs. The clothing men wore also reinforced the desirability of an ideal masculine physique. Anne Hollander argues that the uniform of the suit sexualized the male body, echoing the popularity of neoclassical nudes rather than erasing masculine exhibitionism.[6] The simplicity and tightness of the suit put greater stress on the body underneath as well as the shape of the head and its crowning locks, providing not renunciation but narcissistic and scopic pleasure in being the subject of the gaze. And men did not even need to be looked at by either men or women but could revel in their own narcissism. The male gaze was one of lustful envy when men looked at women, but when they looked at each other or themselves, it was with pure pleasure and vanity.[7]

As the center of both the male and female gaze, young, fashionable men had to achieve a balance in their self-presentation between indifference and artifice. During the Revolution, it was politically savvy for a man "to show that he has wasted as few moments as it was possible at his toilette, and that his mind is bent on higher cares."[8] Men had to create their look (either disheveled or well groomed, depending on the period and political leanings of the individual) without obvious pretense. The new man of the early nineteenth century was not meant to be fashionable and vain. Commentators admitted, however, that this "renunciation" of the toilette caused great frustration. The single man's credo was filled with mixed signals: "What one cannot avoid is the toilette. While acting aloof, one also wants to come off as tender; one wants to be well dressed, one wants to follow fashion or more truly anticipate it."[9]

Authors were acutely conscious of the stigma attached to male coquettes but argued that men should not completely reject grooming. It was important for men not to "affect . . . a philosophical disdain for the toilette or grooming of the hair," since a clean, well-kept exterior indicated internal morality.[10] Doctors were especially worried that men, told to give up cosmetics, might also give up the practices of health and hygiene. As early as the 1770s, Goulin addressed this problem in his medical work aimed at men, by saying, "many people think that all these little details belong only to women and that it is futile for a man to care about them." He stressed that many of these "little details" of the toilette were also indispensable to men. Yet, for men to learn the skills of grooming, they had to turn to his earlier work *Médecin des dames*.[11]

The simplified masculine fashions and the toilette of the revolutionary period were meant to highlight men's natural characteristics and roles, copying English fashions. To be plainspoken, enlightened political orators, men had to be transparent in their feelings and opinions. Transparency implied an end to deceit and the most deceitful aspect of masculine Old Regime dress was the ubiquitous hairpiece. The first step was the simplification of the wig to fit Enlightenment ideals of simple self-presentation. Wigs had stood for respectability, leveling generational differences with powder and creating professional ranks through style. The new simpler, more natural-looking wigs symbolized convenience rather than emulation of the court. Taste masters defined wigs as a means of protecting natural hair and scalp, making them more appropriate than the hair underneath. Men, such as Rousseau, could choose a simpler wig style to convey their rejection of all things aristocratic and artificial.[12] In 1788, Mercier commented that "one no longer wears wigs; the doctor, the surgeons at court wear their hair in a *bourse* (hair bag), or at least use a wig that imitates the natural."[13]

But for Mercier, even natural-looking wigs were not radical enough. He found the fashion for wigs ridiculous and hoped that men would realize the practicality and healthiness of short hair.[14] It was for these reasons that Old Regime soldiers were said to be the first to cut their hair short and go without wigs entirely.[15] When they started wearing their shorn heads without shame, the fashion spread throughout society. Quentin Bell sees this shift as the beginning of the male renunciation of exhibitionism.[16] Men gave up their wigs to proclaim their naturalness and their suitability in the new public sphere. The Revolution further politicized hair, with natural hair representing radicals in the early years and powdered hair proving royalist sympathies by the Directory. The royalist *Incroyables* pulled off the bonnets of Jacobins, while Jacobins tried to tear off their wigs. Despite Robespierre's headpiece, "the cradle of liberty has become the grave of Old Regime lawns."[17]

After the Revolution, obvious wigs were stodgy and old fashioned. They could not be part of the new, youthful, martial society. The younger generation had to destroy the cachet of the wig and powder to assert their social and economic position. In his early nineteenth-century play entitled *Le jeune médecin ou l'influence des perruques,* L. B. Picard depicted with humor the necessity of debunking both the fashions and influence of the older generation. In it, two young men, a doctor and a lawyer, donned wigs and powder to dupe their respectable old-fashioned clientele into thinking they were middle-aged men and thus to be trusted and hired. Their nemesis was an aging aristocratic fop who believed that by wearing a blond hairpiece he could pass for twenty and gain the confidence of the grandmother along with the hand of her granddaughter. When, at the end of the play, the deceit of both parties became clear, the crafty lawyer and doctor asked their client, "So, madame, what is more wrong, the wig that ages us, or the false hair which makes him younger? . . . Is it not more ridiculous to act the young man than to be one? . . . Is not a young man starting his profession worth more than an old man who never knew how to have one?"[18] Youth had possibility, energy, and more important, hair, making youth the winner of lucrative contracts with elderly women and the hand in marriage of young girls. The attempted mimicry of youth by old age remained a joke about bad taste and bad hairdressing. Ultimately, Picard banished both the respectability and deception of the wig in favor of talent and naturalness. By the early nineteenth century, the term *têtes à perruques* implied empty-headed imbeciles who depended on old-fashioned, and no longer meaningful, markers of learning and respectability.[19]

The emasculation of the old aristocratic fop was not only due to his wig and powder but also due to the lack of hair it implied underneath. Wigs in the early nineteenth century signified loss and deception rather than social emulation or convenience. In stories and images, young women accused old men of wearing unfashionable, revolting wigs to disguise the signs of aging: wrinkles, pockmarks, and loss of hair. Nougaret tells of a seventy-year-old baron who attempted to gain the favors of a much younger woman. When he was mockingly rejected, he turned his attentions to her mother. Still found ridiculous, he "redoubled his cares to hide his age, had an even more elegant wig made than his usual one, that, according to him, made him look forty."[20] The mischievous lady, however, saw through his disguise and purposefully knocked off his wig, exposing to all those assembled his bald pate and wisps of white hair.

The masculine coteries who watched the emasculations of their peers were fully aware that this humiliation could just as well happen to them. In an early nineteenth-century print, *Garde à vous: La perruque enlevée,* a woman collecting scraps of paper inadvertently lifts off a man's wig. The man, parodying Corneille, exclaims, "Oh rage, Oh despair! Oh wig, my sweetheart, did you live only for that disgrace!" The wig and the trash are mixed together and the man's dismay is both highly comical and tragic. He has lost his cover to the "vile hook" of a poor old woman who should not have the ability to emasculate a respectable man.[21] In another print from the same period, *L'inconvénient des faux toupets,* a hapless man bowing to the ladies leaves his toupee in his hat (figure 10). Though the women seem to be politely shocked, his well-hatted and bewigged companion ogles and laughs openly at his friend's misfortune. The man who kept his hat on may be impolite, but he nonetheless managed to remain respectable. Men were as vulnerable to the gaze of their competitors as to their potential conquests. For men of the early nineteenth century, fashion

Figure 10. L'incovénient des faux toupets, Bibliothèque nationale estampes

choices were tricky. If they adopted a wig, it signified stodginess and it might fall off inopportunely, but if they wore their naturally thinning hair, they were also left defenseless in a world of new signs.

The Rise and Fall of Powder

The downward fall of the wig took with it the profession of starch makers. Hair and its accessories were an important part of the luxury trades in eighteenth-century France. Wearing wigs and powder had been central to courtly fashion; yet, it was a practice also adopted by the middle classes and urban artisans. In 1769, there were twelve thousand hairdressers and wigmakers in Paris, making it the largest and most contentious luxury trade.[22] The public's dependency on hairdressing and wigs meant that starch makers and perfumers profited from the consumption of perfumed powders along with scented pomades to nourish the hair and keep it clean. When the wig first started going out of fashion, men continued to wear powder on their hair, but eventually natural color triumphed over the uniformity of white. For traditional and older men, even this fashion did not fade, with many continuing to wear wig and powder well after the Revolution. Robespierre wore his wig powdered throughout the Revolution, which, according to Mercier, caused many to repudiate this fashion out of hatred for the Jacobin leader. Because many Jacobins gave up powder as well, no political distinction was made during the Terror between powdered and not.[23]

Whether for political or fashion reasons, the market for powder started to shrink in the 1780s. As a fashion accessory, powder was no longer needed in such large quantities because numerous wigmakers went out of business. Like rouge makers, producers of power attempted to salvage their commerce; yet, they failed to resurrect its popularity. Instead of creating new uses (such as face powder and perfumed clothing powder), most sellers stuck too closely to their dying niche. They also failed to adapt to changing times because they did not address growing concerns regarding the edible qualities of the starch that was the basis for hair powder. By the end of the century, the association of powder with bread production put starch makers too far at odds with both public opinion and the government to institute a successful comeback.

The foremost reason for wearing powder in the eighteenth century was fashion, tied to the court practices and the mimicry of white hair. Powder, however, was also seen as capable of transforming all men into respectable actors, erasing lines of age and rank. With or without a wig, powder was the finishing touch of a man's toilette. To justify this strange fashion, commentators ascribed to powder other functions such as warding off disease. One commentator felt that "the moderate use of perfumed powder in hair is linked as much to health as convenience; and it is regarded as a necessity amongst all polite peoples."[24]

The arguments made for wearing powder quickly became reasons to shun it. The practice of wearing powder was found to be unhygienic and destructive of physical beauty. Le Bègue de Presle condemned the application of hair powder and greases since they "inflame the scalp by blocking the pores of the skin; their putty induces itching, causing humors, pimples." Those who did not comb their hair had the added problem of vermin and other insects inhabiting their scalp.[25] Certain powders, specifically those made with lime, led to hair loss that made wearing wigs even more necessary. Others felt that powder was frivolous and excessively used. One of the petit maître's most ridiculous traits was his powder-covered clothing.[26] Time spent powdering seemed wasted when a simple gust of wind could destroy all the wigmaker's hard work.[27] A well-powdered person could also foul the air, furniture, and clothing.[28] The adoption of natural hair and color was an aesthetic, as well as a hygienic, reform promoted by critics and doctors as part of the larger shift in fashion and behavior.

Yet, it was the association of powder with foodstuffs that caused the greatest difficulties for the industry. Powder was fabricated from starch made primarily from bran and wheat by-products sold by bakers to starch makers. Both during the Old Regime and the Revolution, critics accused starch users of exacerbating bread shortages. As early as 1731, a priest was shocked to find that "the stores of wigmakers were more sprinkled with flour than mills."[29] Mercier railed against the two hundred thousand fashionable people in Paris who whitened their hair with enough wheat to feed ten thousand peasants, calling for a return to natural hair color.[30] The elite's fashion was literally taking food out of the mouths of hungry citizens. Attacks against frivolous uses of wheat were also common among philosophes: "Voltaire and Rousseau, despite their antagonistic views on the social utility of luxury, joined hands to assail the prodigal waste of precious flour in wig preparation and cosmetics."[31]

When wheat became scarce in years of bad harvest, these fears could be embodied in laws. Amid a 1740 food shortage, the Paris Parlement issued a moratorium on selling barley and grain to starch makers, as well as more stringent laws limiting baking white bread.[32] Even in the prosperous harvest year of 1760, a tax was proposed to diminish the purchase of hair powder and to increase the amount of coarse wheat (*blé grossier*) in foodstuffs. The corporation of perfumers fought back, arguing that this law punished the public who employed the leftover parts of grain for their cleanliness and the conservation of their health. They also argued that a tax on the coarser, lesser parts of grain would force perfumers and starch makers to employ finer edible wheat now made more affordable. Finally, perfumers warned that charlatans might react to this ban by producing low-quality and potentially harmful powders from other ingredients.[33]

The perfumers may have exaggerated the benefits of powder, but they were right to fear unofficial attempts to create powder from other sources. Numerous inventors petitioned the government for approvals for new kinds of powder, while others advertised their findings directly to the public. One man had the idea of using a foreign grain, *Nigella* (fennel flower), claiming it could produce whiter powder in greater quantity per acre than wheat.[34] In 1772, another inventor petitioned the Academy of Sciences to fabricate starch from rotten beans. This proposal was rejected by Lavoisier because starch was already made from "rotten wheat, middling (*gruau*), and by-products," not causing the people to suffer from a loss of food. Moreover, the citizens of Paris alone consumed "three million tons of starch" a year, too much to produce from beans alone.[35]

That starch was fabricated from substances seemingly edible only in times of famine did not stop revolutionary officials from discouraging the production of powder. In 1790, the *Société des Amis de la Constitution* of Nice (the local clubs of the Parisian Jacobins) proposed that "curling powder is only a luxury need, Republicans should not know this vice, especially when it diminishes the quality of bread and increases its price." They further proposed a ban on hair powder, starch, and all establishments serving beer made from hops.[36] This proposal was not implemented, but in 1792, the department of Calvados banned the production of beer and starch because of a bad wheat harvest.[37] In a move of patriotic zeal, the Paris section of St. Eustache renounced wearing hair powder en masse.[38] In this state of need, inventors again pressed the government with plans to make powder out of everything from chestnuts to alabaster. This time the government took such proposals seriously and encouraged inventors to replace costly wheat with cheaper vegetable by-products.[39] Yet, in so doing, the revolutionary government was more concerned with maintaining grain stocks than with circumscribing fashions. Popular concerns with hoarding wheat and fears of famine made the production of any type of starch unpopular, whatever its uses. Only when these fears abated was the ban on starch lifted.

Though the laws against starch may never have been strictly enforced, powder producers were directly affected by the Revolution. Citizen Garnier was "forced to cease his business for the duration of the revolutionary laws." When he reopened his shop in 1797, he reassured "merchants and shopkeepers that he was doing all he could to merit their confidence in the accuracy of his operations, the quality of his merchandise, and the moderation of his prices."[40] Though no longer frightened by government reprisals, Garnier realized that powder had lost its popularity and profit. His emphasis on cheapness and quality, and his subsequent pleas to previous customers, indicates just how damaged the hair powder industry had become by the end of the century. Women's new short Titus haircut caused starch sellers to wish toothaches on these fashion victims.[41]

Other powder manufacturers continued to advertise during the Revolution, using the dissolution of the guilds to transform themselves from starch makers to creators of powder (*fabriquants de poudre*), a title previously belonging to perfumers.[42] This newfound freedom, however, did not help artisans sell their now unpopular product. Instead of deflecting criticism with direct references to the debates about foodstuffs, these advertisers adopted the same discourses of medical danger found in rouge advertisements. Of the numerous advertisements for powder during the Revolution, only one makes reference to food shortages.[43] Instead, they alerted customers of adulteration in desperate times. For instance, Besnard "warned consumers about the perils of powders currently sold mixed with drugs."[44] Powder had become a political issue and these advertisements did little to quell criticisms of its role in bread lines. Though hair powder would have gone out of fashion regardless of food shortages, starch producers' unwillingness or inability to address public concerns impeded the adaptation of their businesses. Unlike other cosmetics sellers who deflected criticisms and redefined their products to fit new fashions, starch sellers were not able to save their industry.

By 1798, hair powder had all but disappeared in advertisements and on the heads of the fashionable elite. Though the returning émigrés and the new petits maîtres of the early nineteenth century adopted it, hair powder never returned as a widely acceptable fashion.[45] The disgrace of powder was tied to a combination of factors. The loss of its popularity due to the decline of wigs, the association of starch with food shortages, and the inability of producers to address this problem or alter their product's applications led to an almost complete decline of its commercial potential. The claim, made by retailers, that wearing powder was important to the health of the French people was unpersuasive during the revolutionary years of turmoil and strife. Hair powder was the only beauty product to be a direct victim of the Revolution. The starch makers and those who profited from perfuming powder, to say nothing of the wigmakers, were irretrievably weakened by this change in fashion.

Masculine Vanity and the Cosmetics Market

The decline of the wig and powder created a new set of cosmetic problems for men: visible hair loss. Since nature was to be the dominant aesthetic, men were supposed to accept baldness as a masculine trait, a necessary part of a truthful personality. This acceptance, however, was neither simple nor without casualties. Hair was closely linked to masculine sociability as well as sexual and economic power. French men continued to be perceived in terms of physical traits, judged by their outward appearance and their diminishing pates. A new emphasis on hygiene, exercise, and youth further exacerbated the desire for lively follicles. The bald male head may have been present in the occasional portrait of an intellectual, but in the social salons of Parisian bourgeois and elite society it remained an anathema. So, forced to shun the toilette, men had to take more care of their hair in secretive ministrations. It had to shine and curl at will, representing a fundamental aspect of their masculine identity. As such, it was the hardest aspect of the physical body to tame without resorting to obvious artifice. The hope and promise brought by new cosmetic cures and medical discoveries (still going on today) fed on the general instability in the masculine physique. In case these products failed, men also continued to depend on inventive wigs that might pass as real. In the highly competitive market of the postrevolutionary period, a man's ability to stop the inevitable physical deterioration could symbolize prosperity. Bald by age and nature, the man of nineteenth-century France had to face his public hair on head.

In the late eighteenth and early nineteenth centuries, the medical profession closely scrutinized male hair loss for the first time. Doctors and their patients were keen to find solutions to baldness, made prominent by the loss of wigs. Doctors divided hair loss into two categories: *calvitie,* which was loss due to aging, and *alopécie,* which could be blamed on illness. Most doctors asserted that little could be done for calvitie; at the most, it could be stemmed but not stopped. Its root causes were understood to be the diminishing output of hair follicles due to a decline in bulb vitality. This lack of "nourishing greases which feed the bulbs of the hair" occurred naturally with old age.[46] For men and their physicians the perplexing problem was frustrating bald spots and receding hairlines on men whose aspirations for social integration and seduction were still active, thus neither short-term *alopécie* nor the traditional old-age calvitie. What was especially frightening to commentators, as to many people today, was that men started losing their hair by natural causes in the bloom of youth. The medical student Grellier in his 1806 thesis did not think that there were more bald men than previously and cited common Roman jokes aimed at bald men. Nonetheless, he was concerned that in his Europe "it is almost a deformity" for younger men to lose their hair.[47] As a later commentator quipped, bald men "no longer have the brilliant prerogative of covering this malformation with a laurel wreath" like Cesar or a well-made wig like their own ancestors.[48]

Nineteenth-century doctors associated hair loss with male sexuality but without knowledge of hormones or genetics. In 1809, the doctor Marie de St. Ursin connected sperm with hair strength, arguing that hair fell out during old age because of a decline in "erotic fluid."[49] For him, hair (especially beards) was a sign of masculine potency and strength. If the presence of hair implied masculine potency, then "seminal loses, venereal excesses, or masturbation," as well as syphilis were the main causes for hair loss.[50] Men who wasted their fluid were punished by an early loss of their masculine traits and could only hope to regain them by reforming their ways. Petits maîtres were the perfect example of an extreme lifestyle, mixing luxury, sexual debauchery, and feminine traits and thus the most likely to lose their hair.[51] Yet by 1815, a medical student pointed out that this link between sperm and hair was not borne out in observation because women, children, and eunuchs did not lose their hair. It was not until 1847 that a scientist surmised that the vigorous heads of hair on eunuchs might be linked to their lack of sperm, thus reversing the previous assumption that diminishing potency caused hair loss.[52]

Nineteenth-century scientists may not have had any knowledge of endocrinology but they tried to explain why men were more likely to lose their hair than women. Doctors pointed out that though men lost their hair with old age women were more likely to do so during long spells of illness, specifically during pregnancy.[53] This theory went well with the scientific assumption that the female organism was weaker, easily put upon by strong emotions and sensations. Yet it was specifically feminine sobriety and lack of bad habits that may have made them less likely to face a full calvitie.[54] The most often cited reason for the differences in the sexes was that women took better care of their hair than men and tended, by nature, to have thicker hair. This explanation considered both cultural habits (female vanity) and biology, implying ultimately that men could improve their chances by taking the feminine example of grooming to heart.[55]

Though there was no consensus on the main cause of hair loss, most doctors stressed the need for better hygiene and healthier habits. Goulin, an early advocate of natural styles, argued that the solution for beautiful hair was to reject all Old Regime fashions.[56] Doctors suggested that simpler food, purer air, and moderate pleasures would equal longer, healthier lives and thus stronger capillaries as well.[57] They blamed extremes: too much heat, sadness, emotion, intellectual thought, or sleep.[58] These external sources, when combined with internal causes (such as illnesses and old age), helped doctors explain what they saw as a growing epidemic. Because most of these causes were behavioral, doctors encouraged balding men to change their habits and reform their behavior before it was too late. Men were not to blame for these habits, even when they were sexual, because they were expected of fashionable men. Baldness could be cured by proper hygiene, self-control, and better fashion sense.

Though doctors did not fault men for their hair loss, they did not encourage public baldness because of its popular association with sexual weakness and aging faculties. But the doctors' behavioral cures were neither quick nor decisive, and desperate men wanted promises of results. Their saviors were entrepreneurial inventors all to willing to promote their products as capable of redefining the social makeup of the respectable elite. The bane of the professional physician, these hawkers of potions latched onto the possibility of self-deception among a population of fashion-conscious men. In a world of visible pates, the beauty aid of the early nineteenth was hair lotion. The precursors to shampoos (not used in Europe until the late nineteenth century and brought from India), these products had a multitude of usages. They promised to make hair shiny, to thicken it, and to stop hair loss and were aimed at both men and women. Such products as the *Pommade régénératrice* and *Poudre transmutative* gained popularity with those who wanted their own hair to triumph over wigs.[59] Despite their purported rejection of all toiletries, men gained prominence as consumers of cosmetics since their failures were now on display. Those who made and sold hair products were not so much redefining their goods to fight off criticism, as profiting from the shift toward natural fashions that had doomed other parts of the industry.

Before the development of advertising and the professionalization of medicine in the late eighteenth century, home cures for hair loss were the main solution. In the late seventeenth century, when wigs dominated, advice books provided recipes for ridding oneself of hair as well as regaining it.[60] Those worried about hair loss could try scrubbing their heads with *eau de vie,* honey, eggs, fly cinders, and serpent or bear grease. The marketing and packaging of these cures expanded in the 1770s. Journal advertisements for the sale of greases or oriental creams to cure all aspects of hair loss became common. Such miracles sold for as cheap as two francs a bottle in the 1820s.[61] To distinguish themselves from more feminine cosmetics, hair potions adopted a series of pseudoscientific names. In the pages of advertisements can be found the *Régénérateur, Philocome au quinquina, Huile phénomène,* and *Cosmogène Isnard.* Though advertisements rarely disclosed ingredients, most were likely to be based on vegetable or animal oils with various added perfumes to please the senses.

The most famous brand of hair-loss product was undoubtedly Alex Rowland's Macassar oil. In the early nineteenth century, Macassar represented hope for renewed vitality among European men. First sold in London, it gained approval by the British crown (1809), the Emperor of Russia (1814), the King and Queen of France (1830), and the Emperor of Persia, who "testify their approbation of the discovery . . . with a large order." Rowland had outlets in all major European cities, as well as in Boston, New York, Charleston, Montreal, Quebec, and Philadelphia.[62] Two perfumers, Naquet and Mayer, were the official purveyors of this discovery in Paris. The original ingredients in this marvel were oil of *been* or *ben* (which comes from the moringa tree), "esprit de vin," and flower essences, though Naquet and Mayer added hazelnut oil, an ingredient mimicked by Balzac.[63] Macassar oil represented an exotic solution to a prosaic problem. Named after the city of Macassar on the island of Celebes, it evoked strange foreign lands stamped of respectable British commerce. As with other cosmetics, the appropriation of exotic goods as an essential part of growing European empires was a common motif in hair products. Macassar advertisements promised a wild abundance of hair to civilized men and women.

As a common cure used since the fifteenth century, bear grease evoked the wilderness most directly, commonly that of the backwoods of French Canada.[64] Numerous sellers proclaimed that they were the sole carriers of veritable pure and white "bear grease made without heat by American Indians" at a price of three livres a pot.[65] An early nineteenth-century label depicts two native Canadians tentatively

Figure 11. Pommade et huile de castor, Bibliothèque nationale estampes

prodding a friendly-looking bear. These savages will collect the precious grease (in a scene of carnage purposefully left out), but it was European traders who had the know-how to market it for hair loss. Another advertisement for beaver oil, also known for its positive properties for hair, depicts two natives in full gear with the fruits of their hunt. The primitive, however, was closely linked to the civilizing forces of European commerce. Ancient Greek caryatides and the announcement of a patent integrate the exotic beaver with European standards of science and reliability. Natives may have hunted the animal, but a French inventor and perfumer discovered its use and processed it for sale, making it available widely throughout France and Europe (figure 11). The men (and women) who used these potions would not turn into hairy backwoodsmen or grow hair like a wild animal but rather would gain potency as defined by European standards of beauty and fashion.

To take simple grease and turn it into a sophisticated, fashionable cure, inventors used more than advertisements and evocative images. Inventors wrote brochures and manuals to convince the public of their worth. Hairdressers, perfumers, and wig-makers claimed knowledge about the hygiene and maintenance of the scalp and often used the findings of doctors to support their assertions. Duflos' *Essai sur les cheveux* outlined the reasons for hair loss and then concluded with a discussion of his own cream's nutritive qualities. The wigmaker Villaret claimed his knowledge came from the research of chemists and doctors. He gave advice to men and women on how to care for their hair and even described the inner-workings of the scalp. He advertised his *Crème d'Alibour* amid his lengthy discussions of follicles, asserting that it had the full approval of the Medical Faculty. By the 1830s, this form of promotion had evolved into client testimonies to convince the public. The doctor Oldendorff recounted the tales of real people to illustrate the efficacy of his treatments. He even said that no person should have recourse to wigs since he could prove his *Huile préparatoire* and *Huile définitive* infallible. The hairdresser Obert printed letters from satisfied clients in his treatise, while also advertising his ingenious wigs just in case. He also provided a before and after image of a thirty-five-year-old man's rapid recovery.[66] These sellers hoped that the consumer would prefer their mix of science and guaranteed success to the medical tracts that presented only pessimistic truths about hair loss.

The extravagant promises of hair potions were the target of much criticism and popular satire. In one boulevard theater sketch, Arlequin bought a bottle of Macassar to try on himself, but having accidentally dropped it in a kettle of boiling water, out came twelve wigs! Villaret also recounted the story of a lord who, after using this prodigious oil, lost all his hair and had to adopt a wig for life. He bemoaned, however, that the French did not learn their lesson from this story but instead laughed at the poor lord while still spending good money on this useless cure. He predicted that this continued blind vanity would lead to more wigs and toupees covering bald heads, as well as more "pompous advertisements covering the walls."[67] Theater sketches and adverse publicity mocking the credulity of the public further reinforced the visibility of hair potions.

The popularity and profitability of such cures also worried the medical profession that tried both to discredit and compete with this market. Doctors warned that such seemingly magic potions sold by charlatans were often made of "acid bases or corrosives, inciting itchiness . . . [and] that can have very serious consequences." Goulin recommended that bald men go to a competent wigmaker rather than risk harming their scalps with such malevolent products.[68] Some specialists realized that despite stating that calvitie was not reversible, most men would still buy cures. L'Artois accused his colleagues of ignoring the possibility of cures for too long, leaving it open to charlatans.[69] Though their capillary studies were supposedly rational and scientifically motivated, doctors started promoting the distribution of medically viable potions. Most physicians copied one another's findings to provide clients with reliable pharmaceuticals. The *Pommade de Dupuytren* (a hair specialist) was a widely distributed remedy depending on cantharides (Spanish fly) mixed in animal fat. Another doctor added quinine and opium to this mixture, to neutralize the exciting effect of cantharides on the nervous system.[70] The chemical concoctions touted by doctors may have been more effective than bear grease, but they were undoubtedly more dangerous to the health of the user. Doctors who attacked advertisers of hair potions for endangering the public also participated in the frenzied attempt (whether based on myth or medical research) to control the market for hair loss products and with it the recuperation of masculine dignity.

In tandem with this growing market for hair products, the market for wigs remained an important, albeit reduced, part of fashion production. Since most potions were not known to provide miracles, many men had to turn once again to the promises of false hairpieces. Yet, these hairpieces were not the same as their Old Regime ancestors. A revolution in wigs had occurred. Though late eighteenth-century men had been sold wigs meant to look natural, postrevolutionary men wanted wigs that could actually pass as real hair. A multitude of new inventions—curls inserted inside riding hats, toupees, and false ponytails—emerged to satiate the new fashions and alleviate the ultimate and unforgiving march of aging. Wigs were a private masculine purchase, an essential aspect of the secret toilette the new man publicly denied. Men's wigs and toupees, like cosmetics for women, were highly visible in advertisements of the period but mainly invisible as consumer goods. The best-selling wig stayed put on the gentleman's head while he was bowing to the ladies, transacting important business, or even more risky, engaging in sexual adventures.

False hair was especially important for constructing new and ever-changing hair-styles. In the revolutionary period and Empire, tastes spanned from long curly locks to the short Titus hairstyle, both difficult to manage without the aid of false hair. By the 1820s, men's hairstyles continued to demand wigs. For instance, the hairstyle popular in 1823 was so curled and creped that "one thought that these men had wigs."[71] Men wanted to have "nothing false, at least on the exterior," but everyone knew that the rage was for luxurious curled hairpieces that could be attached to the inside of hats.[72] Each specific lock and where it fell had a name ("the victorious ringlet" or "the seductive hook").[73] Men who lacked the proper virile and sexually enticing curl would understandably resort to art. Artificial hairpieces to create a style justified false hair tresses as objects of fashion.

Other men justified wearing false hair for health reasons. Most nineteenth-century doctors still believed that wigs could protect the head from bad weather and thus illness. "Wigs should not be considered solely objects of the toilette . . . " since "a great number of people are forced by the loss of hair and especially by the vicis-situdes of the atmospheric temperature . . . " to adopt them out of necessity.[74] Men who had lost their hair from "late night work or honorable wounds" could thus don a wig respectably.[75] This reasoning assumed that certain men, especially the elderly, would be better served wearing a false hairpiece than having an uncovered head. As justified by health, the wig could also function as an object of social integration, hid-ing the weaknesses inherent with hair loss.

Despite continued support for wig wearing, the successful wigmaker promoted wigs as a mimicry of the natural, rather than as a social integration tool. Early nineteenth-century wigmakers expanded on earlier inventions to help their products be more realistic. They invented new frames and measured their client's heads for a better fit.[76] Achieving perfection in verisimilitude gained recognition from both con-sumers and the state.[77] One of the most famous inventors in this domain was Allix who was honored with prizes, patents, and public recognition of his art. At the 1819 *Exposition des produits de l'industrie* in the Louvre, his stand was surrounded by "pe-tits maîtres observing the false toupees and the mechanical tufts," all ready to spend large sums on these promising covers. Allix proposed wigs for all seasons and styles, which became synonymous with men's fashion.[78] Allix and his competitors repre-sented the utmost ingenuity in an art that had long been associated with French crafts-men. "Mechanical" hairpieces were sold alongside mechanical clocks and toys, proof of the continued ability of French artisans to amaze and seduce consumers. Though wigmakers would never regain the renown and financial wealth of the Old Regime, in the early nineteenth century, hairpieces remained lucrative for businesspeople who could mask the processes of aging with fashion and scientific invention.

Wigmakers, inventors of potions, and doctors vied with one another for influence over men's heads. As a group, they reinforced the need for a solution to the problem of baldness. Doctors asserted the reasons for the loss, and though less confident about its solutions, took sides on the debate between cosmetic manufacturers and wigmakers. In turn, the scientific language of the medical profession helped those who sold solutions to legitimate their products. Their advertisements made clear that there was something to be done, a purchasable commodity awaiting men who despaired about their lack of hair and thus their lack of masculinity in society. The aggressive presence of hair products in the consumer market of the late eighteenth and early nineteenth centuries did not create the stigma of baldness, but it did guarantee that all elite men (and probably quite a few of the lower classes) knew of the potential solutions that the market could provide them.

Conclusion

In *Cesar Birotteau*, Balzac's perfumer hero was at once a naïve investor and a visionary businessman. His ingenious plan to conquer the French market for cosmetics was to bet on the vanity, not of the fair sex but of men. Thus, Birotteau invented (with the help of a famous chemist) a hair regenerating oil. Birotteau's reasoning behind his cure was that "at a certain age men will do anything to grow hair on their heads when they have none . . . Since the peace, men live more among women, and women do not like bald heads . . . So the demand for that class of article can be explained by the political situation."[79] Peace and vanity in the 1820s was the instigation for increased masculine anxiety, and Birotteau hoped to find financial wealth in a solution. Balzac's perfumer echoed the multitude of advertisements and tracts that proposed to help men with their bald spots. Balzac chose to copy Macassar oil precisely because this product was both so lucrative and so ludicrous. The novel used contemporary personages and products to create a credible criticism of the dangers of rampant capitalism as well as the inherent profitability of masculine vanity in the budding consumer market. Birotteau was at once a bumbling fool whose attempts at social elevation left him open to manipulation and a shrewd reader of inherent masculine weakness and its commercial possibilities.

Birotteau's invention was a simple concoction made with hazelnut oil that he believed must work because medical students used it to make their mustaches thicker.[80] To bolster his specious claim, he turned to the famous chemist Vauquelin. Balzac copied Vauquelin's own scientific study on the composition of hair as the basis for this conversation. Vauquelin at first denied that hazelnut oil would have any special effect. He enlightened Birotteau with the fact that hair was dead and that even the popular Macassar would not bring it back. Nevertheless, the fictional chemist was willing to judge hazelnuts as more suitable than other oils because of their stimulating nature (according to the well-known doctor and researcher on hair, Dupuytren) and gave his name to the marketing of the newly baptized *Huile céphalitique.*[81] Balzac portrayed a world in which specialists and scientists were aware of the false promises made to men by charlatans and perfumers but were also too blasé or too financially implicated to try to stop them. The fictional Vauquelin saw no harm in perpetuating myths and giving hope to consumers.

Melding science and commerce had to be matched by a new means of marketing and advertising. But it was not the elderly perfumer who would revolutionize French consumerism and masculine beauty, but a younger and more creative generation. Balzac made the marketing of *Huile céphalitique* the first national publicity campaign. Birotteau's young assistant, Popinot, and his friends concocted visually dramatic and discursively persuasive billboards to be plastered permanently in the perfume and hairdressing stores of France. They also manipulated the possibilities of a new nationalized press. The inventive young promoter bribed, cajoled, and fêted editors, journalists, and printers to get the product talked about, not just through advertisements, but, more important, through informative and supposedly objective articles. These new entrepreneurs "had the wit to comprehend the influence of journalism and the effect produced upon the public mind by the piston stroke of the reiterated paragraph."[82]

New means of publicity, thus, went hand in hand with the development of a new market, one that was principally aimed at male rather than female consumers. Birotteau's enthusiasm and Popinot's profits matched the success of actual perfumers and physicians. Scientific approval, manipulation of consumer vanity, and commercial acumen came together to make an unbeatable consumer product, a necessity for those with thinning pates, and a highly desirable commodity for the rest. Balzac's view of history, though off by twenty years chronologically, reemphasized a vision of early nineteenth-century France that firmly linked the development of consumerism, not solely with feminine pastimes but also with the weaknesses of men. Balzac's Birotteau realized that "the most certain speculations are those that are based on vanity, self-love, or a regard for appearance. Those sentiments will never be extinct."[83] And those most likely to part with their money because of their vanity were men. A man without hair was a figure of degeneration and impotence. Hair concretely symbolized a man's sexual and financial suitability. Thus, the promise of hair would remain a profitable sector well into our own time.

At the beginning of the eighteenth century, cosmetics (primarily fards) were associated with the court and aristocracy, markers of rank more than signs of beauty. Shops sold a multitude of beauty aids, but many elites still made their beauty products at home. As the century progressed, these same products were diversified (with new names and uses) and sold more cheaply and widely, appealing to an increasingly savvy and financially stable middle and working class. As the new Parisian consumer market of proto-luxuries grew, a shift toward natural fashions also took place. Though critics of luxury justified increased consumerism as part of the redefinition of taste, paint was labeled artifice to be rejected by both women and men. Visible cosmetics symbolized aristocratic deception and the possibility of physical and moral decay, rather than "modernity."

Men and women who bought and wore makeup could not easily escape the barrage of criticism aimed at them from a diversity of voices. Critics sought to excise men from the toilette, simplify women's beauty practices, and reform both genders' behavior in society. The goal was to separate the rabble and the decadent aristocracy from the respectable classes by defining limits to taste and nature. Critics fought a determined battle against the forces of Old Regime fashion by badgering and cajoling wearers of cosmetics, frightening them with the dangers of resisting change. By the end of the century, these critics, on the surface, had won: natural fashion that stressed simplicity and youthful innocence replaced the reign of the coquette, even if it mimicked the previous ideals of beauty. Doctors joined in this chorus of criticisms. The aesthetic of the natural was allied with the medical imperatives of health and hygiene. Newly professionalized physicians positioned themselves as the antithesis to charlatans, ready to protect the buying public from shoddy potions and dangerous recipes.

The attacks on artifice by *philosophes,* moralists, and medical professionals challenged but did not destroy the commerce of beauty. Sellers responded by aggressively adopting the language of their critics and building a new set of associations for their products. Their combination of Enlightened and medical language with promises of personal pleasure helped transformed old cosmetics into new, acceptable purchases. Both male and female sellers helped create new markets by advertising legitimate uses, images, and ingredients for their products. Sellers of cosmetics touted guarantees, effectiveness, and safety. Alongside makers of secret remedies, they petitioned for medical patents, drew on scientific language and altered (or pretended to alter) their ingredients. They renamed their products to associate with Rousseau's cult of the natural. Or, in a move to distance themselves from tainted French products, they evoked Oriental locales, emphasizing exotic (and possibly erotic) possibilities. Demand for wigs declined, benefiting makers of hair products who targeted the well-off and insecure male consumer with promises of hair regeneration.

Retailers rebutted the taint of aristocratic immorality by creating effective counter imagery for their goods. What they did not do was take sides. Marketers did not try to define cosmetics as either solely the markings of the aristocratic courtier (and thus ripe for emulation) or the realm of the new respectable elite. They did not attempt to discipline women's behavior, entering the toilette with only their products and how to apply them. They accepted the premise that the new aesthetic of natural beauty was now the norm, but they offered their very artificial products as a means for achieving it. And, more important, they did not accept the social, moral, and political strictures that were associated with the new fashion. Instead, marketers alluded to utility alongside promises of miracles and personal pleasure. What type of woman or man a buyer transformed into was left to the individual's choice, since sellers simply laid out possible outcomes, not a strict definition of gender roles. Social meaning and rank were mostly left unsaid. The bourgeois matron could coexist alongside the coquette, the actress, or the *petit maître*.

They did, however, want to serve as the main advisors, if not of gender roles, than of the sphere of buying beauty. Creators of new ploys and products responded to their customers' desires, hoping to be able to shape them as well as fulfill them. Advertisers were well aware of the growing public of buyers that demanded more services from their local shops. The publicity of cosmetics, both in newsprint studied here and in less available sources, was directly aimed at effecting these buyers' choices. Buyers needed sellers' advice to make informed choices if they wished to be safe and natural. With this help, women and men could use new and newly redefined products in the privacy of their homes. What these marketers stressed was that giving up all forms of beautification was not necessary or reasonable. Sellers, and increasingly journal articles as well, invited buyers to enter the public sphere of consumerism and vanity sure of their options.

The consumer revolution created a new hierarchy of legitimate voices in which those with access to the market and publicity could triumph over their critics. Store owners had a distinct advantage because they had direct links to their customers, whereas advice writers and journalist could not control how women (and men) used their work. The face-to-face contact enhanced sellers' position as the ultimate definers of fashion and consumption. Other taste masters, however, were not banished from the toilette. Doctors and journalists could compete more effectively by entering the sphere of commerce. Rather than just criticize cosmetics, they had to offer alternatives to undermine the growing power of the market. Doctors were especially connected to cosmetics sales, both through the system of patents and their own forays into remedies. Critics of artifice could position their articles next to advertisements or take on the system of marketing directly. Increasingly, commentators shifted from a focus on the actions of women in private, to the interaction of buyers and sellers in public. The falsity of artifice was joined by the falsity of the market, ready to dupe innocent and wholly natural women into frivolous and even dangerous purchases.

Despite criticisms, publicity and marketing had a growing importance in consumer choices. Daniel Roche argues that the new commercial methods "such as nascent forms of advertising, classified advertisements, and mail-order" proposed "liberation through reading, emancipation through consumption . . . Papers afforded women promotion and independence based on the values of a culture of subversive frivolity."[1] Advertisements provided a space in which buyers could see their desires and concerns reflected alongside articles on changing fashions. Buyers were increasingly educated in the language of natural beauty, participating in "subversive" redefinitions using complex artifice. These redefinitions created a new more powerful relationship between the wearer and their own self-presentation. In this way, the commerce of cosmetics, with its publicity and marketing, played a key role in encouraging individual choice and "liberation" of women (and men) within the limits of acceptable behavior.

Whether marketers succeeded in altering fashion choices and meanings is tested in the actual uses of consumers. Did consumers, faced with the prospect of natural fashion, throw away their bottles or did they continue painting while advocating purity of the face? How did men adapt to the limitations on their toilettes? The answers can be guessed from the previous chapters, despite only indirect anecdotal evidence. The number of advertisements, patents, and visibility of sellers, matched by the increased criticisms, indicates that late eighteenth-century French men and women still wore and owned paint. But how did women feel about their use of paint in this changing world? How did men feel about giving up the pleasures of the toilette? These questions are much more difficult to answer. There are few honest and personal discussions of cosmetics at the height of their use, and there are just as few during their decline. Despite these limitations, a few examples allow a glimpse into how individuals responded to the contradictory demands of the new ideals of beauty.

The most visible consumer for natural fashions and the one with the most influence was undoubtedly Marie Antoinette. She was said to have helped calm the overuse of rouge and beauty patches when she and her ladies at the Petit Trianon adopted more natural styles.[2] Her personal taste, outside court regalia, was for simpler fashions, as depicted in Vigée-Lebrun's portraits. The queen adopted the *robe à chemise,* a style imported from England, which proved popular among her admirers. When the Salon of 1783 exhibited Vigée-Lebrun's portrait of the queen in such a dress and straw hat, the public was so shocked by its immodesty that the picture was removed and replaced by a more formal one.[3] The first portrait, thus, represents the new natural fashion of Rousseau, while the second depicts acceptable court dress. In both portraits, however, Marie Antoinette's cheeks and lips are depicted as rosy red and her skin is pure snow white. The cheek color highlights her cheekbone and flushes down her face, from her ear to jaw line. This is not the perfectly round circles of color found at the beginning of the century, but neither is it much different from the images of royalty since the late reign of Louis XV. This flush of color resembles that of an embarrassed child, rendered uneven by the painter to indicate its naturalness. Yet, nothing in the queen's stance or look link her color to her emotions: her stare is confident and slightly coquettish. Despite the shift in fashions and aesthetics, the queen's rouged cheeks (whether natural or applied) remain similar in purpose and in intensity in both portraits.

The queen's shift to the natural represents the elite's full acceptance of this aesthetic, even while promoting the color of rouged cheeks. The dual portraits of the daughters of the Genevan banker Jacques Rilliet, painted in 1790 by David, underscore how important it was for the once profligate elite, especially those whose wealth was suspect, to redefine themselves as respectable. According to Jerrine Mitchell, these paintings mimicked self-portraits of Vigée-Lebrun that stressed her virtue and talents, traits these aristocrats wished to emulate from their social inferiors. Newly married, the Comtesse de Sorcy (twenty years old and a recent mother) and the Marquise d'Orvilliers (eighteen) are painted wearing the height of fashionable dress and hair, without any sign of their wealth or station.[4] The comtesse wears a *robe à chemise* and a shawl, with her own luxurious curls falling on her shoulders. But her hair is lightly powdered, her cheeks sport round red patches, and her beautiful white complexion matches her dress and hair (see cover art). She is the perfect amalgamation in one person of the ideals of natural fashion and the continued use of rouge and powder. Her sister is less pretty, painted as plumper, ruddier in color, and wearing darker clothing than her almost alabaster sister. This contrast in color created the illusion of "an implied equivalence between appearance and personal identity," distinguishing the sisters from each other.[5] Makeup, or its implication on canvas, could function as a means of defining character, even as critics of artifice hoped it would no longer get in the way of a legible read. Yet, the white face, towering head of curls, and rouged cheeks on the comtesse also evoke an enactment in costume of the new respectable elite by a very young girl. These sisters epitomized youthfulness and its suggestion of true beauty. Married to wealthy, powerful men as teenagers, they hoped to represent elite womanhood through their youthful, natural traits, not despite them. Tellingly, when David painted the comtesse's husband the next year, he is wearing an English-style suit and a lush head of his own hair.[6]

David set the standard for these portraits, and it is difficult to know whether these women dressed in *robe à chemise* in their daily lives. Portraits do not allow us to directly access the thoughts of those who posed about their makeup. Through their memoirs and letters, several key figures of the period have left us with traces of what it meant to live through a revolution in taste. Mlle Clairon, a highly successful actress at the Comédie-Française, helped redefine the use of paint and artifice in theater. Moralists traditionally accused actresses of using their beauty to seduce and corrupt men and thus society.[7] A pornographic tale recounted a fictionalized version of Clairon's early days as an actress, stressing her ability to use makeup to restore her virginity.[8] In her memoirs, written when she was in her late sixties in 1791–92, Clairon hoped to erase her youthful proclivities and solidify her reputation as an actress of great skill and clout, helping improve the status of performers in general. To do so, she deemphasized the importance of beauty in her professional life. When she fought the church over the ban on sacraments for actors and organized a counterfuneral for Crébillon they could attend, she and the other actresses wore no rouge to stress their piety and respectability.[9] She also strongly critiqued the fashion of wearing thick layers of white face paint on stage, arguing that this practice "absorbs the physiognomy, hides from view the precious mobility of the facial muscles . . . " and thus her ability to render emotions and characters to the audience. Yet, she saw no problem with helping nature when it fit the role, softening or darkening her eyebrows and applying powder because these practices did not hide emotions.[10]

Her emphasis on a natural and readable stage physiognomy contradicted her use of rouge in private. In her fifties, she bluntly explained to her lover's wife that he preferred her because "I wear rouge, which gives me a younger and gayer look, and you are of such paleness as to squelch all possible desire."[11] Meaning to offer sympathetic words of advice, the actress fully understood the association of sexuality and artifice, especially for women who were too old to seem naturally beautiful. She had a pragmatic relationship to makeup. She used it when it fit the character she was playing, whether as a mistress or as an actress, as long as it allowed her the ability to express herself honestly. Clairon did not critique women for wearing fard but rather understood that, in social circles that advocated youth and naturalness, most women hoped to please their male companions by painting on their lost youth.

Yet, in her memoirs, she also attempted to depict herself as willingly giving up the coquetry of youth when she reached a respectable retirement age. At age forty, she spotted her first wrinkle and claimed that she soon gave up both her career and her conquests. She never married because men automatically based their love on beauty, and when this beauty faded, "one rarely finds qualities that can console one of its loss."[12] As an actress, however well respected, she depended on her lovers for financial support. Despite her claims, she continued to act privately and attempted to keep her lover faithful with the above-mentioned rouge, even though he eventually left her for a younger woman.[13] Her hope was to gain respect from men, rather than desire, but as a mistress, she had no recourse when her lovers chose to give her neither. Clairon could not imagine a world outside the boundaries of youthful beauty, but she had to keep trying to reproduce it for her own survival. Though her memoirs claim to be advice for how to survive the loss of beauty by emphasizing talent and character, she could not take her own advice to heart. Despite her failures to age gracefully, the section of her memoirs on dealing with wrinkles was reprinted in the *Journal des dames* as advice to young girls. Despite her background as an actress, she had managed through her memoirs to whitewash her past and sell herself as the perfect representation of respectable old age.[14]

The painter Girodet, student of David, provides both a personal commentary on his appearance (specifically his hair) and artistic representations of himself and other men of his generation. From Girodet's earliest portraits during the Revolution to his late work before his death at age fifty-seven in 1824, his hair played a key role in exemplifying his social, political, and professional roles. Girodet was not a typical revolutionary man. He was caught up in the events of the period both as an artist and a freethinker. Yet, his struggle to define his masculinity through his art exemplifies the difficulties presented to men who were trying to both reject Old Regime artifice while remaining consumers of current fashions. In his attempt to create a legacy for himself, Girodet's hair, like that of many men, functioned as "a performance, one that happens at the boundary of self-expression and social identity, of creativity and conformity."[15] As an actor in his own romance, Girodet constantly readjusted his image to fit the masculine roles of the period.

When Girodet arrived in Italy in 1790 to study painting at the French Academy in Rome, he still wore a wig and powder. As a student, however, he fired his wig-maker for lack of funds and decided instead to wear his hair natural and thus short. He was proud of his savings despite being told that "in this new costume, I look like . . . a bust of Brutus who killed Cesar."[16] His friends, however, worried that the conservative Romans would mistake him for a Jacobin. Even the director of the academy advised him to return to powder for his own safety. He admitted that "as soon as I can have the smallest possible pony-tail, that would be for me, an anchor and a protection."[17] Soon after, he was almost killed by a mob of antirepublican Italians and became a revolutionary hero back in France. Girodet's revolutionary experiences confirmed the importance of self-presentation and the symbolic power of fashion.[18]

Girodet's hair problems in Italy only got worse. Rather than grow longer, in 1794 his "beautiful blond hair" started to fall out due to a bout of illness. Fearing it was syphilis, Girodet was ashamed of his symptoms and hid them from his colleagues. They deduced that this early baldness was caused by his rejection of powder and grease, assuming like many that these cosmetics had protective functions. Contrary to his newfound Jacobin values, he was forced to "wear wig."[19] Girodet felt betrayed by his own body, obliging him to create an artificial self in public and most tellingly in painting. In a 1795 self-portrait, Girodet painted himself with a lush, shiny, long, dark head of hair topped by a wide brimmed hat popular in republican circles (figure 12). Emulating the long silky hair of his own *Endymion* (an example of a highly androgynous Romantic male nude), Girodet recreated for himself an idealized masculinity, both in his painting and in the masquerade of wig and dress. The purchase of the wig (and possibly cosmetic hair products), in a period of natural hairstyles, allowed him to play-act the sexually charged role of artist while waiting for his real hair to grow back. Though in life, as in art, he believed that if men were "elegant, without affectation, they will always know how to please," he realized that it was still necessary to borrow artifice to recreate the supposed unkempt beauty of a romantic hero.[20]

As he aged and his career did not have the resonance he hoped for, Girodet's self-portraits became fiercer but no less theatrical. Tellingly when his hair started to fall out, he hid his receding hairline with the use of flying Titus curls, a trick used by many other artists. His last portrait right before his death shows him at his work-table with a quite healthy head of hair. One of his students corrected this vain lie after his death.[21] Though Girodet painted older mentors with obvious hair loss, he was never able to depict himself or his contemporaries with follicular weakness. As a recent essay on his portraits argues, Girodet was no Rousseau. He did not wish to display his inner-self to the world. Rather he created fantasies of his ideal selves.[22] The revolutionary and Napoleonic periods masculinized art and society, tying men to fraternal brotherhood and later militaristic empire. Girodet hoped to enact this highly active masculinity by a continued use of artifice. Natural masculinity (whether neoclassical or Romantic) demanded unkempt beauty and flowing hair. Men were willing to adopt artifice to achieve this ideal despite the costs and the contradictions involved.

Though neither Clairon nor Girodet represent everyday French beauty practices, their memoirs nonetheless point to the ambiguity with which the new models of fashion and taste were adopted.[23] Both played with artifice, while accepting, how-

Figure 12. Anne Louis Girodet De Roussy-Trioson, Self Portrait (1795), Réunion des musées nationaux/Art Resource

ever grudgingly, the changes in aesthetics. Old age was the most difficult aspect of this new natural beauty and both tried to fight off inevitable decline. Their concili-ation of artifice and naturalness signaled the complexity inherent in ideals of trans-parency. Undoubtedly, many other painters of the face found the transition to nat-ural beauty both difficult and unwise.

Never truly scrubbed clean of its marks and vices, the visage remained a complex and ultimately treacherous read at the end of the eighteenth century. As the Baronne d'Oberkirch rightly pointed out, the fad of the natural, meant to define the tastes of the new elite as distinct from the rabble and aristocracy, could just as easily be adopted by courtesans who understood better than anyone the wiles of fashion.[24] This renewed fear of successful emulation was played out in an 1801 directory of Parisian prostitutes. One woman was described as "pretty enough . . . her complexion, like many others, needs the help of art to seem vermillion." Male customers were still assumed to want healthy, though artificial color. Yet, other women are described in the same terms with which Rousseau characterized Julie. For instance, Angélique was "not a perfect beauty," but "she is the only one who has both good physical and moral traits."[25] Both the triumph and ultimate failure of natural beauty can be found in these young women's charms: the moral and aesthetic criteria of transparent beauty had entered the bordello, hitherto the empire of artifice and corruption.

The culture of French beauty by the early nineteenth century contained many modern-day elements. It coexisted with natural fashions, entered the homes of all ranks, was aggressively marketed, and emphasized the possibility of self-fashioning. As the nineteenth century progressed, cosmetics continued to illicit strong opposition alongside more covert forms of support. Makeup became more gendered but did not disappear from view.[26] Unlike England and America, where paint was increasingly associated with prostitution and decadence, in France makeup alongside perfume and creams remained adaptable items within the toilettes of respectable women. Today, the French commerce of beauty, headed by the behemoth L'Oréal, remains associated with the values of its predecessors: medical legitimacy, guaranteed creation of beauty, and pleasurable ownership. Despite the common assumption that it was in the twentieth century that broad use of cosmetics first occurred, eighteenth-century sellers of rouge, creams, and powders had already taken the first step in turning what had been an aristocratic prerogative into an acceptable (if hidden) part of many women and some men's toilettes.

Introduction

1. DeJean, *The Essence of Style;* Weber, *Queen of Fashion.*
2. Wrigley, *The Politics of Appearances,* 230–31; Ribeiro, *The Art of Dress.*
3. Perrot, "La Richesse cachée," 159.
4. On eighteenth-century cosmetics, see Corson, *Fashions in Makeup;* Williams, *Powder and Paint.* On the nineteenth century, see Peiss, *Hope in a Jar;* M. L. Stewart, *For Health and Beauty,* 11–14.
5. McKendrick, Brewer, and Plumb, *The Birth of Consumer Society,* 9; Roche, *The People of Paris,* ch. 5; Pardailhé-Galabrun, *The Birth of Intimacy,* ch. 6; Fairchild, "The Production and Marketing of Populuxe Goods in Eighteenth-Century Paris," in Brewer and Porter, *Consumption and the World of Goods.*
6. Crowston, *Fabricating Women;* Sargentson, *Merchants and Luxury Markets;* Coquery, "Mode, commerce, innovation"; idem, "The Language of Success," 71–89.
7. Lanoë, *La poudre et le fard.*
8. McKendrick et al., *Birth of Consumer Society,* chs. 3, 4.
9. See, for instance, Marc Martin, *Trois siècles de publicité.*
10. C. Jones, "The Great Chain of Buying," 39.
11. Veblen, *The Theory of the Leisure Class;* McKendrick, "The Consumer Revolution of Eighteenth-Century Britain," in McKendrick et al., *Birth of a Consumer Society,* 11.
12. See, among others, Vickery, "Women and the World of Goods," in Brewer and Porter, *Consumption and the World of Goods;* Berg, *Luxury and Pleasure in Eighteenth-Century Britain.*
13. J. Jones, *Sexing la Mode,* 212–13.
14. Maza, "Luxury, Morality, and Social Change," 219. J. Jones makes a similar argument in *Sexing la Mode,* 212.
15. Simmel named this theory the "trickle-down theory" in 1904. McCracken, *Culture and Consumption,* 93; see also Perrot, *Fashioning the Bourgeoisie,* 18. On the theory of distinction, see Bourdieu, *Distinction.*
16. Shovlin, "The Cultural Politics of Luxury in Eighteenth-Century France," 588.
17. Shovlin, *The Political Economy of Virtue,* 133. On England, see R. Jones, *Gender and the Formation of Taste in Eighteenth-Century Britain;* Smith, *Consumption and the Making of Respectability 1600–1800.*
18. Perrot, *Le travail des apparences ou les transformations du corps féminins, XVIIIe–XIXe,* 91; Roche, *La culture des apparence,* 437–40.
19. Festa, "Cosmetic Differences," 27.
20. J. Jones, *Sexing la Mode,* ch. 4.
21. Phillippy, *Painting Women,* 4.
22. Veblen, *Theory of the Leisure Class,* 179–82. On separate spheres for women, see Landes, *Women and the Public Sphere.*
23. Vickery, "Women and the World of Goods," in Brewer and Porter, *Consumption and*

the World of Goods, 280–81. See also Kowaleski-Wallace, *Consuming Subjects.* On men's shopping, see Finn, "Men's Things"; Kwass, "Big Hair," 631–59.

24. Kwass, "Big Hair," 634.

25. Campbell, *The Romantic Ethic and the Spirit of Capitalism,* 158; Kwass, "Ordering the World of Goods: Consumer Revolution and the Classification of Objects in Eighteenth-Century France," 88; Berg, "New Commodities, Luxuries, and Their Consumers in Eighteenth-Century England," in Berg and Clifford, *Consumers and Luxury.*

26. Jaton, "Du corps paré au corps lave," 217–25.

Chapter One · The Practices of Beauty

1. See Pillivuyt, *Histoire du parfum;* Angeloglou, *A History of Make-Up;* Vaultier, "Les soins de beauté en France au XVIIIe siècle: Les Fards," 115–18.

2. Pillivuyt, *Les flacons de la séduction,* 51.

3. Pillivuyt, *Histoire du parfum,* 208.

4. Genlis, *Mémoires,* 1:241.

5. Barbe, *Le parfumeur royal,* 123–36.

6. Barbe, *Le parfumeur français,* 49–71.

7. Corson, *Fashions in Hair,* 275; Pillivuyt, *Les flacons de la séduction,* 41; Caraccioli, *Dictionnaire critique,* 279.

8. Ribeiro, *Art of Dress,* 109.

9. Sabine Sander, e-mail message to author, June 25, 2008. See Sander, "Von den sonderbahren Geheimnüssen des Frauen-Zimmers' zur 'Schwachheit des schönen Geschlechts' Frauen in des Populärmedizin des 18 Jahrhunderts," 75–120.

10. Festa, "Cosmetic Differences," 27, 29.

11. G. F. Coyer, *Les dames anglaises, francisées par les soins d'un abbé* (London: 1769), 15, qtd. in Ribeiro, *The Art of Dress,* 239.

12. *Journal des dames et des modes* 72 (18 Feb. 1798): 13.

13. Macquer, *Dictionnaire portatif des arts et métiers,* 1:348; Jaubert, *Dictionnaire raisonné universel des arts et métiers,* 3:361.

14. Jaubert, *Dictionnaire raisonné universel des arts et métiers,* 4:269.

15. Savary de Bruslon, *Dictionnaire universel de commerce, d'histoire naturelle, et des arts et métiers,* 2:501.

16. Le Camus, *Abdeker, ou l'art de conserver la beauté,* 2:202–3; Pillivuyt, *Les flacons de la séduction,* 52.

17. Lanoë, "La céruse dans la fabrication des cosmétiques sous l'Ancien Régime," 25–26.

18. Lanoë, "L'invention du rouge au XVIIIe siècle," 92–93.

19. ASRM, box 130, dos. 5; ASRM, box 103, dos. 24.

20. Le Camus, *Abdeker, ou l'art de conserver la beauté,* 2:128.

21. Ibid., 2:224; Lanoë, "L'invention," 93.

22. Pillivuyt, *Les flacons de la séduction,* 57–58.

23. AP, D5B6 3108, Letter to Goubault (6 June 1763).

24. Corson, *Fashions in Makeup,* 204.

25. Pillivuyt, *Les flacons de la séduction,* 53.

26. Goulin, *Le médecin des hommes,* 410.

27. *Mercure* (April 1742): 787; *Avant coureur,* no. 4 (22 Jan. 1770): 51.

28. Corson, *Fashions in Makeup,* 202; Angeloglou, *A History of Make-Up,* 76.

29. Corson, *Fashions in Makeup,* 260.

30. ASRM, box 102, dos. 26, no. 1(a).

31. Hornot, *Traité des odeurs,* 146.

32. *Le parfumeur royal ou traité des parfums,* 113.

33. Alletz, *L'Albert moderne;* Buc'hoz, *Toilette de flore.*

34. Poncelet, *Chimie du goût et de l'odorat,* 289.

35. Bruzen de Lamartinière, *Secrets pour conserver la beauté des dames,* 117–20.

36. Hornot, *Traité des odeurs,* 162.

37. Bruzen de Lamartinière, *Secrets pour conserver la beauté des dames,* 126–27.

38. Perrot, *Travail,* 56; *Avant coureur,* no. 44 (2 Nov. 1761): 691.

39. Jaubert, *Dictionnaire raisonné universel des arts et métiers,* 2:22.

40. *Mercure de France* (Sept. 1750): 206.

41. Vigarello, *Le propre et le sale,* ch. 1, 100–101.

42. Pillivuyt, *Les flacons de la séduction,* 20.

43. Roche, *People of Paris,* 158. See also Corbin, *The Foul and the Fragrant.*

44. *Avant coureur,* no. 3 (17 Jan. 1763): 36; *Art du savonnier* (Paris: 1774), 55.

45. Pillivuyt, *Les flacons de la séduction,* 20; Vigarello, *Le propre et le sale,* 122.

46. Vaultier, "Les soins de beauté," 118.

47. Corson, *Fashions in Makeup,* 204, 211.

48. Campan, *Mémoires de la vie privée de Marie-Antoinette,* 140.

49. *Parfums et flacons au XVIIIe siècle.*

50. See Nostradamus, *Excellent et très utile opuscule à tous nécéssaire, de plusieurs exquises recettes . . . fard;* Bourgeois, *Recueil de secrets pour diverses maladies principalement des femmes avec leurs embellissements;* Blegny, *Secrets concernant la beauté et la santé.* On books of secrets, see Flandrin, "Soins de beauté et recueils de secrets"; Ferguson, *Bibliographical Notes on Histories of Inventions and Books of Secrets.*

51. Meyssonnier, *La magie naturelle,* 171.

52. Pillivuyt, *Histoire du parfum,* 145.

53. Meyssonnier, *La magie naturelle,* 163–64.

54. Pillivuyt, *Histoire du parfum,* 145.

55. Meurdrac, *La chymie charitable et facile en faveur des dames,* 251.

56. Lémery, *Nouveau recueil de secrets,* 60.

57. Vaultier, "La parfumerie et les soins de beauté au xviie siècle," 38.

58. Cinquarbre, "Recettes et produits de beauté du début du XIXième siècle," 213.

59. Bruzen de Lamartinière, *Secrets pour conserver la beauté des dames,* 117–20.

60. Ibid., 122–24.

61. Fargeon, *L'art du parfumeur ou Traité complet de la préparation des parfums, cosmétiques, pommades, pastilles, odeurs, etc.,* 132–53.

62. Hornot, *Traité des odeurs,* 195.

63. Ibid., vi–vii.

64. Buc'hoz, *Toilette de flore,* frontispiece, i.

65. Roche, *People of Paris,* 153; Pardailhé-Galabrun, *The Birth of Intimacy,* 139–44.

66. AP, D5B6 1819, fols. 3 and 17 (1738–39).

67. AP, D5B6 996 (1768–1772); D5B6 612 (1771).

68. AP, D5B6 4215 (1784–1785).

69. AP, D5B6 996 (1768–1772).

70. AP, D5B6 2796 (1774).

71. AP, D5B6 2771 (1774–1781).

72. AP, D5B6 4466 (1779–1784).

73. AP, D5B6 30 (1765–1774).

74. AP, D5B6 927, Letter from Tellier (1779); AP, D5B6 3108, Letter to Goubault (1763).

75. AP, D5B6 881 (1786–1787).

76. Lanoë, "L'invention," 100.

77. J. Jones, *Sexing la Modes,* 3–5.

78. AP, D5B6 2796 (1774). From 1726 to 1789, the value of French money did not change: one gold louis equaled twenty-four livres, one livre equaled twenty sols, and one sol equaled twelve deniers.

79. AP, D5B6 996 (1770–1771).

80. AP, D5B6 475; D5B6 2771.

81. *AAAD* (January 1794), 6087; *Mercure de France* (July 1775): 201–2.

82. *Mémoires de la Baronne d'Oberkirch,* 438; AP, D5B6 2771, Loury's account book for 1774–1781.

83. Cochin, *Avis aux dames* (1750), qtd. in Festa, "Cosmetic Differences," 38.

84. Casanova, *Mémoires de Jacques Casanova* (1843) 2:384.

85. Ribeiro, *Dress in Eighteenth-Century Europe 1715–1789,* 202; Roche, *People of Paris,* 75; Labrousse and Fernand Braudel, *Histoire économique et sociale,* 2:669–70.

86. Labrousse and Braudel, *Histoire économique et sociale,* 2:670.

87. Roche, *People of Paris,* 75, 145; Sonenscher, *Work and Wages,* 175.

88. Labrousse and Braudel, *Histoire économique et sociale,* 2:396–97, 705.

89. De Vries, "Between Purchasing Power and the World of Goods," in Brewer and Porter, *Consumption and the World of Goods,* 85–132.

90. Roche, *People of Paris,* ch. 5, 94.

91. Mercier, *Tableau de Paris,* ch. 491, 1:1341.

92. Roche, *People of Paris,* 155.

93. Restif de la Bretonne, *Les nuits de Paris,* no. 207, p. 934.

94. Restif de la Bretonne, *Les nuits de Paris,* qtd. in J. Jones, *Sexing la Mode,* 154.

95. Mercier, *Tableau de Paris,* ch. 820, 2:938.

96. Isherwood, *Farce and Fantasy,* 222.

97. Mercier, *Nouveau Paris,* ch. 95, 3:100.

98. Casanova, *Mémoires de Jacques Casanova de Seingalt* (1900) 2:302.

99. Restif de la Bretonne, *Les nuits de Paris,* no. 121, p. 837.

100. Vaublanc, *Souvenirs,* 255–56; Casanova, *Mémoires de Jacques Casanova de Seingalt* (1900) 2:390.

101. Fersen, *Le Comte de Fersen à la cour de France,* xvii–xviii.

102. Walpole, Letter to Richard West, 2 April 1739, in *Letters of Horace Walpole,* 1:27.

103. D'Assailly, *Fards et beautés ou l'éternel féminin,* 129.

104. Mercier, *Tableau de Paris,* ch. 883, 2:1117.

105. Qtd. in Festa, "Cosmetic Differences," 33.

106. Diderot, "Salon of 1761," qtd. in Rand, "Love, Domesticity, and the Evolution of Genre Painting in Eighteenth-Century France," *Intimate Encounters,* 8.

107. See *The Stolen Kiss* (1759–1760), *Blindman's Buff* (1753–1756), *The Love Letter* (1769–1770), and The Progress of Love Series (1771–1773).

108. See Chardin, *The Good Education* and *The Kitchen Maid* both reproduced in Rand, *Intimate Encounters.*

109. See Posner, "The Duchess de Velours and Her Daughter," 131–41.

110. Over three hundred Carmontelle portraits are at the Condé Musée, Chateau de Chantilly.

111. Jean Mark Nattier, *Marie Leszcynska, Queen of France* (1748), Versailles; *Comtesse de Tessin* (1741), Musée du Louvre.

112. Jean-Baptiste Greuze, *Madame Léger de Sorbet* (1749); Joseph Siffred Duplessis, *Madame Lenoir,* Musée du Louvre; Jacques Louis David, *Marie-Josephe Buron* (1769), Art Institute of Chicago.

113. Mercier, *Tableau de Paris,* ch. 883, 2:1117.

Chapter Two · A Market for Beauty

1. Remy Saisselin, *The Enlightenment against the Baroque,* 65.

2. Gail Bossenga, "Protecting Merchants," 703.

3. Fairchild, "The Production and Marketing of Populuxe Goods in Eighteenth-Century Paris," in Brewer and Porter, *Consumption and the World of Goods.*

4. Sewell, *Work and Revolution in France,* 27.

5. Sonenscher, *Work and Wages,* 213, 216–18.

6. Vindry, *Naissance et développement de la parfumerie contemporaine,* 98–99; Rasse, *La cité aromatique,* 15.

7. Franklin, *Les corporations ouvrières de Paris du XIIe au XVIIIe siècle,* 546.

8. "Statuts de la communauté des marchands gantiers, poudriers, parfumeurs de la ville, fauxbourgs et banlieues de Paris, 18 Mars 1656," *Statuts de la communauté des marchands gantiers, poudriers, parfumeurs de la ville, fauxbourgs et banlieue de Paris* (Paris: 1772), 17.

9. Rasse, *La cité aromatique,* 16.

10. For a history of the mercer's guild, see Sargentson, *Merchants and Luxury Markets.*

11. Franklin, *Dictionaire historique des arts, métiers et professions,* 354; "Sentence de Police . . . , 18 Janvier 1754," *Statuts,* 368–69.

12. Gamel Seguir de L'Étang, *Mémoire pour le sieur Bougy* (1776), qtd. in Le Tulzo, "La Corporation des parfumeurs au XVIIIième siècle," 27.

13. Le Tulzo, "La Corporation des parfumeurs au XVIIIième siècle," 28.

14. "Arrêt du Parlement qui défend aux perruquiers de vendre aucune marchandise de l'état de gantier-parfumeur, 18 Mai 1726," *Statuts,* 276–77.

15. "Sentence de police . . . qui déclare bonne et valable la saisie faite sur le sieur Lesage, maître amidonier, 7 Mai 1751," *Statuts,* 351–52. See also "Remonstrens très humblement des

jurés de la communauté des maîtres et marchands gantiers . . . ," BN, Ms Joly de Fleury 263, fol. 174 (1748).

16. "Arrest du Parlement servant de réglement entre les communautés des maîtres et marchands gantiers, parfumeurs et des maîtres vinaigriers, 14 Aout 1756," *Statuts,* 387–96.

17. See, for example, "Sentence de Police . . . contre Bottereau, marchand mercier, et Lorraine, marchand forain de la ville de Grasse, 17 Avril 1703," *Statuts,* 210–11.

18. *Mercure de France* (Jan. 1775): 219–20.

19. *AAAD* (13 Feb. 1758): 102.

20. *AAAD* (28 June 1769): 588.

21. Lanoë, "La céruse," 30.

22. Kaplan, *La fin des corporations,* 232.

23. J. Jones, "Coquettes and Grisettes," 40.

24. Crowston, *Fabricating Women,* 65–66.

25. J. Jones, *Sexing la mode,* 162–63. Kowaleski-Wallace argues that in England the sexual relationship was between male sellers and female buyers. Kowaleski-Wallace, *Consuming Subjects,* 86–87.

26. Lanoë, "La Céruse," 25.

27. For instance, Pierre Joseph Buc'hoz was a doctor (*Toilette de flore*) and Antoine Hornot (Dejean, pseud.) was a distiller (*Traité des odeurs*).

28. Le Tulzo, "La Corporation des parfumeurs au XVIIIième siècle," 124–27.

29. Ibid., 92.

30. On arguments for the guilds, see Sewell, *Work and Revolution in France,* 63, 77.

31. Kaplan, *Fin des corporations,* xiv, 109–11.

32. AP, D5B6 2796 (1773–1777).

33. AP, D5B6 927 (1781).

34. Celnart, *Manuel du parfumeur,* 7–8.

35. Pillivuyt, *Histoire du parfum,* 157.

36. Oberkirch, *Mémoires de la Baronne d'Oberkirch,* 438.

37. Augarde, "Noël Gérard et le Magasin Général à l'Hôtel Jabach," in Fox and Turner, *Luxury Trades and Consumerism in Ancient Régime Paris,* 169–71.

38. Fairchild, "The Production and Marketing of Populuxe Goods in Eighteenth-Century Paris," in Brewer and Porter, *Consumption and the World of Goods,* 242.

39. Hermand, fils, *Mémoire pour marchands contre forains,* 16.

40. 5 November 1784 entry. Cradock, *Journal de Mme Cradock,* 97.

41. Sargentson, *Merchants and Luxury Markets,* 128–29, 130.

42. 1778 almanach, qtd. in Sargentson, *Merchants and Luxury Markets,* 123.

43. Bel Air, *Manuel des élégants et des élégantes,* 93.

44. Le Tulzo, "La corporation des parfumeurs au XVIIIième siècle," 43–48.

45. Lacroix, *Le dixhuitième siècle,* 244.

46. Le Tulzo, "La corporation des parfumeurs au XVIIIième siècle," 106–7.

47. Coquery, *L'hôtel aristocratique,* 79.

48. Le Tulzo, "La corporation des parfumeurs au XVIIIième siècle," 52.

49. *AAAD* (9 Oct. 1779): 2251.

50. AN, MC et/cxxii/788, "Louis Philippe Dulac, Inventaire d'après décés, 1775."

51. AP, D4B6 76, dos. 5083.

52. Le Tulzo, "La corporation des parfumeurs au XVIIIième siècle," 54.

53. Ibid., 17–18, 90, 92.

54. *AAAD* (11 Nov. 1792): 4968.

55. *Gazette du commerce* (28 Dec. 1773): 831; *Journal de politique et de littérature* (5 Dec. 1774): 198–99; *AAAD* (27 May 1780): 1213; AN, F/12/1473.

56. *Journal de politique* (5 Jan. 1775): 37–38.

57. *Journal des dames* (March 1775): 398.

58. *Mercure* (Jan. 1775): 219–20.

59. Caraccioli, *Dictionnaire critique,* 2:192; Le Tulzo, "La corporation des parfumeurs au XVIIIième siècle," 130.

60. AP, bankruptcy series D4B6, D5B6, D11U3.

61. See AP, D4D6 80, dos. 5334 (1781).

62. Coquery, *L'hôtel aristocratique,* 170–73.

63. AP, D4B6 92, dos. 6299; AP, D4B6 74, dos. 4868 (1779).

64. Hoffman, Postel-Vinay, and Rosenthal, *Priceless Markets,* chs. 5–7.

65. Pillivuyt, *Les flacons de la séduction,* 31; AN, F/12/874, Auguste Fréderic Fargeon, Faillite (7 Jan. "La corporation des parfumeurs au XVIIIième siècle," 1817); AN, F/12/874, Antoine Louis Fargeon, Faillite (Feb. 1818).

66. AP, D5B6 5299 (1784–86); AP, D4B6 97, dos 6792 (1786); AN, F/12/1473; AAAD (13 April 1782): 872; AAAD (3 Feb. 1787): 348.

67. Kaplan, *Fin des corporations,* 230, 229.

68. Le Tulzo, "La corporation des parfumeurs au XVIIIième siècle," 43–45.

69. *Avant coureur,* no. 33 (15 Aug. 1767): 516.

70. Watin-Augouard, *Il n'y a que Maille,* 29.

71. Gontaut-Biron, *Mémoires de la Duchesse de Gontaut, 1773–1836,* 8.

72. *L'année littéraire,* 7 (1767): 136.

73. Mercier, *Tableau de Paris,* ch. 547, 2:40; Mercier, *Brouette du vinaigrier.*

74. Mercier, *Tableau de Paris,* ch. 547, 2:40.

75. *L'année littéraire,* 7 (1767): 138; Mercier, *Tableau de Paris,* ch. 774, 2:798.

76. See *Affiches de provinces* (Oct. 1779); *Mercure* (Jan. 1771, Jan. 1772, March 1776, March 1777); *Avant coureur* (Dec. 1770, Dec. 1783); *AAAD* (Dec. 1770, Oct. 1782, Nov. 1785).

77. *AAAD* (24 May 1754): 796; *Mercure* (June 1754): 213.

78. *Mercure* (April 1762): 210.

79. *Mercure* (Feb. 1760): 254–55.

80. Charbon, *Au temps des malles-poste et des diligences,* 17–18, 20, 27.

81. Hohenberg, "Urban Manufactures in the Proto-Industrial Economy," in Berg, *Markets and Manufacture in Early Industrial Europe,* 170–71, and Berg, "Markets, Trade and European Manufacture," in Berg, *Markets and Manufacture in Early Industrial Europe,* 6.

82. Mercier, *Nouveau Paris,* ch. 221, 5:202.

83. Balzac, *César Birotteau,* 25, 6.

84. Neuville, *Mémoires du Baron Hyde de Neuville,* 1:355.

85. AN, F/7/6396; Lenotre, *Vieilles maisons, vieux papiers,* 2:184–92; Watin-Augouard, *Il n'y a que maille,* 30; Balzac, *César Birotteau,* 8.

86. Mercier, *Nouveau Paris,* ch. 122, 4:35–36.

87. Greer, *Incidence of Emigration during the French Revolution,* 134.

88. *AAAD* (13 March 1797): 2815.

89. *AAAD* (24 Oct. 1792): 4455; *AAAD* (13 Aug. 1794): 8830.

90. Duval, *Souvenirs de la Terreur,* 42–44.

91. *Le Mois,* no. 9 (1799), 306.

92. Mercier, *Nouveau Paris,* ch. 221, 5:198–200.

93. *AAAD* (21 Aug. 1795): 6840.

94. *AAAD* (16 Sept. 1791): 6450.

95. *Almanach de Paris* (Paris: 1789, 1798).

96. *Almanach du commerce de Paris* (Paris: 1789, 1798, 1809).

97. *Paris et ses modes ou les soirées parisiennes* (1803), 191.

98. AN, D16u3/1, Marque de fabrique, registre de dépots (27 Oct. 1806).

99. AN, F/12/2248, Letter from Laugier to S. M. L'empereur (11 Feb. 1811).

100. Payen, *Rapport du Jury départemental de la Seine sur les produits de l'industrie admis au concours de l'exposition publique de 1827,* 1:217–18.

101. Vindry, *Naissance et développement de la parfumerie contemporaine,* 99.

102. Celnart, *Manuel du parfumeur,* 9–10.

103. Héricart de Thury, *Rapport du jury d'admission des produits de l'industrie du département de la Seine à l'exposition du Louvre,* 206–7; Moléon [Tuleu] and Le Normand, *Description des expositions des produits de l'industrie française,* 181.

Chapter Three · *Advertising Beauty*

1. Caraccioli, *Dictionaire critique, pittoresque et sententieux,* 1:4.

2. Mercier, *Tableau de Paris,* ch. 307, 1:803–4.

3. CCIP, X-3 (6), *Grands gardes et gardes des marchands des six corps de Paris,* "À Monsieur le lieutenant géneral de police" (1762).

4. Ibid.

5. Marc Martin, *Trois siècles de publicité,* 22–23, 25.

6. When referring to the genre of publicity sheets, I will use the term *affiches.* For all the name changes, see Morag Martin, "Consuming Beauty," 66n8.

7. C. Jones, "Great Chain of Buying," 17–18.

8. For histories of the press, see Censer, *The Press in the Age of Enlightenment;* Popkin, *Revolutionary News.*

9. For a study of later nineteenth-century perfumers' marketing methods, see Briot, "César Birotteau et ses pairs: poétiques et mercatique des parfumeurs dans le Paris du XIXième siècle," in Blonde et al., *Marchands et consommateurs.*

10. P. Stewart, "Affiches de province," 1:85.

11. Marc Martin, *Trois siècles de publicité,* 39.

12. *Affiches de Paris* (28 Oct. 1788): 2993.

13. Marc Martin, *Trois siècles de publicité,* 40–41; *AAAD* (19 June 1797); *Petites affiches, annonces et avis divers* (30 June 1797): 1.

14. Marc Martin, *Trois siècles de publicité,* 26; C. Jones, "Great Chain of Buying," 17.

15. Marc Martin, *Trois siècles de publicité*, 37.

16. C. Jones, "Great Chain of Buying," 18. For a discussion of reading, see Gough, *The Newspaper Press in the French Revolution*, 217–18.

17. Censer, *The Press in the Age of Enlightenment*, 186, 216; Descombes, "La publicité dans la presse parisienne 1777–8, 1787–8," 39; Baruch, *Simon Nicolas Henri Linguet*, 109.

18. *Année littéraire* (1763).

19. C. Jones, "Great Chain of Buying," 19.

20. Restif de la Bretonne, *Les nuits de Paris*, no. 359, 1074.

21. Gough, *The Newspaper Press in the French Revolution*, 219–20.

22. Feltaine, *De la publicité commerciale*, 73.

23. Ibid.

24. Datz, *Histoire de la publicité*, 1:189.

25. Mart***, *La voix des commerçans, artisans et d'un grand nombre d'autres citoyens*, 14, 2, 4.

26. Marc Martin, *Trois siècles de publicité*, 57.

27. *Ancien album* (5 Jan. 1828): 187–90.

28. Feltaine, *De la publicité commerciale*, 69.

29. Marc Martin, *Trois siècles de publicité*, 58, 60. See also Hahn, "Street Picturesque."

30. I have examined all available issues of the *Affiches* from 1750 to 1799, the *Mercure* from 1750 to 1780, and a selection of other short-lived journals such as the *Avant coureur* and the *Journal des dames*. I found 1,680 advertisements for cosmetics.

31. Marc Martin, *Trois siècles de publicité*, 62.

32. *AAAD* (13 Aug. 1785): 2181.

33. Walsh, "Advertising and Marketing in Eighteenth-Century London," 88–89, and Coquery, "French Court Society and the Advertising Art," 99–101, both in Wischermann and Shore, *Advertising and the European City;* Scott, "The Waddesdon Manor Trade Cards," 97.

34. Marc Martin, *Trois siècles de publicité*, 34–35, 40; Descombes, "La Publicité dans la presse parisienne 1777–8, 1787–8," 146.

35. C. Jones, "Great Chain of Buying," 19, 25; Censer, *The Press in the Age of Enlightenment,* 65, 78–79.

36. Todd, "French Advertising in the Eighteenth Century," 533; C. Jones, "Great Chain of Buying," 22.

37. Todd, "French Advertising in the Eighteenth Century," 532.

38. The average number of cosmetics advertisements per year in the 1750s was nine, but by the 1780s, this number increased to twenty-three, and by the 1790s, it was seventy-three. Morag Martin, "Consuming Beauty," 77.

39. Ibid., 75–77.

40. McKendrick, "George Packwood and the Commercialization of Shaving," in McKendrick, Brewer, and Plumb, *The Birth of Consumer Society;* Walsh, "Advertising and Marketing in Eighteenth-Century London," in Wischermann and Shore, *Advertising and the European City,* 81; Mui and Mui, *Shops and Shopkeeping in Eighteenth-Century England*, 247.

41. AP, D4B6/97/6792; AP, Y-1744 (April 1783).

42. Watin-Augouard, *Il n'y a que Maille*, 19.

43. AN, V/3/193, "Lettres de privilège pour les marchands" (Dec. 1776); ibid. (1727–1773).

44. *Mercure de France* (Jan. 1771): 215.

45. *Almanach dauphin* (1773, 1776).

46. *Avant coureur,* no. 47 (23 Nov. 1772): 739.

47. AN, F/12/1473. For other uses of patrons, see Coquery, *L'hôtel aristocratique,* 99–102.

48. Sewell, *Work and Revolution in France,* 71–72.

49. *Avant coureur,* no. 4 (25 Jan. 1762): 53.

50. *AAAD* (12 July 1791): 2543.

51. *AAAD* (11 Dec. 1797): 1532.

52. *AAAD* (suplément 21 Dec. 1786): 3373.

53. *Petite Affiche* (27 Jan. 1809): 426.

54. *AAAD* (14 Sept. 1796): 7083.

55. *Journal des dames* (April 1775): 397–98.

56. AN, F/12/1473. See also *AAAD* (6 Aug. 1790): 2338.

57. *Gazette d'agriculture, commerce, arts et finances* (23 Jan. 1770): 63; *AAAD* (1 Dec. 1781): 2764.

58. *Journal de politique* (25 Nov. 1774): 155.

59. *Journal des dames* (July 1775): 111.

60. *Mercure* (April 1769): 204; *Mercure* (Jan. 1771): 215.

61. *AAAD* (1 Nov. 1791): 3971.

62. *Avant coureur,* no. 48 (26 Nov. 1770): 760.

63. *Magasin des modes nouvelles* (May 1789): 125.

64. *Mercure* (July 1775): 201–2.

65. Jeze, *État ou tableau de la ville de Paris* (Paris: 1760), 311.

66. *Gazette du commerce* (28 Dec. 1773): 831.

67. *AAAD* (13 Oct. 1794): 8417.

68. AN, F/12/1473.

69. Watin-Augouard, *Il n'y a que Maille,* 22.

70. *AAAD* (4 Nov. 1797): 860–61.

71. *Magasin des modes nouvelles* (March 1788): 92–93.

72. On criticisms of the kings, see Chartier, *The Cultural Origins of the French Revolution;* Hunt, *The Family Romance of the French Revolution.*

73. *Mercure* (Jan. 1771): 215.

74. *AAAD* (24 Nov. 1774): 939.

75. *AAAD* (4 Nov. 1797): 860–61.

76. *Avant coureur,* no. 33 (15 Aug. 1767): 516.

77. Kwass, "Ordering the World of Goods," 88.

78. *Journal de politique* (25 Nov. 1774): 155.

79. *Année littéraire* (1771): 143.

80. J. Jones, *Sexing la mode,* 184; Crowston, *Fabricating Women,* 70.

81. C. Jones, "Great Chain of Buying," 26.

82. Dulac, *Almanach des adresses de tous les commerçans de Paris pour l'année 1818,* introduction.

83. Bourdet, *Soins faciles pour la propreté de la bouche,* 29.

84. See, for instance, Duflos, *Essai sur les cheveux;* Mayer, *Quelques réflexions sur la manière de maintenir à la beauté les charmes primitifs de la jeunesse.*

85. Auffray, *Idées partriotiques sur la nécéssité de rendre la liberté au commerce,* 10–11.

86. McKendrick, "George Packwood," in McKendrick, Brewer, and Plumb, *The Birth of Consumer Society,* 148.

Chapter Four · Maligning Beauty

1. Roche, *La culture des apparences,* 491.
2. Shovlin, *Political Economy of Virtue,* 132–33, 120.
3. Goodman, *The Republic of Letters,* 6.
4. For a recent revision of the separate spheres theory, see Hesse, *The Other Enlightenment.*
5. Phillippy, *Painting Women,* 15.
6. Festa, "Cosmetic Differences," 31.
7. Braunschvig, *La femme et la beauté,* 80.
8. Grenaille, *L'honneste fille,* 20.
9. Fitelieu, *La contre-mode,* 20.
10. Phillippy, *Painting Women.*
11. La Peyre, *Les moeurs de Paris,* 50.
12. "An Essay on Fashions, Extracted from the Holland Spectator," *Gentleman's Magazine* 6 (July 1736), 377; and Montagu, *Complete Letters of Lady Mary Wortley Montagu,* ed. Robert Halsband (Oxford: Clarendon Press, 1965), 1:39–40, both qtd. in Festa, "Cosmetic Differences," 29, 27.
13. Mercier, *Tableau de Paris,* ch. 498, 1:1364; Perrot, *Travail,* 41–42.
14. Festa, "Cosmetic Differences," 37.
15. Favre, "Le Petit pot de rouge de Junon," in *Quatre heures de la toilette des dames,* 41.
16. On the Rococo aesthetic, see Sheriff, *Fragonard, Art, and Eroticism;* Hyde, "The 'Makeup' of the Marquise," 3.
17. Favre, *Quatre heures de la toilette des dames,* preface, 18.
18. Casanova, *Memoirs* (1990), 2:390.
19. See Phillippy, *Painting Women,* 23–25.
20. Lichtenstein, *The Eloquence of Color,* 191.
21. Guibert, *Poésie et oeuvres diverses,* 89.
22. Caraccioli, *La critique des dames et des messieurs à leur toilette,* 6; Phillippy, *Painting Women,* 31.
23. Roche, *La culture des appearances,* 384–85.
24. *Tableau général du goût, des modes et costumes,* 259.
25. Bractéole, *Éloge philosophique de l'impertinence,* 149.
26. *Éloge des coëffures,* 9.
27. Barthe, *La jolie femme ou la femme du jour,* 1:52.
28. Quinault, *La mère coquette ou les amans brouillés,* 31.
29. *Cinq années littéraires,* 4:14.
30. *Le babillard,* 3:29.
31. Touchard-Lafosse, *L'oeil-de-boeuf,* 4:336.
32. Genlis, *Manuel de la jeune femme,* 63; Caraccioli, *Dictionnaire critique,* 1:76.
33. *Mercure de France,* (14 Aug. 1779): 50.

34. Genlis, *Manuel de la jeune femme,* 63.

35. Mercier, *Tableau de Paris,* ch. 628, 2:344.

36. Nougaret, *Paris ou le rideau levé,* 31.

37. Casanova, *Mémoires de Jacques Casanova de Seingalt* (1900), 2:324.

38. Nougaret, *La faiblesse d'une jolie femme,* 1:1.

39. Masson de Morvilliers, avocat, "À une vieille coquette—ode anacréontique," *Mercure* (August 1779): 50. Printed also in the *Journal des dames* (August 1775).

40. A Viennese law forbade makeup in 1766, and there was a plan for a similar law in England in 1770. Williams, *Powder and Paint,* 74.

41. Nougaret, *Paris ou le rideau levé,* 79–82.

42. Nougaret, *Astuces et tromperies de Paris,* 3:77–79.

43. Du Coudray, *Le luxe, poème en six chants,* 59.

44. Caraccioli, *Dictionnaire critique,* 1:134, 3:296.

45. De Bellegarde, *Modèles de conversations pour les personnes polies,* qtd. in Vaultier, "Les soins de beauté," 115.

46. Caraccioli, *Jouissance de soi-même,* 324.

47. Mercier, *Tableau de Paris,* ch. 883, 2:1118.

48. Lichtenstein, *The Eloquence of Color,* 187.

49. La Salle, *Almanach de la civilité française,* 19–20.

50. Moreau le Jeune, *Suite pour monument du costume,* 47; Moreau le Jeune, *Les petites parties et les grands costumes;* Caraccioli, *Livre des quatre couleurs,* 46–47.

51. Diderot, *Les bijoux indiscrets,* 2:270. For a similar seventeenth century description, see Dancourt, *L'est des coquettes,* 20, 30.

52. Caraccioli, *Livre des quatre couleurs,* 75, 87.

53. *Papillotage,* 29. See also Nougaret, *Mille et une folies,* 2:4; Caraccioli, *Livre à la mode,* 85.

54. Cochin text in Moreau le Jeune, *Suite pour monument du costume,* 53; Mercier, *Tableau de Paris,* ch. 92, 1:234–35.

55. Caraccioli, *La critique des dames et des messieurs,* 12.

56. Bastide, *Les confessions d'un fat,* 27.

57. Caraccioli, *Dictionnaire critique,* 2:96.

58. Bractéole, *Éloge philosophique de l'impertinence,* 151.

59. Mercier, *Tableau de Paris,* ch. 32, 1:94.

60. Restif de la Bretonne, *La femme dans les trois états,* pt. 1, 8.

61. Lacqueur, *Making Sex.* For a discussion of both cross-dressing and gender roles in the eighteenth-century, see Kates, *Monsieur d'Eon Is a Woman.*

62. Restif de la Bretonne, *Les nuits de Paris,* no. 189, 919.

63. Gaudet, *Bibliothèque des petits maîtres,* 149.

64. Restif de la Bretonne, "Le mari invisible," *Les contemporaines,* 4:509.

65. Countess de Getnon-Ville, *L'épouse rare,* 56, 71–72, 134.

66. Caraccioli, *Jouissance de soi-même,* 336.

67. *Encyclopédie méthodique,* 4:401.

68. *Festa,* "Cosmetic Differences," 35.

69. Genlis, *Manuel de la jeune femme,* 38.

70. M. le Général, "La coquette démasquée," *Mercure* (April 1774): 57.

71. On pornography, see Hunt, *Eroticism and the Body Politic.*

72. Nougaret, *Les dangers de la séduction,* 1:38, 52.

73. Ibid., 2:2.

74. Fauchery, *La destinée féminine dans le roman Européen du xviii siècle,* 181.

75. "Lettre d'une Italienne à l'auteur du journal," *Journal des dames* (Feb. 1775): 217.

76. Restif de la Bretonne, *Les françaises,* 1:18.

77. Caraccioli, *Dictionnaire critique,* 1:25–26; Caraccioli, *La critique des dames et des messieurs,* 8.

78. Lichtenstein, *The Eloquence of Color,* 189.

79. Rousseau, *Julie ou la nouvelle Héloise,* 367.

80. Nougaret, *Les dangers de la séduction,* 2:71.

81. "Lettre de Madame Cor . . . à Monsieur d'Auln sur la manière de mettre le rouge," *Journal des dames* (June 1761): 281–82.

82. *Mémoires of the Princess de Palatine,* qtd. in Pillivuyt, *Les flacons de la séduction,* 58.

83. J. Jones, *Sexing la mode,* 148.

84. Caraccioli, *Les entretiens du Palais Royal,* 17–18.

85. Boureau-Deslandres, *Lettre sur le luxe,* 20.

86. Perrot, *Le travail des apparences,* 48.

87. J. Jones, *Sexing la mode,* 212.

88. Mercier, *Tableau de Paris,* ch. 418, 1:1156. For more on the luxury debates, see Shovlin, *The Political Economy of Virtue;* Maza, "Luxury, Morality, and Social Change."

89. Chevrier, *Les ridicules du siècle,* 22.

90. Caraccioli, *Jouissance de soi-même,* 323.

91. "Sur le bal de l'Opéra," in Delacroix, *Le spectateur français avant la Révolution,* 422.

92. Roche, *La culture des apparences,* 492–94.

93. J. Jones, *Sexing la mode,* 213.

94. See Maza, "Luxury, Morality, and Social Change," 219–25.

95. *Courtine and Haroche, Histoire du visage,* 132.

96. Hutcheson, *Recherches sur l'origine des idées que nous avons de la beauté,* 32. For a subjective view, see Gerard, *Essais sur le goût.*

97. De Marcenay de Ghuy, *Essai sur la beauté,* 17–18.

98. Pernety, *La connaissance de l'homme moral,* 1:176.

99. Rousseau, *Confessions,* t. IV, 139.

100. Lennox, *Sophie ou le triomphe des grâces sur la beauté,* 26.

101. M.D., Avocat au parlement de Rennes, "Lisette," *Mercure* (June 1780): 49–51.

102. Anonymous poem to Mlle Doligny at her début, *Journal des dames* (Dec. 1764): 6.

103. Quinault, *La mère coquette ou les amans brouillés,* 26.

104. *Mercure* (Jan. 1769): 22–23.

105. Favre, *Quatre heures de la toilette des dames,* 48–49. See also *Mercure* (Jan. 1769): 22–23.

106. Caraccioli, *La critique des dames et des messieurs,* 8.

107. Delacroix, *Le spectateur français avant la Révolution,* 175.

108. Boudier de Villemert, *L'ami des femme,* 131.

109. Rousseau, *Julie ou la nouvelle Héloise,* 373–76.

110. Rousseau, *Emile,* 498, 465.

111. Genlis, *Manuel de la jeune femme,* 398.

112. Choderlos de Laclos, *De l'éducation des femmes,* 34, 81–82.

113. Ibid., 78–79.

114. Boudier de Villemert, *L'ami des femme,* 120.

115. d'Abrantès, *Une soirée chez Madame Geoffrin,* 119.

116. Charleval and St. Pavin, *Poésies de Charleval et St. Pavin,* 64.

117. Nougaret, *Les dangers de la séduction,* 1:5. See also Caraccioli, *Jouissance de soi-même,* 297.

118. Gaudet, *Bibliothèque des petits maîtres,* 84.

119. Mercier, *Tableau de Paris,* ch. 157, 1:371.

120. Schwartz, *The Sexual Politics of Jean-Jacques Rousseau,* 72, 75–78.

121. J. Jones, *Sexing la mode,* ch. 4.

122. Burollet, *Musée Cognacq-Jay,* 128–29. The engravings are in Salaman, *French Colour Prints of the Eighteenth Century.*

Chapter Five • Domesticating Beauty

1. *Affiches Parisiennes ou Gazette de France* 247 (4 Sept. 1818): 1033; Jean-Baptiste Mège, *Alliance d'hygie et de la beauté.*

2. On female literacy, see Roche, *People of Paris,* 199–203.

3. Chaptal de Chanteloup, *Eléments de chymie,* 2:278–79; Angeloglou, *A History of Make-Up,* 75.

4. Foucault, "The Politics of Health in the Eighteenth Century," in *The Foucault Reader,* 273–90, 279–84. See also Foucault, *Birth of the Clinic;* Duden, *The Woman beneath the Skin,* 3–4, 14–15.

5. Perrot, *Travail,* 75.

6. Wilson, *Women and Medicine in the French Enlightenment,* 95.

7. Foucault, "Truth and Power," 119.

8. Wilson, *Women and Medicine in the French Enlightenment,* 5–6. See also Jordanova, *Sexual Visions.*

9. Perrot, *Travail,* 79; Roche, *La culture des apparences,* 441–43; Vigarello, *Le propre et le sale,* 116–17.

10. Tissot, *Essai sur les maladies des gens du monde,* 108.

11. Corbin, *The Foul and the Fragrant,* 71–85.

12. Phillippy, *Painting Women,* 24.

13. Berriot-Salvadore, *Un corps, un destin,* 95.

14. Nostradamus, *Excellent et très utile opuscule à tous nécéssaire;* Meyssonnier, *Recueil de secrets pour la conservation de la beauté.*

15. See de Renou, *Oeuvres pharmaceutiques,* 80.

16. Ramsey, "The Popularization of Medicine in France 1650–1900," 107, 113.

17. Brockliss and Jones, *The Medical World of Early Modern France,* 668.

18. Lémery, *Cours de chymie contenant la manière de faire les opérations qui sont en usage dans la médecine,* 108, 115.

19. Marie de Saint-Ursin, *L'ami des femmes ou lettres d'un médecin,* 288–89.

20. *Mercure de France* (March 1773): 193–94.

21. Marie de Saint-Ursin, *L'ami des femmes ou lettres d'un médecin,* 301.

22. Buc'hoz, *Toilette de flore,* 198; Jaubert, *Dictionnaire raisonné universel des arts et métiers,* 3:362–63.

23. Retz, *Nouvelles ou annales de l'art de guérir,* 5:532.

24. Jaubert, *Dictionnaire raisonné universel des arts et métiers,* 4:270.

25. Macquer, *Dictionnaire portatif des arts et métiers,* 349.

26. Le Bègue de Presle, *Le conservateur de la santé ou avis sur les dangers qu'il importe à chacun d'éviter,* 350.

27. Le Camus, *Abdeker, ou l'art de conserver la beauté,* 1:203–4.

28. Bourdet, *Soins faciles pour la propreté de la bouche,* 11.

29. See Jones, "Pulling Teeth in Eighteenth-Century Paris," 100–45.

30. Bourdet, *Soins faciles pour la propreté de la bouche,* 29.

31. Le Bègue de Presle, *Le conservateur de la santé,* 340; Vigarello, *Le propre et le sale,* 146.

32. Roussel, *Système physique et moral de la femme,* 128.

33. Deshais-Gendron, *Lettre à monsieur,* 20.

34. Ibid., 24.

35. Roussel, *Système physique et moral de la femme,* 126.

36. Banau, *Histoire naturelle de la peau,* xv–xvi.

37. Choderlos de Laclos, *Dangerous Acquaintances,* 428.

38. Casanova, *Mémoires de Jacques Casanova* (1843), 52.

39. See Peter, "Les médecins français face au problème de l'inoculation variolique et de sa diffusion, 1750–1790," 251–64.

40. Mercier, *Tableau de Paris,* ch. 342, 1:927.

41. Jaubert, *Dictionnaire raisonné universel des arts et métiers,* 4:545.

42. Virard, *Essai sur la santé des filles nubiles,* 32.

43. Retz, *Nouvelles ou annales de l'art de guérir,* 5:532.

44. Tissot, *Essai sur les maladies des gens du monde,* 265. On Tissot and makeup, see Simon-Mazoyer, "Le conflit entre les excès de la mode et de la santé au XVIIIe siècle, l'habillage du visage," 41–53.

45. *Le parfumeur royal ou traité des parfums,* 143.

46. Hornot, *Traité des odeurs,* v–vi.

47. Caron, *Toilette des dames ou Encyclopédie de la beauté,* 29–30; Fargeon, *L'art du parfumeur ou Traité complet de la préparation des parfums,* 2.

48. Article by Jaucourt in Diderot and Le Rond d'Alembert, *Encyclopédie,* 4:291–92. The *Encyclopédie* provided recipes for cosmetics. See Dock, *Women in the Encyclopédie,* 66–67.

49. Jaubert, *Dictionnaire raisonné universel des arts et métiers,* 4:362–63, 271.

50. *Feuille sans titre* (10 Feb. 1777): 38–39.

51. "Lettre sur les dangers du fard," *Journal des dames* (August 1761): 189.

52. Le Camus, *Abdeker,* 1:22.

53. Jean Goulin, *Le médecin des dames ou l'art de les conserver en santé,* xi. Some of the works listed by Goulin are Marie Meurdrac, *La chymie charitable;* Le Camus, *Abdeker;* Hornot, *Traité des odeurs.*

54. Jordanova, *Sexual Visions,* 27–29.

55. Le Camus, *Abdeker,* 1:172–74; Marie de Saint-Ursin, *L'ami des femmes ou lettres d'un médecin,* 302; Hornot, *Traité des odeurs,* 167.

56. Wilson, *Women and Medicine in the French Enlightenment,* 13.

57. Marie de Saint-Ursin, *L'ami des femmes ou lettres d'un médecin,* 27–77, 278.

58. Goulin, *Médecin des dames,* 429–30.

59. Deshais-Gendron, *Lettre à monsieur,* 26.

60. Hornot, *Traité des odeurs,* 139.

61. See, for instance, Delindre, *L'art de se faire aimer de sa femme.*

62. Caron, *Toilette des dames ou Encyclopédie de la beauté,* 116.

63. *Journal des dames* (June 1761): 279.

64. Knibiehler and Fouquet, *La femme et les médecins,* 86–87.

65. Steinbrügge, *The Moral Sex,* 43.

66. Knibiehler and Fouquet, *La femme et les médecins,* 91.

67. Lemaire, *Le dentiste des dames,* 125.

68. Veblen, *The Theory of the Leisure Class,* 81–85.

69. Marie de Saint-Ursin, *L'ami des femmes ou lettres d'un médecin,* 209.

70. Le Camus, *Abdeker,* 1:5.

71. Isoré, "De l'existence des brevets d'invention en droit français avant 1791," 94; Hilaire-Pérez, "Invention and the State in Eighteenth-century France," 923.

72. BN, Ms Joly de Fleury, 2543, *État des particuliers;* Roze de Chantoiseau, *Essai sur l'almanach général d'indication d'adresse . . . des six corps arts et métiers;* ASRM, boxes 97 and 107, and manu 16.

73. C. Jones, "Médecins du Roi at the End of the Ancien Regime and in the French Revolution," 210. For more information on these groups, see Brockliss and Jones, *The Medical World of Early Modern France,* 627–28, 760–82; Ramsey, "Traditional Medicine and the Medical Enlightenment."

74. "Arrêt du conseil d'état du roi concernant les remèdes pour la distribution desquels on demanderait des lettres patentes, brevets ou permission," *Avis au public concernant les remèdes pour lesquels on demande des permissions ou brevets.*

75. ASRM, manu. 14–16, boxes 96–107; *Second avis au public concernant les remèdes pour lesquels on demande des permissions ou brevets; Troisième avis au public concernant les remèdes pour lesquels on demande des permissions ou brevet; avec un état contenant la suite de ceux que la Société Royale de Médecine a examinés et rejettés.*

76. Ramsey, "Traditional Medicine," 223.

77. ASRM, manu. 14–15 (14 Feb. 1783); (20 Feb. 1781); (1786).

78. ASRM, box 103, dos. 7; box 100, dos. 39; box 103, dos. 19; box 97, dos. 75.

79. ASRM, box 101, dos. 49.

80. ASRM, manu. 14–15.

81. ASRM, box 101, dos. 3.

82. ASRM, manu. 14–15 (28 Oct. 1781).

83. ASRM, box 100, dos. 28.

84. ASRM, box 97, dos. 14.

85. ASRM, box 101, dos. 3.

86. AN, F/12/1473, 7 March 1772.

87. ASRM, box 103, dos. 71.

88. Lavoisier, "Rapport sur le rouge végétal, 26 July 1775," in *Oeuvres de Antoine Lavoisier,* 4:227–28.

89. *Affiches de province* (9 Aug. 1775): 127.

90. *Affiches de province* (9 Aug. 1775): 127; *Journal de politique* (March 1777): 386–87.

91. *Troisième avis au public,* 1.

92. *AAAD* (11 Aug. 1790): 2410.

93. *Dictionnaire du commerce et des marchandises,* 1:361–62. For an analysis of the changing conceptions of property, see Sewell, *Work and Revolution in France,* 114–42.

94. Hilaire-Pérez, "Invention and the State in Eighteenth-century France," 928–29.

95. AN, F/12/1024/a, Ministre de l'Intérieur (1814–16).

96. AN, F/12/2267, Ministre de l'Intérieur (Nov.–Dec. 1821). For a review of the process, see *Dictionnaire du commerce,* 1:362.

97. INPI, Goubet, 22 April 1813.

98. INPI, Charles Jean Baptiste Vauquelin, 16 August 1812.

99. See, for instance, INPI, Chammas, 1825.

100. *Affiches de Provence, Aix* (8 Nov. 1778): 353.

101. *Affiches de Provence, Aix* (14 Nov. 1778): 358–59.

102. Qtd. by Laubriet, introduction to *César Birotteau,* by Balzac, cix–cx.

103. Balzac, *César Birotteau,* 108. See also Mercier, *Tableau de Paris,* ch. 924, 2:1228–29.

104. *Petites affiches de Paris* (22 Jan. 1809): 344.

105. *Gazette de France,* no. 247 (4 Sept. 1818): 1034–35.

106. M. L. Stewart, *For Health and Beauty,* 37, 197.

Chapter Six · *Selling Natural Artifice*

1. *AAAD* (20 March 1781): 79.

2. ASRM, box 97, dos. 35.

3. ASRM, box 100, dos. 27.

4. This figure comes from an analysis of the files of the ASRM for cosmetic patents compared with advertisements in major journals.

5. See *Mercure* (June 1775): 221.

6. ASRM, box 103, dos. 5.

7. Cézan and Saint-Ildephont, "Remèdes approuvés par la faculté de médecine," 212–13.

8. ASRM; BN, Ms Joly de Fleury, *État des particuliers,* 2543; *Avis au public concernant les remèdes;* Roze de Chantoiseau, *Essai sur l'almanach général;* Falvy, *Contribution à l'histoire de quelques remèdes secrets,* 98–105.

9. ASRM, box 101, dos. 65; box 102, dos. 75; box 98, dos. 2.

10. *AAAD* (13 Feb. 1788): 438; *AAAD* (20 March 1781): 79; *Journal de la côte d'or* (26 Aug. 1811): 556; INPI, Durochereau, 1816.

11. 1772 advertisement in Deshais-Gendron, *Lettre à monsieur.*

12. *Journal de politique* (March 1777): 386–87; *AAAD* (3 July 1775): 746; *Affiches de province* (9 Aug. 1775): 127.

13. *Avant coureur,* no. 6 (29 Jan. 1774): 1.

14. *Avant coureur* (1770): frontispiece.

15. *Journal de politique* (March 1777): 386. See also *Journal de politique* (December 1774): 198–99; (November 1777): 489.

16. *Avant coureur,* no. 46 (18 Nov. 1765): 715.

17. *Mercure* (December 1750): 210.

18. On medical language in advertising, see C. Jones, "Great Chain of Buying," 32–33.

19. *AAAD* (30 June 1797): 5110.

20. *Avant coureur,* no. 6 (29 Jan. 1774): 1.

21. *Avis divers* (11 Feb. 1777): 181; *Mercure* (Jan 1771): 215; *Avant coureur* (11 Jan. 1768): 20–21.

22. *AAAD* (26 Dec. 1801): 1517; *Avant coureur,* no. 17 (27 April 1761): 259; *AAAD* (27 Oct. 1777): 1354; *Avant coureur,* no. 13 (26 March 1770): 197; *Avant coureur,* no. 4 (23 Jan. 1764): 53.

23. *AAAD* (1 Dec. 1781): 2764; *Avant coureur,* no. 18 (30 April 1764): 278; *Journal des dames* (14 June 1800): 435; *AAAD* (22 Aug. 1776): 814; *Mercure* (March 1771): 193.

24. *Avant coureur,* no. 18 (1 May 1769): 277.

25. *AAAD* (1 Nov. 1791): 3971; *Avant coureur,* no. 31 (1 Aug. 1763): 490; *Gazette d'agriculture, commerce, arts et finances* (23 Jan. 1770): 62.

26. *AAAD* (1 Dec. 1781): 2764; *Mercure* (April 1770): 217; Grimod de la Reynière, *Almanach des gourmands* (1805), 236, quoted in Watin-Augouard, *Il n'y a que Maille,* 33.

27. *Gazette d'agriculture, commerce, arts et finances,* no. 57 (17 July 1770): 534.

28. INPI, Goubet (1813).

29. *AAAD* (18 June 1798): 5251.

30. *L'indiscret* (20 July 1823): 176; *Petit courier des dames* (30 Nov. 1823): 83–84; Corson, *Fashions in Makeup,* 297, 318.

31. *Affiches de Provence* (1 Aug. 1770): 123–24.

32. *Journal des dames* (28 Feb. 1799): 493.

33. *Petit magasin des modes* (Paris: s.d.): 11.

34. *Journal des dames* (29 May 1799): 145–46.

35. *Journal des dames* (26 March 1815): 341–43.

36. Kleinert, *Le "Journal des dames et des modes,"* 71.

37. *Observateur des modes,* no. 45 (1820): 31–32.

38. Goncourt and Goncourt, *Histoire de la société française sous le directoire,* 410; Cinquarbre, "Recettes et produits de beauté du début du XIXième siècle," 211. Karen Halttunen dates this change to the 1830s for America. Halttunen, *Confidence Men and Painted Women,* 57, 73.

39. *Journal des dames* (11 Dec. 1801): 121. See also *Journal des dames* (2 Dec. 1803): 110.

40. For instance, *Journal des dames* (27 Oct. 1797): 5–6.

41. *Journal de la Côte-d'Or* (11 July 1811): 446.

42. Clavelin, *Petites étrennes récréatives de la mode,* 100.

43. J. Jones, "Repackaging Rousseau," 963.

44. Kleinert, *Le "Journal des dames et des modes,"* 120.

45. AN, F/12/1473, Edict du Roi (1778), 92.

46. *Annales politiques, civiles et littéraires du 18ième siècle* (Aug. 1780): 364–67.

47. Elbée, *La véritable ressource que l'on peut tirer du rouge,* 7.

48. Ibid., 13.

49. *Journal de politique* (March 1777): 386–87; *Annales politiques* (Aug. 1780): 364–67.

50. AN, F/12/992, "Mémoire" (1780).

51. AN, F/12/992, Du Frésne, "Lettre à M. de Montaran" (7 May 1780).

52. AN, F/12/1473 (12 Dec. 1787).

53. AN, F/12/1473, Collin, "Lettre au Controlleur général" (Nov. 1787).

54. AN, F/12/1473, Guérin, "Lettre au Ministre d'art et de manufacture" (3 July 1796).

55. AN, F/12/1473, Ministre d'art et de manufacture, Letter to Guérin (14 Aug. 1796).

56. Root, *The Fountain of Privilege,* 131–33; Lewis, "Producers, Suppliers and Consumers," in Fox and Turner, *Luxury Trades and Consumerism in Ancient Régime Paris,* 292–95.

57. Kaplan, *Fin des corporations,* 108–9.

58. Ibid., 519–23.

59. AN, F/12/1473, "Mémoire" (n.d.).

60. J. Jones, *Sexing la mode,* 138.

61. On the awareness of clothing and fashion trades, see J. Jones, *Sexing la mode,* 114.

Chapter Seven · Selling the Orient

1. Behdad, "The Eroticized Orient," 109; Grosrichard, *Structure du serial,* 176.

2. Stein, "Amédée Van Loo's *Costume turc.*"

3. Delpierre, *Dress in France in the Eighteenth Century,* 67–68.

4. Stein, "Madame de Pompadour and the Harem Imagery of Bellevue," 30.

5. Stein, "Amédée Van Loo's *Costume turc,*" 433.

6. Behdad, "The Eroticized Orient," 109; Grosrichard, *Structure du sérail,* 155.

7. Behdad, "The Eroticized Orient," 112.

8. Du Vignau, Sieur des Joannots, *Secrétaire turc* (Paris 1688), qtd. in Grosrichard, *Structure du Serail,* 176.

9. Petit, *Le miroir,* 18.

10. Said, *Orientalism,* 3.

11. Kahf, *Western Representations of the Muslim Woman,* 137.

12. Yeazell, *Harems of the Mind,* 8.

13. Kahf, *Western Representations of the Muslim Woman,* 6–7.

14. For a comic example, see Auger, *Arlequin odalisque.*

15. See Marmontel, "Soliman II," 1761 in *Trois contes moraux;* Favart, "Les Trois sultanes," 1761, in Petitot, *Répertoire du théatre français;* Yeazell, *Harems of the Mind,* 155–57.

16. Kra, "The Role of the Harem in Imitations of Montesquieu's *Lettres persanes,*" 273. See also Douthwaite, *Exotic Women,* ch. 2; Göçek, *East Encounters West.*

17. Montesquieu, *Persian Letters,* letter 26, 77.

18. Ibid., 76–77; letter 7, 47.

19. Lowe, *Critical Terrain: French and British Orientalisms,* 70.

20. Montesquieu, *Persian Letters,* letters 54, 96.

21. Ibid., letter 54.

22. Kra, "The Role of the Harem in Imitations of Montesquieu's *Lettres persanes,*" 276.

23. Douthwaite, *Exotic Women,* 94.

24. Sedaine de Sarcy, *Le sérail à l'encan,* 8, 13, 34–36, 38, 54.

25. Ibid., 23–24; Douthwaite, *Exotic Women,* 110–15.

26. Le Camus, *Abdeker,* 1:80–81.

27. Gwilliam, "Cosmetic Poetics," 145.

28. Le Camus, *Abdeker,* 1:27–28, 42–43, 163.

29. Gwilliam, "Cosmetic Poetics," 149.

30. Douthwaite, *Exotic Women,* 18.

31. Le Camus, *Abdeker,* 1:159.

32. D'après Voltaire, *L'odalisque,* 1796, in *Les maîtres de l'amour,* 230, 233, 234, 237, 239, 242, 247–48. For other pornographic lessons, see Yeazell, *Harems of the Mind,* 115–18.

33. Voltaire, *L'odalisque,* 247–48.

34. Blancard, *Manuel du commerce des Indes,* 158, 174, 178, 168, 318; Desmet-Grégoire, *Le divan magique,* 57. See also Masson, *Histoire du commerce français dans le Levant au XVIIIe siècle,* 468–69, 505–6.

35. Raybaud, *Observations sur l'extraction des huiles essentielles,* 4.

36. Balzac, *César Birotteau,* 40.

37. Ibid., 33–34.

38. *Journal de politique* (25 Nov. 1774): 155.

39. *AAAD* (3 Jan. 1792 supplément): 42.

40. *AAAD* (30 Jan. 1794): 5919.

41. *Mercure* (July 1770): 212.

42. *AAAD* (30 Jan. 1794): 5919.

43. *Journal de politique* (25 Nov. 1774): 155.

44. *Avis divers* (21 Jan. 1777): 84.

45. *Journal encyclopédique,* no. 1332 (1775): 757–58; Bachaumont, *Mémoires secrétes,* 156, qtd. in Stein, "Amédée Van Loo *Costume turc,*" 433.

46. D'Arcier, *Les agents de Napoléon en Egypte 1801–1815,* 156.

47. *Code du commerce* (Paris: 1829), 181–84.

48. Virey, *De la femme sous ses rapports physiologique, moral et littéraire,* 15.

49. *Journal des dames* (15 Aug. 1810): 358.

50. Virey, *De la femme sous ses rapports physiologique,* 22.

51. D'Arcier, *Les agents de Napoléon en Egypte,* 156.

52. Malo, *Bazar Parisien* (1821), 226.

53. *Le bouquet, Album des modes et des nouveautés* (May 1827): 76.

54. *AAAD* (29 May 1805): 9833.

55. *Paris et ses modes* (August 1821): 153–55.

56. *AAAD* (1 Jan. 1807): 7.

57. *AAAD* (1803–1811).

58. Said, *Orientalism,* 83–84.

59. INPI, Bacheville (1820).

60. Paul de Kock, "Aisha," *Mercure galant* 1 (1841): 10–12.

61. See INPI, Mayer and Naquet patent request (1821).

62. For a similar questioning of racial integration, see Gwilliam, "Cosmetic Poetics," 153–59. On cosmetics, race, and empire, see Coleman, "Janet Schaw and the Complexions of Empire," 169–93.

Chapter Eight · *Selling Masculinity*

1. Flügel, *The Psychology of Clothes,* 110–19.

2. Hunt, "Freedom of Dress in Revolutionary France," 237.

3. On bourgeois masculinity, see Perrot, *Travail* and *Fashioning the Bourgeoisie.*

4. Kuchta, *The Three-Piece Suit and Modern Masculinity,* 176.

5. Rauch, *Le premier sexe,* 51.

6. Hollander, *Sex and Suits,* 100.

7. Lajer-Burcharth, *Necklines,* 183, 189–90, 197; Solomon-Godeau, *Male Trouble,* ch. 2.

8. Williams, qtd. in Ribeiro, *The Art of Dress,* 85.

9. "La Vie de garcon," *Journal des dames* (20 Nov. 1815): 506.

10. Villaret, *L'art de se coiffer,* 1.

11. Goulin, *Médecin des hommes,* 409, 163–34.

12. Kwass, "Big Hair," 644–45, 657.

13. Mercier, *Tableau de Paris,* ch. 870, 2:1089.

14. Mercier, *Tableau de Paris,* ch. 870, 2:1091.

15. Revolat, *Nouvelle hygiène militaire ou Préceptes,* 106–7.

16. Bell, *On Human Finery,* 126.

17. Deguerle, *Éloge des perruques,* 22.

18. Picard, *Le jeune médecin ou l'influence des perruques,* 40.

19. Simonnin, *Le mariage de Charles Collé,* 26.

20. Nougaret, *Paris ou le rideau levé,* 13.

21. BHVP 115659, *Garde à vous, no. 1, La perruque enlevée.*

22. Assailly, *Fards et beautés,* 136. For a history of the wigmakers, see Gayne, "The Wigmakers, the Public, and the State."

23. Mercier, *Nouveau Paris,* ch. 168, 4:200–201.

24. Sobry, *Le mode français,* 419–20.

25. Le Bègue de Presle, *Le conservateur de la santé,* 210, 340.

26. Gaudet, *Bibliothèque des petits maîtres,* 149.

27. Mercier, *Tableau de Paris,* ch. 32, 1:94.

28. Vaublanc, *Souvenirs,* 263–64, 266.

29. Bibliothèque de l'Arsenal, Manuscrit Bast. 10027, no. 229, anonymous letter to Hérault, 20 April 1731, qtd. in Kaplan, *The Bakers of Paris and the Bread Question 1700–1775,* 596.

30. Mercier, *Tableau de Paris,* ch. 32, 1:95. See also Mercier, *Nouveau Paris,* ch. 168, 4:199.

31. Kaplan, *The Bakers of Paris,* 24.

32. Ibid., 544.

33. "Représentations . . . au sujet de l'impôt sur l'amidon et la poudre à poudrer, 24 Mars 1760," *Statuts,* 383–86.

34. *Avant coureur,* no. 11 (13 March 1769): 165.

35. Lavoisier, "Rapport sur l'établissement d'une fabrique d'amidon, 25 Nov. 1772," in *Oeuvres de Lavoisier,* 4:135.

36. AN, F/12/1473, Membre . . . de la société républicaine de Nice . . . "Lettre à la Commission du Commerce" (14 Aug. 1790).

37. AN, F/12/1500 (1792).

38. Quicherat, *Histoire du costume*, 623.

39. AN, F/12/1473 (1794; 1796).

40. *AAAD* (18 Sept. 1795): 7167; *AAAD* (23 July 1797): 5015.

41. Henrion, *Encore un tableau de Paris*, 8.

42. For instance, *AAAD* (16, 18 July 1795).

43. *AAAD* (24 Oct. 1798): 585.

44. *AAAD* (25 Aug. 1795): 6944.

45. For ridicules against powder, see Bel Air, *Manuel des élégants et des élégantes*, 13; Mullot, *L'art de la parure ou la toilette des dames*, 86.

46. *Annuaire des modes* (March 1814): 62; Grellier, *Dissertation sur les cheveux*, 15.

47. Grellier, *Dissertation sur les cheveux*, 21.

48. Duflos, *Essai sur les cheveux*, 8.

49. Marie de Saint-Ursin, *Gazette de santé* (11 April 1809): 86.

50. Oldendorff, *Traité anatomique, physiologique et pathologique du systéme pileux*, 8, 40.

51. *L'observateur des modes*, no. 46 (1820): 32.

52. Bienvenu, *Essai sur la systeme pileux*, 35; Obert, *Traité des maladies des cheveux*, 21.

53. Langlebert, *Études sur l'alopécie*, 23.

54. *L'observateur des modes*, no. 412 (1818): 52.

55. Oldendorff, *Traité anatomique*, 25.

56. Goulin, *Médecin des hommes*, 412–13.

57. Dupont de L'ain, *Études médicales sur les quatre ages de la vie*, 170.

58. Villaret, *Les métamorphoses de la chevelure*, 5–6.

59. *Journal des dames* (20 Dec. 1815): 560.

60. Ruscelli, *Secrets du Seigneur Alexis Piedmontais*, 569.

61. Villaret, *Art de se coiffer*, 194.

62. Rowland, *Treatise on the Human Hair*, 13, 19.

63. INPI, Naquet et Mayer, 1817, 1820.

64. Segrave, *Baldness*, 3.

65. *AAAD* (2 Jan. 1781): 13.

66. Villaret, *Art de se coiffer*, 193; Oldendorff, *Traité anatomique*, 60, 1; Obert, *Traité des maladies des cheveux*, 57–62.

67. Villaret, *Métamorphoses*, 122–23, 120–21.

68. Goulin, *Médecin des hommes*, 411, 412.

69. L'Artois, *Mémoire sur le traitement propre à prévenir et arrêter la chute des cheveux*, 4.

70. Langlebert, *Études sur l'alopécie*, 27.

71. *L'indiscret* (15 Dec. 1823): 403.

72. *Nouveau journal des dames* (25 Dec. 1821): 275.

73. Duchesne, *De la nécessité de la coiffure pour les hommes*, 8.

74. *Journal des dames* (31 May 1808): 238; AN, F/12/1013 (1808).

75. *L'observateur des modes* 2, no. 7 (1818): 97.

76. INPI, Palette (1811); INPI, Pascal (1825); INPI, Dufour (1821).

77. INPI, Souchard (1822).

78. AN, F/12/1027b (10 June 1817); *Folies parisiennes* (1819): 157; *Paris et ses modes* (1821): 43.

79. Balzac, *César Birotteau*, 19.

80. Balzac, *César Birotteau*, 84–85. For a similar concoction, see INPI, Aubril (1817).

81. Vauquelin, *Extrait d'un mémoire sur les cheveux lu à l'institut national le 3 mars* (Paris: 1806); Balzac, *César Birotteau*, 120–23.

82. Balzac, *César Birotteau*, 200.

83. Ibid.

Conclusion

1. Roche, "Between a 'Moral Economy' and a 'Consumer Economy': Clothes and Their Function in the Seventeenth and Eighteenth Centuries," in Fox and Turner, *Luxury Trades and Consumerism,* 228.

2. Vaublanc, *Souvenirs,* 254; Weber, *Queen of Fashion,* 146.

3. Sheriff, *The Exceptional Woman,* ch. 5.

4. Mitchell, "Picturing Sisters, 179.

5. Ibid., 183.

6. Bordes, "Jacques-Louis David's Anglophilia on the Eve of the French Revolution," 486–87.

7. Berlanstein, "Women and Power in Eighteenth-Century France: Actresses at the *Comédie-Française,*" in Adams, Censer, and Graham, *Visions and Revisions of Eighteenth-Century* France, 178–84, on Clairon, 166–68.

8. Gaillard de la Bataille, *Histoire de Mlle Cronel.*

9. McManners, *Abbés and Actresses,* 5.

10. Clairon, *Mémoires de Mademoiselle Clairon,* 270–80.

11. Ibid., 139.

12. Ibid., 192.

13. Ibid., 149.

14. *Journal des dames* (5 Feb. 1808): 52.

15. Powell and Roach, "Big Hair," 83.

16. Letter to Dr. Trioson, 1 Feb. 1792, qtd. in part in Bruno Chenique, *La Vie d'Anne-Louis Girodet de Roussy (1767–1824), essai de biochronologie,* CD Rom in Bellenger, *Girodet, 1767–1824,* 223.

17. Letter to Dr. Trioson, 27 March 1792, in Coupin, *Oeuvres posthumes,* 2:413.

18. On hair length during the Revolution, see Wrigley, *The Politics of Appearances,* 233–34.

19. *Oeuvres posthumes,* 1:xlvj; Letter to Jacques Louis David, 20 May 1794, Besançon, Bibliothèque municipale, MS 1441, 434–35, qtd. in Ledbury, "Unpublished letters to Jacques-Louis David from his pupils in Italy," 296–300.

20. Coupin, *Oeuvres posthumes,* 1:391.

21. Girodet, *Autoportrait,* private collection; Paul Claude Michel Carpentier, *Portrait of Girodet after His Self-Portrait,* Musée Magnin.

22. Jean-Loup Champion, "A Theater of Mirrors: Girodet's Self-Portraits," in Bellenger, *Girodet,* 107.

23. For an in-depth look at Mlle Clairon, see Morag Martin, "Casanova and Mlle Clairon."

24. Oberkirch, *Mémoires de la Baronne d'Oberkirch,* 302.

25. *Nouvelle liste des plus jolies femmes publiques de Paris,* 39, 9–10.

26. M. L. Stewart, *For Health and Beauty,* 11–13.

Primary Sources

ABBREVIATIONS FOR ARCHIVES, LIBRARIES, AND JOURNALS

AAAD   *Annonces, affiches et avis divers* 1751–1811
AN   Archives nationales
ANM   Académie nationale de médecine
AP   Archives de Paris
ASRM   Archives de la société royale de médecine
BHVP   Bibliothèque historique de la ville de Paris
BN   Bibliothèque nationale de France
CCIP   Archives de la chambre de commerce et d'industrie de Paris
INPI   Institut national de la propriété industrielle
MC   Minutier central

PERIODICALS

Affiches de Provence, feuille hebdomadaire d'Aix. Aix, 1778.
Affiches de Toulouse. Toulouse, 1781.
Affiches Parisiennes ou Gazette de France. Paris, 1818–1819.
Ancien album. 1828.
Annales politiques, civiles et littéraire du 18ième siècle. Londre, 1777–1784.
L'année littéraire. Paris, 1754–1790.
Annonces, affiches et avis divers. Versailles: Jacques Guerin, 1751–1782.
Annonces, affiches et avis divers (de province). Paris, 1752–1784.
Annonces, affiches et avis divers ou Journal général de France. Paris, 1783–1811.
Annuaire des modes de Paris, ou almanach des modes. Paris, 1814–1822.
L'avant coureur, feuille hebdomadaire où sont annoncés les objets particuliers des sciences et des arts.
    Paris, 1759–1774.
Avis divers. Paris, 1777–78.
Aviseur national. Paris, 1792–1793.
Le babillard. Paris, 1778–1779.
Le bouquet, Album des modes et des nouveautés, 1827.
Cinq années littéraires. Paris, 1745–1752.
Feuille sans titre. Amsterdam, 1777.
Folies parisiennes. Paris, 1819
Gazette d'agriculture, commerce, arts et finances. Paris, 1763–1783.
Gazette de santé. Paris, 1773–1829.
Gazette du commerce. Paris, 1763–1769.
L'indiscret, Journal des nouveautés, des modes, des arts, de la littérature et des théatres. Paris, 1823.
Journal de la Côte-d'Or. Dijon, 1796–1863.
Journal de politique et de littérature. Bruxelles, 1774–1778.

Journal des dames. The Hague, January 1759–June 1778.

Journal des dames et des modes. Paris, 1797–1837.

Le magasin des modes nouvelles françaises et anglaises. Paris, 1786–1789.

Mercure de France. Geneva: Slatkine Reprints, 1971, 1732–1803.

Mercure galant, Revue des modes, théâtres, littérature. 1841.

Nouveau journal des dames. Paris, 1821.

L'observateur des modes. Paris, 1818–1823.

Paris et ses modes. Paris, 1821.

Petites affiches, annonces et avis divers ou journal général de France. Paris, 1797.

Petites affiches de Paris ou journal général d'annonces, d'indication et de correspondance. Paris, 1799–1811.

Petit courier des dames. Paris, 1821–1865.

Tableau général du goût, des modes et costumes. Paris, 1797.

OTHER PRINTED WORKS

Alletz, Auguste. *L'Albert moderne.* 1768.

Almanach dauphin ou tablettes royales. Paris, 1772, 1776, 1777, 1789.

Almanach de Paris. Paris, 1789, 1798.

Almanach du commerce de Paris. Paris, 1798–1838.

Almanach historique et commercial du Palais-royal. Paris, 1827.

Art du savonnier. Paris, 1774.

Auffray, Jean. *Idées partriotiques sur la nécéssité de rendre la liberté au commerce.* Lyon, 1762.

Auger, Louis Simon. *Arlequin odalisque.* Paris, 1799.

Avis au public concernant les remèdes pour lesquels on demande des permissions ou brevets. Paris, 1778.

Balzac, Honoré de. *César Birotteau.* 1837. Vol. 4. *La Comédie humaine.* Translated by W. P. Trent. New York: Century Co., 1909.

Banau, J. B. *Histoire naturelle de la peau.* Paris, 1802.

Barbe, Simon. *Le parfumeur français.* Lyon: Thomas Amaurly, 1693.

———. *Le parfumeur royal.* Paris, 1699.

Barthe, Th. (d'après Barbier). *La jolie femme ou la femme du jour.* Paris, 1769.

Bastide, Jean François. *Les confessions d'un fat.* Paris, 1749.

Baumé, Antoine. *Élemens de pharmacie théorique et pratique.* Paris, 1762.

Bienvenu, R. *Essai sur le système pileux.* Paris, 1815.

Bel Air [pseud.]. *Manuel des élégants et des élégantes.* Paris, 1805.

Blancard, Pierre. *Manuel du commerce des Indes.* Paris, 1806.

Blegny, Nicolas. *Secrets concernant la beauté et la santé.* 2 vols. Paris: Laurent D'houry, 1688–89.

Boudier de Villemert, Pierre-Joseph. *L'ami des femme ou la morale du sexe.* Paris, 1759.

Bourdet, Bernard. *Soins faciles pour la propreté de la bouche, pour la conservation des dents et pour faire éviter aux enfants les accidents de la dentition.* Paris, 1771.

Boureau-Deslandres, François André. *Lettre sur le luxe.* Paris, 1745.

Bourgeois, Loyse, dite Boursier. *Recueil de secrets pour diverses maladies principalement des femmes avec leurs embellissements.* Paris, 1635.

Bractéole [Maimieux, Joseph de]. *Éloge philosophique de l'impertinence.* Paris, 1788.

Bruzen de Lamartinière, Aut. Aug. *Secrets pour conserver la beauté des dames.* Paris, 1777.

Buc'hoz, Pierre-Joseph. *Toilette de flore.* Paris: Valade, 1771.

Butini, Jean-François. *Traité de luxe.* Geneva, 1774.

Campan, Jeanne Louise Henriette Genest. *Mémoires de la vie privée de Marie Antoinette reine de France et de Navarre.* Paris, 1823.

Cantillon, Richard. *Essai sur la nature du commerce en général.* Paris, 1755.

Caraccioli, Louis Antoine de. *La critique des dames et des messieurs à leur toilette.* Paris, 1770.

———. *Dictionnaire critique pittoresque et sententieux.* 3 vols. Lyon: Benot Duplain, 1768.

———. *Les entretiens du Palais Royal.* Utrecht: Buisson, 1786.

———. *Jouissance de soi-même.* Autrecht: H Spruit, 1759.

———. *Livre à la mode.* Paris, n.d.

———. *Livre des quatre couleurs.* Aux quatre élements: Quatre saisons, 1760.

Caron, Auguste. *Toilette des dames ou Encyclopédie de la beauté.* Paris, 1806.

Casanova, Giacomo. *Mémoires de Jacques Casanova de Seingalt.* 4 vols. Paris: Paulin, 1843.

———. *Mémoires de Jacques Casanova de Seingalt écrits par lui-même.* 8 vols. Paris: Garnier Frères, 1900.

———. *Memoirs.* Translated by Arthur Machen. 6 vols. London: G. P. Putnam's Sons, 1900.

Celnart, Elisabeth Felicie. *Manuel des dames.* Paris, 1833.

———. *Manuel du parfumeur.* Paris: Roret, 1834.

Cézan, Louis-Alexandre de, and Guillaume-Réné Lefebvre de Saint-Ildephont. "Remèdes approuvés par la facultés de médecine." *État de médecine, chirurgie, pharmacie.* Paris, 1776.

Chaptal de Chanteloup, Jean Antoine Claude, comte. *Eléments de chymie.* 3 vols. Paris: Deterville, 1796.

Charleval, Jean Louis, and Denis Sanguin St. Pavin. *Poésies de Charleval et St. Pavin.* Amsterdam, 1759.

Chevrier, François Antoine. *Les ridicules du siècle.* London, 1752.

Choderlos de Laclos, Pierre Ambroise Françoise. *Dangerous Acquaintances.* Translated by Richard Aldington. 1782. Reprint, London: Routledge, 1924.

———. *De l'éducation des femmes.* 1785. Reprint, Paris: A Messein, 1903.

Clairon, Claire Josephe Hippolyte Legris de Latude. *Mémoires de mademoiselle Clairon.* Paris, 1798.

Clavelin, G. *Petites étrennes récréatives de la mode.* Paris, 1821.

Clément, Jean Marie Bernard. *Satire sur les abus du luxe.* Geneva, 1770.

Code du commerce, manuel complet d'industrie commerciale, par l'auteur du code de la conversation. Paris, 1829.

Coupin, P. A., ed. *Oeuvres posthumes de Girodet-Trioson, peintre d'histoire; suivies de sa correspondances.* 2 vols. Paris, 1829.

Cradock, Anna Francesca. *Journal de Mme Cradock, voyage en France, 1783–1786.* Translated by O. Delphin Balleyguier. Paris, 1896.

D'abrantès, Duchesse. *Une soirée chez Mme Geoffrin.* Bruxelles: Société générale d'imprimerie, 1837.

Dancourt, Florent Carton. *L'est des coquettes: comédie.* Paris, 1691.

Deguerle, Akerlio. *Éloge des perruques.* Paris, 1799.

Delacroix, Jacques Vincent. *Le spectateur français avant la Révolution.* Paris, 1793, 1796.

De La Salle, Jean Baptiste. *Almanach de la civilité française.* Paris, 1714.

Delindre, J. B. *L'art de se faire aimer de sa femme.* Paris, 1799.

Deshais-Gendron, Louis-Florent. *Lettre à monsieur*** sur plusieurs maladies des yeux causées par l'usage du rouge et du blanc.* Paris, 1760.

Dictionnaire du commerce et des marchandises. 2 vols. Paris, 1839.

Diderot, Denis. *Les bijoux indiscrets.* 2 vols. Paris, 1748.

Diderot, Denis, and Jean Le Rond d'Alembert, eds. *Encyclopédie ou dictionnaire raisonné des sciences, des arts et des métiers.* 17 vols. Paris, 1751–1777.

Duchesne. *De la nécessité de la coiffure pour les hommes distingués; ses rapports avec la civilisation.* Paris, 1829.

Du Coudray, Alexandre Jacques Louis. *Le luxe, poème en six chants.* Paris, 1773.

Duflos, L. J. *Essai sur les cheveux.* Paris: Chez l'auteur, 1812.

Dulac, H. *Almanach des adresses de tous les commerçans de Paris pour l'année 1818.* Paris, 1818.

Dupont de L'ain. *Études médicales sur les quatre ages de la vie.* Paris, 1830.

Duval, Georges. *Souvenirs de la Terreur.* Paris: Werdet Editeur, 1841.

Elbée, Chevalier de. *La véritable ressource que l'on peut tirer du rouge.* n.p., n.d.

Éloge des coëffures adressé aux dames par un chevalier de l'ordre de St-Michel. Paris, 1782.

Encyclopédie méthodique. Paris: Panckouke, 1783.

Fargeon, D. J. *L'art du parfumeur ou traité complet de la préparation des parfums, cosmétiques, pommades, pastilles, odeurs, etc.* Paris, 1801.

Favart, Charles-Simon. "Les trois sultanes." 1761. In *Répertoire du théatre français,* ed. M. Petitot. Vol. 22. Paris, 1804.

Favre, Abbé de. *Quatre heures de la toilette des dames, poème érotique en quatre chants.* Paris, 1779.

Fersen. *Le Comte de Fersen à la cour de France.* Paris, 1877.

Fitelieu, Sieur de Rodolphe et du Montour. *La contre-mode.* Paris, 1642.

Gaillard de la Bataille. *Histoire de Mlle Cronel,* dite Frétillon, *actrice de la Comédie de Rouen, écrite par elle-même.* 5 vols. La Haye, 1772.

Gaudet, François Charles. *Bibliothèque des petits maîtres ou mémoires pour servir à l'histoire du bon ton et de l'extrêmement bonne compagnie.* Paris, 1762.

Genlis, Stéphanie Felicité Comtesse de. *Manuel de la jeune femme, Guide complet de la maîtresse de maison.* Paris, 1829.

———. *Mémoires.* 9 vols. Paris, 1825.

Gerard, Alexandre. *Essais sur le goût . . . augmenté de trois dissertations sur le même sujet par Mrs. de Voltaire, d'Alembert et de Montesquieu, traduit sur la seconde édition anglaise par M.E.* Paris, 1766.

Getnon-Ville, Comtesse de. *L'épouse rare, ou modèle de douceur, de patience et de constance.* Paris, 1789.

Gontaut-Biron, Marie Josephine Louise de Montaut de Navailles. *Mémoires de la Duchesse de Gontaut 1773–1836.* Paris: Plon, 1891.

Goulin, Jean. *Le médecin des dames ou l'art de les conserver en santé.* Paris, 1771.

———. *Le médecin des hommes depuis la puberté jusqu'a l'extrême vieillesse.* Paris, 1772.

Grellier, L. *Dissertation sur les cheveux, presentée et soutenue à l'école de médecine de Paris, le 20 Fevrier 1806*. Paris, 1806.

Grenaille, François Sr. De. *L'honneste fille*. Paris, 1640.

Guibert. *Poésie et oeuvres diverses*. Amsterdam, 1764.

Heinzemann, Johann. *Voyage d'un Allemand à Paris*. Lausanne, 1800.

Henrion, Charles. *Encore un tableau de Paris*. Paris, 1799.

Héricart de Thury, Louis-Etienne-François. *Rapport du jury d'admission des produits de l'industrie du département de la Seine à l'exposition du Louvre*. Paris, 1819.

Hermand, fils. *Mémoire pour marchands contre forains*. Paris, 1758.

Hornot, Antoine [Dejean]. *Traité des odeurs suite du traité de la distillation*. Paris, 1764.

Hutcheson, Francis. *Recherches sur l'origine des idées que nous avons de la beauté*. Translated from English. Amsterdam, 1749.

Jaubert, L'Abbé. *Dictionnaire raisonné universel des arts et métiers*. 4 vols. Paris: Didot Jeune, 1772.

Jeze. *État ou tableau de la ville de Paris*. Paris, 1760.

Kotzebue, Auguste. *Souvenirs de Paris*. Paris, 1805.

Langlebert. *Études sur l'alopécie ou chute temporaire et prémature des cheveux*. Paris, 1847.

La Peyre. *Les moeurs de Paris*. Amsterdam, 1747.

L'Artois, L. de. *Mémoire sur le traitement propre à prévenir et arrêter la chute des cheveux*. Paris, n.d.

La Salle, Jean Baptiste de. *Almanach de la civilité française*. Paris, 1714.

Lavoisier, Antoine. *Oeuvres de Antoine Lavoisier*. 6 vols. Paris, 1864–1893.

Le Bègue de Presle, Achille-Guillaume. *Le conservateur de la santé, ou avis sur les dangers qu'il importe à chacun d'éviter*. Paris, 1763.

Le Camus, Albert. *Abdeker, ou l'art de conserver la beauté*. 2 vols. Paris, 1754.

Lemaire, Joseph. *Le dentiste des dames*. Paris, 1812.

Lémery, Nicolas. *Cours de chymie contenant la manière de faire les opérations qui sont en usage dans la médecine . . . 1677*. Reprint, Paris, 1756.

———. *Nouveaux recueil de secrets et curiositez les plus rares. 1684*. Reprint, Amsterdam, 1709.

Lennox, Sarah, imitation of, in French. *Sophie ou le triomphe des grâces sur la beauté*. London, 1770.

Macquer, Philippe. *Dictionnaire portatif des arts et métiers, contenant en abrégé l'histoire, la description et la police des arts et métiers*. 2 vols. Paris, 1766.

Malo, Charles. *Bazar Parisien, ou choix raisonné des produits de l'industrie parisienne*. 3 vols. Paris, 1821–1824.

Marcenay de Ghuy, M. *Essai sur la beauté*. Paris, 1770.

Marie de Saint-Ursin, P. J. *L'ami des femmes ou lettres d'un médecin, concernant l'influence de l'habillement des femmes sur leurs moeurs et leur santé . . . suivies d'un appendix contenant des recettes cosmétiques et curatives*. Paris, 1804.

Marmontel, Jean-François. *Trois contes moraux*. Paris: Éditions Gallimard, 1994.

Mart***. *La voix des commerçans, artisans et d'un grand nombre d'autres citoyens ou exposé*. Paris, 1814.

Mayer. *Quelques réflexions sur la manière de maintenir à la beauté les charmes primitifs de la jeunesse*. Paris, 1823.

Mège, Jean-Baptiste. *Alliance d'hygie et de la beauté, ou l'art d'embellir d'après les principes de la physiologie précédé d'un discours sur les caractères physiques et moraux de la femme, ses prérogatives et ses devoirs, et sur les moeurs et les coutumes des Anciens.* Paris, 1818.

Mercier, Louis Sébastien. *Brouette du vinaigrier.* Paris, 1778.

———. *Nouveau Paris.* 6 vols. Paris, 1798.

———. *Tableau de Paris.* 2 vols. Amsterdam: Mercure de France, 1994.

Meurdrac, Marie. *La chymie charitable et facile en faveur des dames.* Paris, 1666.

Meyssonnier, Lazare, *La magie naturelle.* Lyon, 1650.

———. *Recueil de secrets pour la conservation de la beauté.* Paris, 1661.

Moléon, Jean-Gabriel Victor de, and Louis Sébastien Le Normand. *Description des expositions des produits de l'industrie française.* Paris, 1824.

Montesquieu, Charles de Secondat, baron de. *Persian Letters.* Translated by C. J. Betts. 1721. Reprint, New York: Penguin Books, 1973.

Moreau le Jeune, Jean-Michel. *Suite pour monument du costume.* Paris, 1777.

Moreau le Jeune et Restif de la Bretonne. *Les petites parties et les grands costumes de la dernière cour en France.* Paris, n.d.

Mullot, Charles. *L'art de la parure ou la toilette des dames.* Paris, 1811.

Neuville, Hyde de. *Mémoires du Baron Hyde de Neuville.* Paris, 1888.

Nicolai, Friedrich. *Recherches historiques sur l'usage des cheveux postiches et des perruques dans les temps anciens et modernes.* Translated by Hendrik Jansen. Paris, 1809.

Nougaret, Pierre Jean Baptiste. *Astuces et tromperies de Paris.* 3 vols. Paris, 1799.

———. *Les dangers de la séduction et les faux pas de la beauté.* 2 vols. Paris, 1796.

———. *La faiblesse d'une jolie femmes ou mémoires de Madame de Vilfranc écrits par elle-même.* 2 vols. Amsterdam, 1779.

———. *Mille et une folies.* 4 vols. Paris, 1771.

———. *Paris ou le rideau levé.* Paris, An VIII.

Nostradamus, Michel de. *Excellent et très utile opuscule à tous nécéssaire, de plusieurs exquises recettes . . . fard.* Lyon, 1555.

Nouvelle liste des plus jolies femmes publiques de Paris. Paris, 1801.

Oberkirch, Henriette Louise von Waldner. *Mémoires de la Baronne d'Oberkirch.* Paris: Mercure de France, 1970.

Obert, L. A. *Traité des maladies des cheveux, de la barbe et du système pileux en général.* Paris, 1847.

Oldendorff, Max. *Traité anatomique, physiologique et pathologique du système pileux et en particulier des cheveux et de la barbe.* Paris, 1831.

Le papillotage, ouvrage comique et moral. Rotterdam, 1767.

Le parfumeur royal ou traité des parfums. Paris, 1761.

Paris et ses modes ou les soirées Parisiennes. Paris, 1803.

Payen, Anselme. *Rapport du jury départemental de la Seine sur les produits de l'industrie admis au concours de l'Exposition publique de 1827.* 2 vols. Paris, 1829–1832.

Pernety, Antoine Joseph. *La connaissance de l'homme moral.* 2 vols. Berlin, 1776.

Petit, Antoine. *Le miroir, comédie en un acte et en vers.* Paris, 1747.

Picard, L. B. *Le jeune médecin ou l'influence des perruques.* Paris, 1807.

Poncelet. *Chimie du goût et de l'odorat.* Paris, 1755.

Quinault, Philippe. *La mère coquette ou les amans brouillés.* Paris, 1769.

Raybaud, Pierre. *Observations sur l'extraction des huiles essentielles.* Paris, 1834.

Renou, Jean de. *Oeuvres pharmaceutiques.* Lyon, 1626.

Restif de la Bretonne, Nicolas-Edme. *Les contemporaines, ou aventures des plus jolies femmes.* 8 vols. Paris, 1780–1782.

———. *La femme dans les trois états.* London, 1773.

———. *Les françaises, ou XXXIV exemples choisis dans les moeurs actuelles.* 4 vols. Paris, 1786.

———. *Les nuits de Paris.* Paris, 1788–1789. In *Paris le jour, Paris la nuit.* Ed. Daniel Baruch. Paris: Robert Laffont, 1990.

———. *Le paysan perverti.* Amsterdam, 1776.

Retz, Noël. *Nouvelles ou annales de l'art de guérir.* 7 vols. Paris, 1789–1791.

Revolat, Étienne-Benoît. *Nouvelle hygiène militaire, ou préceptes sur la santé de l'homme de guerre considéré dans toutes ses positions.* Lyon, 1803.

Rousseau, Jean-Jacques. *Confessions.* 1782. Reprint, New York: Modern Library, 1945.

———. *Emile.* 1762. Reprint, Paris: Garnier Frères, 1961.

———. *Julie ou la nouvelle Héloise.* 1761. Reprint, Paris: Garnier-Freres, 1880.

Roussel, Pierre. *Système physique et moral de la femme ou tableau philosophique.* Paris, 1775.

Rowland, Alex. *Treatise on the Human Hair.* Lyon, 1841.

Roze de Chantoiseau, Mathurin. *Essai sur l'almanach général d'indication d'adresse personnelle et domicile fixe des 6 corps arts et métiers.* Paris, 1769.

———. *Tablettes royales de renommée ou almanach général d'indication des négocians, artistes célèbres et fabricans des six corps, arts et métiers . . . de Paris et autres villes du royaume . . .* Paris, 1773.

Ruscelli, Girolamo. *Secrets du Seigneur Alexis Piedmontais.* 1555. Reprint, Rouen, 1691.

Savary de Bruslon, Jacques. *Dictionnaire universel de commerce, d'histoire naturelle, et des arts et métiers.* 3 vols. Paris, 1723–1730.

Second avis au public concernant les remèdes pour lesquels on demande des permissions ou brevets. Paris, 1779.

Sedaine de Sarcy, Jean-François. *Le sérail à l'encan, comédie en 1 acte.* 1781. Reprint, Amsterdam, 1788.

Simonnin, Antoine Jean-Baptiste. *Le mariage de Charles Collé.* Paris, 1809.

Sobry, Jean François. *Le mode français: Discours sur les principaux usages de la nation française.* London, 1786.

Statuts de la communauté des marchands gantiers, poudriers, parfumeurs de la ville, fauxbourgs et banlieue de Paris. Paris: Vallade, 1772.

Tissot, S. A. D. *Essai sur les maladies des gens du monde.* Paris, 1771.

Torche, Antoine. *La toilette galante de l'amour.* Paris, 1670.

Touchard-Lafosse, G. *L'oeil-de-boeuf: Chroniques pittoresques et critiques.* 1771. Reprint, Paris: Gustave Barba, 1845.

Troisième avis au public concernant les remèdes pour lesquels on demande des permissions ou brevet; avec un état contenant la suite de ceux que la Société Royale de Médecine a examinés et rejettés. Paris, 1782.

Vaublanc, Vincent-Marie Viénot, Comte de. *Souvenirs.* Paris, 1838.

Vauquelin, Baptiste Nicolas Louis. *Extrait d'un mémoire sur les cheveux lu à l'institut national le 3 mars.* Paris, 1806.

Villaret, P. *L'art de se coiffer soi-même—réflexions sur tout ce qui doit composer la toilette des dames—recettes diverses.* Paris, 1828.

———. *Les métamorphoses de la chevelure ou moyens hygièniques de se préserver des cheveux blancs et de se délivrer des cheveux roux suivies d'un aperçu sur la calvitie.* Paris, 1829.

Virard. *Essai sur la santé des filles nubiles.* London, 1776.

Virey, Julien Joseph. *De la femme sous ses rapports physiologique, moral et littéraire.* 1810. Reprint, Paris, 1825.

Voltaire [François Marie Arouet]. "Le mondain." 1736. In *Complete Works of Voltaire.* Oxfordshire: Voltaire Foundation, 1974.

[Voltaire]. *L'odalisque.* 1796. In *Les maîtres de l'amour: L'oeuvre de Voltaire.* Paris: Bibliothèque des curieux, 1923.

Walpole, Horace. *Letters of Horace Walpole.* Helen Toynbee, ed. Oxford: Clarendon Press, 1903–1905.

Secondary Sources

Adams, Christine, Jack R. Censer, and Lisa Jane Graham, eds. *Visions and Revisions of Eighteenth-Century France.* University Park: Pennsylvania State University Press, 1997.

Angeloglou, Maggie. *A History of Make-up.* London: Macmillan, 1970.

Assailly, Gisèle de. *Fards et beautés ou l'éternel féminin.* Paris: Hachette, 1958.

Baruch, Daniel. *Simon Nicolas Henri Linguet, ou, L'irrécupérable.* Paris: Éditions François Bourin, 1991.

Behdad, Ali. "The Eroticized Orient: Images of the Harem in Montesquieu and His Precursors." *Stanford French Review* 13, nos. 2–3 (1989): 109–26.

Bell, Quentin. *On Human Finery.* 1947. Reprint, London: Alison and Busby, 1992.

Bellenger, Sylvain, ed. *Girodet, 1767–1824.* Paris: Musée du Louvre, 2005.

Berg, Maxine. *Luxury and Pleasure in Eighteenth-Century Britain.* Oxford: Oxford University Press, 2005.

———, ed. *Markets and Manufacture in Early Industrial Europe.* London: Routledge, 1991.

Berg, Maxine, and Helen Clifford, eds. *Consumers and Luxury: Consumer Culture in Europe, 1650–1850.* Manchester: Manchester University Press, 1999.

Berriot-Salvadore, Evelyn. *Un corps, un destin, la femme dans la médecine de la Renaissance.* Paris: Honoré Champion, 1993.

Blonde, Bruno, Eugénie Briot, Natacha Coquery, and Laura Van Aert, eds. *Marchands et consommateurs: Les mutations de l'Europe moderne. Angleterre, France, Italie, Pays-Bas.* Tours: Presses universitaires François Rabelais, 2005.

Bossenga, Gail. "Protecting Merchants: Guilds and Commercial Capitalism in Eighteenth-Century France." *French Historical Studies* 15, 4 (Fall 1988): 693–703.

Bordes, Philippe. "Jacques-Louis David's Anglophilia on the Eve of the French Revolution." *Burlington Magazine* 134, no. 1073 (August 1992): 482–90.

Bourdieu, Pierre. *Distinction: A Social Critique of the Judgment of Taste.* Translated by Richard Nice. Cambridge, MA: Harvard University Press, 1984.

Braunschvig, Marcel. *La femme et la beauté, le rôle de la beauté dans la nature.* Paris: Armand Collin, 1929.

Brewer, John, and Roy Porter, eds. *Consumption and the World of Goods.* London: Routledge, 1993.

Brockliss, Laurence, and Colin Jones. *The Medical World of Early Modern France.* Oxford: Clarendon Press, 1997.

Burollet, Thérèse. *Musée Cognacq-Jay; peintures et dessins.* Paris: Les Presses Artistiques, 1980.

Campbell, Colin. *The Romantic Ethic and the Spirit of Capitalism.* Oxford: Blackwell, 1987.

Censer, Jack. *The Press in the Age of Enlightenment.* London: Routledge, 1994.

Charbon, Paul. *Au temps des malles-poste et des diligences: Histoire des transports publics et de poste du XVIIe au XIXe siècle.* Paris: J.-P. Gyss, 1979.

Chartier, Roger. *The Cultural Origins of the French Revolution.* Translated by Lydia G. Cochrane. Durham, NC: Duke University Press, 1991.

Cinquarbre, Pierre. "Recettes et produits de beauté du début du XIXième siècle." *Congrés des sociétés savantes* (1985): 211–13.

Coleman, Deirdre. "Janet Schaw and the Complexions of Empire." *Eighteenth-Century Studies* 36, no. 2 (2003): 169–93.

Coquery, Natacha. *L'hôtel aristocratique: Le marché du luxe à Paris au XVIIIe siècle.* Paris: Publications de la Sorbonne, 1998.

———. "The Language of Success: Marketing and Distributing Semi-luxury Goods in Eighteenth-Century Paris." *Journal of Design History* 17, no. 1 (2004): 71–89.

———. "Mode, commerce, innovation: la boutique parisienne à la fin du XVIIIe siècle. Aperçu sur les stratégies de séduction des marchands parisiens de luxe et de demi-luxe." In *Les chemins de la nouveauté: Innover, inventer au regard de l'histoire,* edited by Liliane Hilaire-Pérez and Anne-Françoise Garçon. Paris: Éditions du CTHS, 2003.

Corbin, Alain. *The Foul and the Fragrant.* Translated by Miriam L. Kochan, Roy Porter, and Christopher Predergast. Cambridge: Harvard University Press, 1986.

Corson, Richard. *Fashions in Hair: The First Five Thousand Years.* London: Peter Owen, 1965.

———. *Fashions in Makeup: From Ancient to Modern Times.* New York: Universe Books, 1972.

Courtine, Jean-Jacques, and Claudine Haroche. *Histoire du visage.* Paris: Payot et Rivages, 1994.

Crowston, Clare. *Fabricating Women: The Seamstresses of Old Regime France, 1675–1791.* Durham, NC: Duke University Press, 2001.

D'Arcier, Amaury Faivre. *Les agents de Napoléon en Egypte 1801–1815.* Paris: Centre d'études napoléoniennes, 1990.

Datz, P. *Histoire de la publicité depuis les temps les plus reculés jusqu'à nos jours.* Paris, 1894.

DeJean, Joan. *The Essence of Style: How the French Invented High Fashion, Fine Food, Chic Cafes, Style, Sophistication, and Glamour.* New York: Free Press, 2005.

Delpierre, Madeleine. *Dress in France in the Eighteenth Century.* Translated by Caroline Beamish. New Haven, CT: Yale University Press, 1997.

Descombes, Alain. "La publicité dans la presse parisienne 1777–8, 1787–8." Mémoire de maîtrise Université de Paris I, 1992.

Desmet-Grégoire, Hélène. *Le divan magique: L'Orient Turc en France au XVIIIe siècle.* Paris: Hartmattan, 1994.

Dock, Terry Smiley. *Women in the Encyclopédie: A Compedium.* Potomac, MD: Studia Humanitatis, 1983.

Douthwaite, Julia V. *Exotic Women: Literary Heroines and Cultural Strategies in Ancien Régime France.* Philadelphia: University of Pennsylvania Press, 1992.

Duden, Barbara. *The Woman beneath the Skin: A Doctor's Patients in Eighteenth-century Germany.* Translated by Thomas Dunlap. Cambridge, MA: Harvard University Press, 1991.

Falvy, Huguette. *Contribution à l'histoire de quelques remèdes secrets.* Paris, 1947.

Fauchery, Pierre. *La destinée féminine dans le roman européen du dix-huitième siècle, 1713–1807; essai de gynécomythie romanesque.* Paris: A. Colin, 1972.

Feltaine, E. *De la publicité commerciale, annonces, commerciales et industrielles.* Caen: E. Lanier, 1903.

Ferguson, John. *Bibliographical Notes on Histories of Inventions and Books of Secrets.* 2 vols. London, 1959.

Festa, Lynn. "Cosmetic Differences: The Changing Faces of England and France." *Studies in Eighteenth-Century Culture* 34 (2005): 25–54.

Finn, Margot. "Men's Things: Masculine Possessions and the Consumer Revolution." *Social History* 25, no. 2 (May 2000): 133–55.

Flandrin, Jean-Louis. "Soins de beauté et recueils de secrets." In *Les soins de beauté: Moyen âge, début des temps modernes: actes du IIIe Colloque international, Grasse (26–28 Avril 1985),* edited by Denis Menjot. Nice: Université de Nice, 1987.

Flügel, John Carl. *The Psychology of Clothes.* London: Hogarth Press, 1966.

Foucault, Michel. *Birth of the Clinic: An Archaeology of Medical Perception.* Translated by A. M. Sheridan. London: Tavistock, 1973.

———. "The Politics of Health in the Eighteenth Century." In *The Foucault Reader,* ed. Paul Rabinow. London, Penguin, 1984.

———. "Truth and Power." In *Power/Knowledge: Selected Interviews and Other Writings 1972–1977,* edited by Colin Gordon. New York: Pantheon Books, 1980.

Fox, Robert, and Anthony Turner, eds. *Luxury Trades and Consumerism in Ancient Régime Paris: Studies in the History of the Skilled Workforce.* Aldershot, UK: Ashgate, 1998.

Franklin, Alfred. *Les corporations ouvrières de Paris du XIIe au XVIIIe siècle.* Paris: Firmin Didot, 1884.

———. *Dictionnaire historique des arts, métiers et professions.* Paris: Leon Willem, 1906.

Gayne, Mary. "The Wigmakers, the Public, and the State: Cultural and Material Production of Eighteenth-Century French Hairstyles." PhD diss., Cornell University, 2007.

Göçek, Fatma Müge. *East Encounters West: France and the Ottoman Empire in the Eighteenth Century.* New York: Oxford University Press, 1987.

Goncourt, Edmond, and Jules Goncourt. *Histoire de la société française sous le directoire.* Paris, 1855.

Goodman, Dena. *The Republic of Letters: A Cultural History of the French Enlightenment.* Ithaca, NY: Cornell University Press, 1994.

Gough, Hugh. *The Newspaper Press in the French Revolution.* London: Routledge, 1988.

Greer, Donald. *Incidence of Emigration during the French Revolution.* Gloucester, MA: Peter Smith, 1966.

Grosrichard, Alain. *Structure du sérail: La fiction du despotisme asiatique dans l'occident classique.* Paris: Éditions du Seuil, 1979.

Gwilliam, Tassie. "Cosmetic Poetics: Coloring Faces in the Eighteenth Century." In *Body and Text in the Eighteenth Century,* edited by Veronica Kelly and Dorothea Von Mücke. Stanford, CA: Stanford University Press, 1994.

Hahn, Haejeong Hazel. "Street Picturesque: Advertising in Paris, 1830–1914." PhD diss., University of California, Berkeley, 1997.

Halttunen, Karen. *Confidence Men and Painted Women: A Study of Middle-Class Culture in America, 1830–1870.* New Haven, CT: Yale University Press, 1982.

Hannaway, Caroline. "Medicine, Public Welfare, and the State in Eighteenth-Century France." PhD diss., Johns Hopkins University, 1974.

Hesse, Carla. *The Other Enlightenment: How French Women Became Modern.* Princeton, NJ: Princeton University Press, 2001.

Hilaire-Pérez, Liliane. "Invention and the State in Eighteenth-Century France." *Technology and Culture* 32, no. 4 (October 1991): 911–31.

Hoffman, Philip, Gilles Postel-Vinay, and Jean-Laurent Rosenthal. *Priceless Markets: The Political Economy of Credit in Paris 1660–1870.* Chicago: University of Chicago Press, 2000.

Hollander, Anne. *Sex and Suits: The Evolution of Modern Dress.* New York: Knopf, 1995.

Hunt, Lynn, ed. *Eroticism and the Body Politic.* Baltimore: Johns Hopkins University Press, 1991.

———. *The Family Romance of the French Revolution.* Berkeley: University of California Press, 1992.

———. "Freedom of Dress in Revolutionary France." In *From the Royal to the Republican Body,* edited by Sara E. Melzer and Kathryn Norberg. Berkeley: University of California Press, 1998.

Hyde, Melissa. "The 'Makeup' of the Marquise: Boucher's Portrait of Pompadour at Her Toilette." *Art Bulletin* 82 (Sept. 2000): 453–75.

Isherwood, Robert. *Farce and Fantasy: Popular Entertainment in Eighteenth-Century Paris.* New York: Oxford University Press, 1986.

Isoré, Jacques. "De l'existence des brevets d'invention en droit français avant 1791." *Revue historique de droit français et étranger* 4, no. 16 (1937): 94–103.

Jaton, Anne-Marie. "Du corps paré au corps lavé: une morale du costume et de la cosmétique." *Dixhuitième siècle* (1986): 215–26.

Jones, Colin. "Great Chain of Buying: Medical Advertisement, the Bourgeois Public Sphere and the Origins of the French Revolution." *American Historical Review* 101, no. 1 (Feb. 1996): 13–40.

———. "Médecins du Roi at the End of the Ancien Regime and in the French Revolution." In *Medicine in the courts of Europe 1500–1837,* edited by Vivienne Nutton. London: Routledge, 1990.

———. "Pulling Teeth in Eighteenth-Century Paris." *Past and Present* 166 (Feb. 2000): 100–45.

Jones, Jennifer. "Coquettes and Grisettes: Women Buying and Selling in Ancien Régime Paris." In *The Sex of Things: Gender and Consumption in Historical Perspective,* edited by Victoria de Grazia. Berkeley: University of California Press, 1996.

———. "Repackaging Rousseau: Femininity and Fashion in Old Regime France." *French Historical Studies* 18, no. 4 (Fall 1994): 939–67.

———. *Sexing la Mode: Gender, Fashion, and Commercial Culture in Old Regime France.* Oxford: Berg Press, 2004.

Jones, Robert. *Gender and the Formation of Taste in Eighteenth-Century Britain.* Cambridge: Cambridge University Press, 1998.

Jordanova, Ludmilla. *Sexual Visions: Images of Gender in Science and Medicine between the Eighteenth and Twentieth Centuries.* Madison: University of Wisconsin Press, 1989.

Kahf, Mohja. *Western Representations of the Muslim Woman.* Austin: University of Texas Press, 1999.

Kaplan, Steven Laurence. *The Bakers of Paris and the Bread Question 1700–1775.* Durham, NC: Duke University Press, 1996.

———. *La fin des corporations.* Translated by Béatrice Vierne. Paris: Fayard, 2001.

Kates, Gary. *Monsieur d'Eon Is a Woman: A Tale of Political Intrigue and Sexual Masquerade.* New York: Basic Books, 1995.

Kleinert, Anne Marie. *Le "Journal des dames et des modes" ou la conquête de l'Europe féminine.* Stuttgart: Jan Thorbecke, 2001.

Knibiehler, Yvonne, and Catherine Fouquet. *La femme et les médecins.* Paris: Hachette, 1983.

Kowaleski-Wallace, Elizabeth. *Consuming Subjects: Women, Shopping and Business in the Eighteenth Century.* New York: Columbia University Press, 1996.

Kra, Pauline. "The Role of the Harem in Imitations of Montesquieu's *Lettres persanes.*" *Studies on Voltaire and the Eighteenth-Century* 182 (1979): 273–83.

Kuchta, David. *The Three-Piece Suit and Modern Masculinity. England, 1550–1850.* Berkeley: University of California Press, 2002.

Kwass, Michael. "Big Hair: A Wig History of Consumption in Eighteenth-Century France." *American Historical Review* 111, no. 3 (June 2006): 631–59.

———. "Ordering the World of Goods: Consumer Revolution and the Classification of Objects in Eighteenth-Century France." *Representations* 82 (Spring 2003): 87–116.

Labrousse, C. E., and Fernand Braudel. *Histoire économique et sociale.* 2 vols. Paris: Presses Universitaires de France, 1970.

Lacqueur, Thomas. *Making Sex: Body and Gender from the Greeks to Freud.* Cambridge, MA: Harvard University Press, 1990.

Lacroix, Paul. *Le dixhuitième siècle—Institution, usage et coutumes.* 1875. Reprint Paris, 1979.

Lajer-Burcharth, Ewa. *Necklines: The Art of Jacques-Louis David after the Terror.* New Haven, CT: Yale University Press, 1999.

Landes, Joan. *Women and the Public Sphere in the Age of the French Revolution.* Ithaca, NY: Cornell University Press, 1988.

Lanoë, Catherine. "La céruse dans la fabrication des cosmétiques sous l'Ancien Régime." *Technique et culture* 38 (2001): 17–33.

———. "L'invention du rouge au XVIIIe siècle: cosmétique populaire ou objet de luxe?" In

Les chemins de la nouveauté: Innover, inventer au regard de l'histoire, edited by Liliane Hilaire-Pérez and Anne-Françoise Garçon. Paris: Éditions du CTHS, 2003.

———. *La poudre et le fard: Une histoire des cosmétiques de la Renaissance aux Lumière.* Paris: Champ Vallon, 2008.

Laubriet, Pierre. Introduction to *César Birotteau,* by Honoré de Balzac. Paris: Garnier, 1964.

Lecomte, Jules. *Monde illustré* (3 Dec. 1859).

Ledbury, Mark. "Unpublished letters to Jacques-Louis David from his pupils in Italy." *Burlington Magazine* 42, no. 1166 (2000): 296–300.

Lenotre, G. (Théodore Gosselin). *Vieilles maisons, vieux papiers.* 2 vols. Paris, 1903.

Le Tulzo, Chrystelle. "La corporation des parfumeurs au XVIIIième siècle." Mémoire de maîtrise Université de Paris I, 1991.

Lichtenstein, Jacqueline. *The Eloquence of Color: Rhetoric and Painting in the French Classical Age.* Translated by Emily McVarish. Berkeley: University of California Press, 1993.

Lowe, Lisa. *Critical Terrain: French and British Orientalisms.* Ithaca, NY: Cornell University Press, 1991.

Martin, Marc. *Trois siècles de publicité.* Paris: Odile Jacob, 1992.

Martin, Morag. "Consuming Beauty: The Commerce of Cosmetics in France, 1750–1800." PhD diss., University of California, Irvine, 1999.

———. "Casanova and Mlle Clairon: Painting the Face in a World of Natural Fashion." *Fashion Theory Journal* 7, no. 1 (March 2003): 57–78.

———. "Doctoring Beauty: The Medical Control of Women's *Toilettes* in France, 1750–1820." *Medical History* 49 (Spring 2005): 351–68.

Masson, Paul. *Histoire du commerce français dans le Levant au XVIIIe siècle.* 1896. New York: Burt Franklin, 1967.

Mauzi, Robert. *L'idée du bonheur.* Paris: Armand Colin, 1969.

Maza, Sarah. "Luxury, Morality, and Social Change: Why There Was No Middle-Class Consciousness in Pre-revolutionary France." *Journal of Modern History* 69 (June 1997): 199–229.

McCracken, Grant. *Culture and Consumption: New Approaches to the Symbolic Character of Consumers Goods and Activities.* Bloomington: Indiana University Press, 1988.

McKendrick, Neil, John Brewer, and J. H. Plumb. *The Birth of Consumer Society: The Commercialization of Eighteenth-Century England.* London: Europa, 1982.

McManners, John. *Abbés and Actresses: The Church and the Theatrical Profession in Eighteenth-Century France.* New York: Oxford University Press, 1986.

Mitchell, Jerrine. "Picturing Sisters: 1790 Portraits by Jacques-Louis David." *Eighteenth-Century Studies* 31, no. 2 (1997–98): 175–97.

Mui, Hoh-Cheung, and Lorna H. Mui. *Shops and Shopkeeping in Eighteenth-Century England.* Kingston: McGill-Queen's University Press, 1989.

Ogura, Tadao, ed. *La mode en France 1715–1815, De Louis XV à Napoléon I.* Translated by Rose Marie Fayolle. Paris: Bibliothèque des Arts, 1990.

Pardailhé-Galabrun, Annik. *The Birth of Intimacy: Privacy and Domestic Life in Early Modern Paris.* Translated Jocelyn Phelps. Philadelphia: University of Pennsylvania Press, 1988.

Parfums et flacons au XVIIIe siècle. Grasse: Musée international de la parfumerie, 1994.

Peiss, Kathy. *Hope in a Jar: The Making of America's Beauty Culture*. New York: Metropolitan Books, 1998.

Perrot, Philippe. "La richesse cachée: Pour une généalogie de l'austérité des apparences." *Communications* 46 (1987): 157–79.

———. *Fashioning the Bourgeoisie: A History of Clothing in the Nineteenth Century*. Translated by Richard Bienvenu. Princeton, NJ: Princeton University Press, 1994.

———. *Le travail des apparences ou les transformations du corps féminins, XVIIIe–XIXe siècles*. Paris: Seuil, 1984.

Peter, J. P. "Les médecins français face au problème de l'inoculation variolique et de sa diffusion, 1750–1790." *La médicalisation en France du XVIIIième au début du XXième siècle*. Colloque de l'Université de Rennes-II. In *Annales de Bretagne et des Pays de l'Ouest* 86, 1979.

Phillippy, Patricia. *Painting Women: Cosmetics, Canvases, and Early Modern Culture*. Baltimore: Johns Hopkins University Press, 2006.

Pillivuyt, Ghislaine. *Les flacons de la séduction: l'art du parfum au XVIIIe siècle*. Lausanne: La Bibliothèque des Arts, 1985.

———. *Histoire du parfum de l'Egypte au XIXe siècle: Collection de la parfumerie Fragonard*. Paris: Denoël, 1988.

Popkin, Jeremy. *Revolutionary News: The Press in France, 1789–1799*. Durham, NC: Duke University Press, 1990.

Posner, Donald. "The 'Duchess de Velours' and Her Daughter: A Masterpiece by Nattier and Its Historical Context." *Metropolitan Museum Journal* 31 (1996): 131–41.

Powell, Margaret K., and Joseph Roach. "Big Hair," *Eighteenth-Century Studies* 38, no. 1 (Fall 2004): 79–99.

Quicherat, J. *Histoire du costume en France depuis les temps les plus reculés jusqu'à la fin du xviii siècle*. Paris, 1875.

Ramsey, Matthew. "The Popularization of Medicine in France 1650–1900." In *The Popularization of Medicine 1650–1850*, edited by Roy Porter. London: Routledge, 1992.

———. "Traditional Medicine and the Medical Enlightenment: The Regulation of Secret Remedies in the Ancien Regime." In *La medicalisation de la société francaise, 1770–1830*, ed. Jean-Pierre Goubert. Waterloo, Ontario: Historical Reflections Press, 1982.

Rand, Richard, ed. *Intimate Encounters: Love and Domesticity in Eighteenth-Century France*. Princeton, NJ: Princeton University Press, 1997.

Rasse, Paul. *La cité aromatique: Pour le travail des matières odorantes à Grasse*. Nice: Éditions Serre, 1987.

Rauch, André. *Le premier sexe: Mutations et crise de l'identité masculine*. Paris: Hachette, 2000.

Ribeiro, Aileen. *The Art of Dress: Fashion in England and France 1750 to 1820*. New Haven, CT: Yale University Press, 1995.

———. *Dress in Eighteenth-century Europe 1715–1789*. London: B. T. Batsford, 1984.

Roche, Daniel. *La culture des apparences: Une histoire du vêtement (XVIIe–XVIIIe siècle)*. Paris: Fayard, 1989.

———. *La France des lumières*. Paris: Fayard, 1993.

———. *The People of Paris: An Essay in Popular Culture in the 18th century*. Translated by Marie Evans. Berkeley: University of California Press, 1987.

Root, Hilton. *The Fountain of Privilege, Political Foundations of Markets in Old Regime France and England.* Berkeley: University of California Press, 1994.

Said, Edward. *Orientalism.* New York: Vintage, 1979.

Saisselin, Remy. *The Enlightenment against the Baroque.* Berkeley: University of California Press, 1992.

Salaman, Malcolm C. *French Colour Prints of the Eighteenth Century: An Introductory Essay.* Philadelphia: J. B. Lippincott, 1913.

Sander, Sabine, "Von den sonderbahren Geheimnüssen des Frauen-Zimmers' zur 'Schwachheit des schönen Geschlechts' Frauen in des Populärmedizin des 18 Jahrhunderts,." In *Die Grenzen des Anderen: Medizingeschichte aus postmoderner Perspektive,* edited by Thomas Schnalke and Claudia Wiesemann, 75–120. Köln: Böhlau, 1998.

Sargentson, Carolyn. *Merchants and Luxury Markets: The Marchands Merciers of Eighteenth-Century Paris.* London: Victoria and Albert Museum, 1996.

Schwartz, Joel. *The Sexual Politics of Jean-Jacques Rousseau.* Chicago: University of Chicago Press, 1984.

Scott, Katie. "The Waddesdon Manor Trade Cards: More Than One History." *Journal of Design History* 17, no. 1 (2004): 91–104.

Segrave, Kerry. *Baldness: A Social History.* Jefferson, NC: McFarland, 1996.

Sewell, William. *Work and Revolution in France: The Language of Labor from the Old Regime to 1848.* Cambridge: Cambridge University Press, 1980.

Sheriff, Mary. *Fragonard, Art, and Eroticism.* Chicago: University of Chicago Press, 1990.

———. *The Exceptional Woman: Elisabeth Vigée-Lebrun and the Cultural Politics of Art.* Chicago: University of Chicago Press 1996.

Shovlin, John. "The Cultural Politics of Luxury in Eighteenth-Century France." *French Historical Studies* 23, no. 4 (Fall 2000): 577–606.

———. *The Political Economy of Virtue: Luxury, Patriotism and the Origins of the French Revolution.* Ithaca, NY: Cornell University Press, 2006.

Simon-Mazoyer, Solange. "Le conflit entre les excès de la mode et de la santé au XVIIIe siècle, L'habillage du visage." In *La médecine des lumières, Tout autour de Tissot,* edited by Vincent Barras and Micheline Louis-Courvoisier. Geneva: *Bibliothèque d'Histoire des Sciences,* 2001.

Smith, Woodruff D. *Consumption and the Making of Respectability 1600–1800.* New York: Routledge, 2002.

Solomon-Godeau, Abigail. *Male Trouble: A Crisis in Representation.* New York: Thames and Hudson, 1997.

Sonenscher, Michael. *The Hatters of Eighteenth-Century France.* Berkeley: University of California Press, 1987.

———. *Work and Wages: Natural Law, Politics, and the Eighteenth-Century French Trades.* Cambridge: Cambridge University Press, 1989.

Stein, Perrin. "Amédée Van Loo's *Costume turc:* The French Sultana." *Art Bulletin* 78, no. 3 (Sept. 1996): 417–38.

———. "Madame de Pompadour and the Harem Imagery of Bellevue." *Gazette des Beaux-Arts* 123 (Jan. 1994): 29–45.

Steinbrügge, Lieselotte. *The Moral Sex: Woman's Nature in the French Enlightenment.* Translated by Pamela E. Selwyn. New York: Oxford University Press, 1995.

Stewart, Mary Lynn. *For Health and Beauty: Physical Culture for French Women 1880s–1930s.* Baltimore: Johns Hopkins University Press, 2001.

Stewart, Philip. "Affiches de province," in *Dictionnaire des journaux 1600–1789.* 2 vols. Edited by Jean Sgard. Paris: Universitas, 1991.

3000 Ans de parfumerie: Parfums, savons, fards, et cosmétiques de l'antiquité à nos jours. Grasse: Musée d'Art et d'Histoire, 1980.

Todd, Christopher. "French Advertising in the Eighteenth Century." *Studies on Voltaire and the Eighteenth Century* 266 (1989): 513–47.

Uzanne, Octave. *La femme et la mode.* Paris: Maison Quentin, 1893.

Vaultier, Roger. "La parfumerie et les soins de beauté au XVIIe siècle." *La France du Parfum* 2, no. 10 (Paris, 1950): 38–42.

———. "Les soins de beauté en France au XVIIIe siècle: les fards." *Pro-Medico* 4 (1984): 115–18.

Veblen, Thorstein. *The Theory of the Leisure Class.* 1899. Reprint, New York: Penguin, 1994.

Vigarello, Georges. *Le propre et le sale: L'hygiène du corps depuis le Moyen Age.* Paris: Éditions du Seuil, 1985.

Vindry, George. *Naissance et développement de la parfumerie contemporaine—3000 ans de parfumerie.* Paris, 1980.

Watin-Augouard, Jean. *Il n'y a que Maille . . . Three Centuries of Culinary Tradition.* Paris: Editions SPSA, 2000.

Weber, Caroline. *Queen of Fashion: What Marie Antoinette Wore to the Revolution.* New York: Holt, 2006.

Williams, Neville. *Powder and Paint: A History of the English Woman's Toilet.* London: Longmans, Green, 1957.

Wilson, Lindsay. *Women and Medicine in the French Enlightenment: The Debate over "Maladies des Femmes."* Baltimore: Johns Hopkins University Press, 1993.

Wischermann, Clemens, and Elliott Shore, eds. *Advertising and the European City: Historical Perspectives.* Aldershot: Ashgate, 2000.

Wrigley, Richard. *The Politics of Appearances: Representations of Dress in Revolutionary France.* Oxford: Oxford University Press, 2002.

Yeazell, Ruth Bernard. *Harems of the Mind: Passages of Western Art and Literature.* New Haven, CT: Yale University Press, 2000.

The letter *f* following a page number denotes a figure.